William Stevenson

Pencilings By The Way, in England, Scotland, Ireland, France, Switzerland, Germany, and Belgium (1881)

William Stevenson

**Pencilings By The Way, in England, Scotland, Ireland, France, Switzerland, Germany, and Belgium (1881)**

ISBN/EAN: 9783743346031

Manufactured in Europe, USA, Canada, Australia, Japa

Cover: Foto ©Andreas Hilbeck / pixelio.de

Manufactured and distributed by brebook publishing software (www.brebook.com)

William Stevenson

**Pencilings By The Way, in England, Scotland, Ireland, France, Switzerland, Germany, and Belgium (1881)**

# SIGHTS AND SCENES

IN

# EUROPE;

OR,

## PENCILINGS BY THE WAY,

In England, Scotland, Ireland, France, Switzerland, Germany, and Belgium,

DURING A SHORT TOUR IN THE SUMMER AND AUTUMN OF 1881.

BY

WILLIAM STEVENSON.

*ILLUSTRATED.*

FLINT, MICH.:
M. S. ELMORE & CO.—SPERRY & BUSHNELL,
PUBLISHERS.
1882.

EDDY PRINTING AND PUBLISHING HOUSE, FLINT.

# PREFACE.

This volume is the outgrowth of a series of letters, written to the *Flint Citizen*, from England, Scotland, Ireland, France, Switzerland, Germany and Belgium. While the matter has been arranged in more convenient form, the order of events is strictly adhered to, and what was written in the hurry of continuous travel and sight seeing has been carefully revised.

It is claimed that books describing European travel can possess neither novelty nor interest, so thoroughly has the subject been exhausted. The interest manifested in these letters, as first published, would indicate that the claim is not well founded. A pampered literary taste may reject plain description, and demand spicy caricatures, dramatic incidents, or a narrative in which the places visited are merely used as threads on which to string witticisms. Ordinary readers, however, will continue to derive satisfaction from familiar descriptions of European countries and scenes, as told by a plain matter of fact person, whose tastes and sympathies are more likely to accord with theirs than the scintillations of the literary sensationalist, or professional joker.

The author claims neither excellency of style, nor originality of thought; he freely admits his indebtedness to the guide books—not having taken the census of a single European city, or measured one of its cathedrals—and yet, from his standpoint, sees no occasion to offer a single apology for the publication of this book, or for the character of its contents.

Flint, Michigan, October, 1882.     W. S.

# CONTENTS.

## CHAPTER I.
### THE OCEAN VOYAGE.

Departure—Life at Sea—The Horizon—Sunday—A Hymn—Sabbath Services—A Gale—Not a Hymn—Ocean Experiences—The Ocean—Its Teachings—Neptune—Amusements—Story of the "Eastern Monarch"—Capt. Johnson—Scotch Coast—Firth of Clyde—"How is Garfield?"—Passing the Customs—Ashore at Greenock..........................................................11

## CHAPTER II.
### GLASGOW—BIRTH PLACE OF BURNS.

Glasgow—Cathedral—Necropolis—University—Public Buildings and Parks—Streets — Prices — Rail to Ayr — Burns' Cottage — Kirk Alloway — Tam O'Shanter—Mungo's Well — Bridge of Doon —"Bonny Doon"— Burns' Monument—Museum—Highland Mary—The Kirk-yard—The "Twa Brigs"—Burns—His Writings—Whittier's Estimate............................22

## CHAPTER III.
### EDINBURGH.

Edinburgh—Scott's Monument—The Castle—Regalia of Scotland—Mons Meg—Barracks—St. Giles—Jenny Geddes—Parliament House—Engine—John Knox's House—The Cannongate—Streets and Closes—Holyrood Abbey—Holyrood Palace—Gallery of Portraits—Audience Chamber—Queen's Bedroom—Supper Room—The Grassmarket—Greyfriars' Churchyard—The New Town—Antiquarian Gallery—Calton Hill—The View—Leith—Newhaven Fishwives—Scotch Women—Business Habits......................34

## CHAPTER IV.
### MELROSE ABBEY—ABBOTSFORD.

To Melrose—The Abbey—Scott's Stone—The Wizard's Grave—Tombs—Chapel—Sculptures—The Monks—Village of Melrose—To Abbotsford—House and Grounds—The Entrance—Hall—Rooms—Armory—Library—Study—Museum—Suggested Memories........................................................52

## CHAPTER V.

### LONDON.

Melrose to London—A Station Dining-room—London—The Old City—Modern London—The Albert Memorial—The American Exchange—Charing Cross—Trafalgar Square—The National Gallery—Whitehall—Parliament House—Victoria Tower—Hall, Chambers, Galleries, etc—House of Lords—House of Commons—Clock Tower—Great Tom of Westminster—Westminster Hall—St. Margaret's Church...................................................62

## CHAPTER VI.

### LONDON.

Westminster Abbey—Anticipations—First Impressions—History—A City of the Dead—Poet's Corner—Monuments and Memorials—Henry VII's Chapel—Chapel of Edward the Confessor—Coronation Chair—Musings and Recollections—Outside Surroundings.................. .. ........................81

## CHAPTER VII.

### LONDON.

The Strand—Somerset House—Law Courts—Temple Bar—Fleet Street—Temple Gardens—Ludgate Hill—St. Paul's Church—Sabbath Services—Monuments—Crypt—Tombs of Wellington and Nelson—Whispering Gallery—In the Ball—Paternoster Row—Newgate—St. Sulpice's—London Stone—The Monument—Billingsgate—Tower of London—St. Thomas' Tower—White Tower—Chapel of St. John—Horse Armory—Crown Jewels—Tower Palace—Prisoners of the Tower—Beauchamp Tower—Inscriptions—Chapel of St. Peter—Ancient Scaffold—Anne Boleyn, Lady Jane Grey, etc.—By the Traitor's Gate................................................96

## CHAPTER VIII.

### PARIS.

A Channel Steamer—Dieppe—Normandy—Arrival in Paris—An Election—Place de la Concorde—Dinner—A Traveler's French—Sunday Night in Paris—The New Opera House—Grand Foyer—The Madelaine—Hotel des Invalides—Arc de Triumphe—Buttes Chaumont—Pere la Chaise—Cathedral of Notre Dame—The Pantheon—Parisian Churches—The Music—In the Streets—An American Girl................. ........................123

## CHAPTER IX.

### PARIS.

Champs Elysees—Bois de Boulogne—Palace of St. Cloud—Versailles—Grand Trianon—State Carriages—Dejeuner—The Grand Palace—Grand Apartments—Paintings—Theater and Church—Sevres and its Museum—Hotel de Ville—Halles Centrales—The Tuileries—Place du Carrousel—The Luxembourg—The Louvre—Galleries — Egyptian Department—Museum of Curiosities—Place de la Bastille—Porte St. Martin—Column Vendome—Gobelins—Jottings—Taxation—Future of Paris ........................149

## CHAPTER X.

### SWITZERLAND.

Paris to Berne—Berne—The Cathedral Terrace—Alpine View—Organ Concert—The Streets—Swiss People—The Bears of Berne—Lake Thun—Interlaken—The Jungfrau—Swiss Houses—Religious Service—Sunday Afternoon—Lake Brienz—Brunig Pass—Lake Lucerne—Lucerne—A Fine Organ—The Lion of Lucerne—Vitznau—Rigi Railroad—View from the Summit—William Tell—Protestant and Catholic—The Common Pasturage............178

## CHAPTER XI.

### GERMANY—BELGIUM.

Lucerne to Strasburg—Strasburg—The Cathedral—The Famous Clock—A Legend—St. Thomas' Church—Streets and Fortifications—Mayence—The Cathedral—Market and Streets—The Rhine—Cities, Villages, Castles, and Scenery—Cologne—The Cathedral—Shrine of the Three Kings—St. Ursula—Bones and Relics—Brussels—Hotel de Ville—Statues and Streets—Waterloo—Antwerp—The Cathedral—Rubens' Famous Picture—Antwerp to London................................................................193

## CHAPTER XII.

### LONDON.

An English Sabbath—Spurgeons' Tabernacle—The Great Preacher—Tower Hill—Royal Exchange—Bank of England—Mansion House—Guildhall—Bow Church—Smithfield—Hyde Park—Parks and Gardens—St. James' Palace—Buckingham Palace—Apsley House—Underground Railroad—Cabs—Omnibuses—St. Giles'—Houndsditch .........................222

## CHAPTER XIII.

### LONDON.

Methodist Ecumenical Conference—City Road Chapel—Opening Services—Bishop Simpson's Sermon—Methodism in England—Relics—Bunhill Fields—Windsor Castle—St. George's Hall—St. George's Church—Memorial Chapel—Round Tower—South Kensington Museum—Courts and Galleries—Museum of Patents—The Crystal Palace—Interior—English Courts—Old Jewry—Tourists—Books of Travel............................................243

## CHAPTER XIV.

### LONDON—LIVERPOOL.

The British Museum—Library—Books and Manuscripts—Coins—Ornaments and Gems—Egyptian and Assyrian Remains—Rosetta Stone—Elgin Marbles, etc.—Madame Tussaud's—The Thames—Greenwich—Victoria Embankment—The Obelisk—Temperance—Taxes, etc.—Liverpool—Docks—Public Buildings—Streets.................................................................263

## CHAPTER XV.

### IRELAND.

Ireland—The Jaunting Car—Belfast—Dromore—Anticipations and Disappointment—The Old Cathedral—Grave by the Laggan—Statistics—An Excursion—Downpatrick—Newcastle—Rostrevor—Newry—Drogheda—The River Boyne—Dublin—Its People—Public Buildings—The Castle—Churches—Glasnevin—Kingston—Athlone, etc.—Condition of the Country—Tenant Farmers—Land League—The Irish People—Notes by the Way, etc.... 290

# SIGHTS AND SCENES IN EUROPE.

## CHAPTER I.

### THE OCEAN VOYAGE.

Departure—Life at Sea—The Horizon—Sunday—A Hymn—Sabbath Services—A Gale—Not a Hymn—Ocean Experiences—The Ocean—Its Teachings—Neptune—Amusements—Story of the "Eastern Monarch"—Capt. Johnson—Scotch Coast—Firth of Clyde—"How is Garfield?"—Passing the Customs—Ashore at Greenock.

"If not on board at 7 o'clock to-morrow morning you will get left," said the New York agent of the State Line Steamship Florida, as I purchased my ticket at the office on Broadway. I was careful to be on board an hour before that time, and as the bells of the city rang out the hour of seven the huge vessel quietly moved from the dock, the immense screw beginning its revolutions, to continue I hope till we reach the city of Glasgow. That the great ship with its valuable cargo and stores, and still more precious living freight, should start on its three thousand mile trip with the promptness of an express train surprised me. The leave takings were hardly observable, but few of the passengers residing in New York or its vicinity, and our departure was business-like, with but little suggestive of tears or romance. The magnitude and possibilities of my undertaking, however, impressed me seriously as soon as I discovered the ship to be in motion, and I felt myself a wanderer on the face of the earth, or rather, of the great deep. The man who can lightly assume the risk of a trip to Europe I do not envy, nor should I be surprised if his family were equally indifferent to his return.

Our sail out of New York Bay to Sandy Hook was like a river excursion, even the swell of the broad Atlantic was not unpleasant, and the passengers as they became acquainted exchanged congratulations on the prospect of a pleasant voyage. Ship life at its best, and with a calm sea, is wonderfully restful—nothing to do, and a total indisposition to doing anything. To kill time various games are resorted to on deck, but the voyager finds it difficult to interest himself and prefers lolling in an easy chair, gazing listlessly at the water, to be aroused occasionally by a school of porpoises or a passing ship.

We read of the "boundless ocean," and imagine a vast expanse of water reaching as far as the eye can see, and yet our ideas as to how much water is in sight may be very far from correct. Owing to the convexity of the earth's surface, the distance to the horizon is governed by the elevation of the observer. From the upper deck of an ocean steamer, with the eye twenty-five feet above the water, the distance is six miles, and the ship is apparently sailing day after day in the center of a small lake twelve miles in diameter, and this is all of the "boundless ocean" that can possibly be seen unless we climb higher. Were the eye six feet above the water the horizon would be three miles distant, and if thirty-two inches above the water the distance would be two miles.

There are twenty-two first-cabin passengers, among them an Irish lord, an Episcopal rector from New York, the president of a Methodist college and the chaplain of a New England reform school. The ladies are agreeable and intelligent, and some of them quite proficient in music. There is a convenient music room with piano, and when the sea is favorable we are entertained with sweet sounds. On Saturday evening it seemed most natural to attend choir meeting, and although an extra roll of the ship would occasionally unseat the pianist, I considered the meeting a success. The Sabbath opened most auspiciously, the weather was all that could be desired, and it was pleasant to observe that the passengers of all grades, as well as the ship's crew, had put on their best attire in honor of the day. During the morning hours I sat on deck watching the busy waves, their white crests dancing in the bright sunlight, and wrote in my note book a

HYMN FOR THE SEA.

Eternal Father, Sovereign Lord,
  Whose glory fills the skies,
To Thee, from all that dwell below,
  Let highest praise arise.

Thy hand the moving waters spread,
  The winds obey Thy will,
And ocean's troubled, heaving breast
  Thy mighty arm can still.

To Thee, we trust our feeble breath,
  Our ways are in Thy hand,
Thy watchful care will safely keep—
  Secure on sea as land.

Eternal Father, Sovereign Lord,
  Accept the praise we bring,
And when we stand on crystal sea
  A nobler song we'll sing.

At 11 o'clock we had Episcopal service in the cabin, to which all the passengers were summoned by the ringing of the ship's bell. Our rector from New York, a clerical looking man, appeared in "surplice and band" and read the beautiful Episcopal service from the English prayer book, furnished in quantities by the captain, careful however to Americanize it where it appeared to him necessary, and to interject a fervent prayer for the recovery of President Garfield. The sermon was appropriate, the choir did remarkably well, and the ocean conducted itself admirably. I call the rector's sermon appropriate because it had no reference to "the dangers by which we are surrounded." That congregation, far from home and friends, did not need to be told that there is but an iron plate between them and death, or that in case of fire most of them would perish, or that in crossing the Banks next day in a fog we might strike an iceberg and all go to the bottom. A narrow minded man might have considered it a glorious opportunity to deal out the "terrors of the Lord," and a very small man might have succeeded in frightening the timid ones almost out of their wits, but our genial rector did no such thing, and therefore I think his sermon was *singularly* appropriate to the occasion. In the afternoon we had Methodist service on deck, and in the evening an interesting praise meeting in the music room.

On Monday the wind had increased to a gale, and the large ship was tossed on the ocean as if a row boat, the waves dashing over the sides and keeping the decks constantly wet. Most of the passengers became sea sick. Very early in the storm I began to feel serious, and like a boy in trouble, I wanted to "go home." That being impossible I determined to reside permanently in Europe, if I lived to reach the other side, and in a short time did n't care a cent where I went or stayed. During semi-lucid intervals I took to scribbling rhyme. Should it seem to follow too closely some other lunatic's attempt in the same direction, I can only—like Dr. Lorimer—plead "saturation," as there was no conscious plagiarism in inditing the following, which is

### NOT A HYMN.

O, the sea, the silver sea!
Smiling like a winsome maiden,
Bearing hopes with joys o'erladen;
  O, the sea!

O, the sea, the noble sea!
Now its liquid waves are swelling,
Of its mighty conquests telling;
  O, the sea!

O, the sea, the merry sea!
Fun to see a fellow walking;
Well,—*I can't* - there's no use talking;
   O, the sea!

O, the sea, the awful sea!
Sudden pains my stomach retching,
As I pass, the hand rail catching;
   O, the sea!

\*     \*     \*     \*     \*

O, the sea, the horrid sea!
Worse than wine this cursed mocker—
Dinner gone to Jones' locker;
   O, the sea!

O, the sea, the cruel sea!
If on thee again a rover,
Hope some one will throw me over;
   O, the sea!

The stars are intended to indicate an intermission of five minutes, or less, to attend to an act of charity, popularly and humorously called at sea "feeding the fishes."

Ocean experiences have been often related, and some may think they have so far lost their interest by repetition that they should be omitted altogether. But the great American dailies, that reflect so truly the popular taste, do not reason in this way. They spare no expense to collect for their Saturday editions, by special reporters and by telegraph, the hangings of the previous day throughout the length and breadth of the great republic—and there is more sameness in hangings than in ocean voyages. The hero of the occasion always rests well the night before, and no matter how many or aggravated his crimes, graciously forgives everybody, invariably closing his pious valedictory with a general and cordial invitation to the lookers-on to meet him in the happy hunting grounds. Now in an ocean voyage the experiences, and the degrees of misery, are various. Sometimes the vessel pitches and sometimes it rolls, the most agreeable form of either being that which is absent. You seldom strike the deck twice at the same angle, and it is now the soup and now the coffee you receive in your bosom at the table. While sea sickness may, in most cases, present the same general features, there is a wonderful variety in the remedies employed. Among those recommended to me I may mention eating heartily and fasting, cathartics and emetics, homeopathic appo-morphia and allopathic blue-pill, sitting on deck and remaining in my berth, brandy and gruel, beef tea and salt pork, painting myself with collodion and wearing a liver pad!

The gymnastics practised on deck are surprising, but those performed in the state room are on the whole more difficult, and introduce, as the circus bills say, "novel and startling effects." Making your morning ablution holding on with one hand, and marking with your feet the segment of a circle around the corner where the wash basin is anchored, with all the variations which your cramped position imposes, is a severe test of piety. The effort to undress and stow yourself away on the rocking and pitching shelf where your nights are spent is a serious and sometimes difficult matter. The state room door and berth act as "buffers," between which you are tossed back and forth like a shuttlecock.

But there is one cause of discomfort that never ceases. That immense auger, the screw, began at New York to bore a hole to Glasgow, 3,000 miles distant. It revolves about fifty times a minute, and with a monotonous and exasperating regularity, giving a peculiar and disagreeable throb or pulsation to the whole ship. At night especially, with nothing to distract the attention, it is to the nervous a cause of great irritation. One of the dreariest of sounds is the wash of the sea against the ship's sides, as heard from the berths, with nothing but the iron plates between. Even the storm that sends the waves with powerful strokes as with a mighty hammer to break in the ship's sides, is a welcome relief from the monotonous swash of the ordinary sea.

There is nothing joyous or assuring in the ocean, however we may admire its ever changing forms and hues. It is the emblem of remorseless power, not of mercy or favor. The study of nature on land may leave impressions of the Divine goodness, but on the ocean, never. "Cruel as the grave" would be more forcible if rendered "cruel as the sea." The grave but furnishes a cherished resting place for the remains of our loved ones. The sea receives their living forms in its chill embrace to engulph them forever. "Mother earth" seems the natural home for the remains of her sons, but what so dreary and repulsive as a burial at sea? Its winds recall not nodding branches or rustling leaves; they bear no fragrance of woods and flowers. Theirs to sound the requiem of departed hopes, or

"Mock the cry
Of some strong swimmer in his agony"

However it may be with sailors, there is with the ordinary landsman an ever present sense of danger. He looks down through a grating on deck thirty or forty feet and discovers that the bottom of the ship is a mass of fire, confined in furnaces it is true, but still fire; and grimy and sweating men ascending from the fiery region to cool themselves remind him of possible danger from that element. The boats swung so as to be lowered in the least possible time suggest danger by water. Indeed, every precautionary arrangement, and they are numerous, as well as every special care on the part of officers and crew speak of possible peril. Poets may invest the sea with all sorts of foolish romance, to the great deception of landsmen, but the only real comfort of an ocean voyage is its successful termination. The man who wrote of "a home on the rolling deep" must, if not an arrant hypocrite, have been brought up in a poor house or under the eagle eye of a step mother with more bantlings of her own than she could care for. "Home" and the "rolling deep" are the antipodes of each other.

Neptune I am afraid must look with contempt on the mortals that cross his domain; the tottering step, woe-begone look, and forebodings of danger that affect the greater number must give him a poor opinion of human nature. And then, if he keeps a stenographer—if all the solemn vows made at sea are recorded! Good heavens what a possibility! As a party interested, and on behalf of all that "go down to the sea in ships," I protest against the jurisdiction, and competency of the record—on shore. I am afraid the Irishman who promised the Virgin to devote a large sum to charitable uses if safely landed, and when reminded by a companion of his promise replied, "An' faith the Vargin Mairy 'll nivir ketch me at say agin," is but a type of the majority.

On shipboard many expedients are resorted to, to interest and amuse. During the fine weather, games of "shovel board" and "ring toss" were played on deck. Since that time, music, recitations, riddles and story-telling have relieved somewhat the dreariness of the cabin. A story told by a lady from Chatham, Ontario, interested me very much.

"In 1858 the Eastern Monarch left England for Australia, with two hundred and fifty emigrant passengers, of all ages. At sea the vessel was discovered to be on fire, and on an ocean where- for the preceding ten days not a vessel had been seen. A panic ensued, the sailors making for the boats, with the intention of deserting the ship and leaving the emigrants to their fate. The captain coolly presented his pistols, with the emphatic declaration that the first man who attempted to lower a boat would be a dead man on the spot, and that *his* orders must be implicitly obeyed.

Order was restored, the hatches battened down to confine the fire, and everything possible done for its extinguishment, but to no purpose. It was the third day since the fire had been discovered and the flames were bursting from their confinement. A sailor on the look-out reported no sail in sight. In this, their great extremity, an old woman of seventy years exclaimed, "I see a ship!" and sure enough a distant vessel greeted their eyes, and proved to be the ship Merchantman from England for India with troops. She came to their aid, and every passenger was removed in safety from the ship, which was now in flames. After this it was thirteen days before the Merchantman sighted another vessel."

The lady who told us the story was especially interested in it from the fact that her son was at the time second officer on board the Merchantman. After we had in turn commended the noble conduct of the captain who stood so bravely by his emigrant passengers, one of the stewards, who had listened to the story, quietly remarked, "That man is Captain Johnson of our ship." This proved to be true; our social kind hearted captain was the hero of the Eastern Monarch. Queen Victoria gave him a gold watch, and the Royal Humane society a gold medal. Frank Leslie published his portrait, but as he was at that time a young man and his picture in the illustrated weekly represented him as a gray-beard, he rather holds a grudge against the publisher.

For six days we had clouds and fog, and during all that time our captain was unable to catch a glimpse of the sun. Running by what is called "dead reckoning" is not considered one of the exact sciences, and it was a great relief when we sighted the lighthouse on Tory Island, on the north-west coast of Ireland. Passing between the Irish Island of Rathlin and a Scotch promontory known as the

Mull of Cantire, we entered the Firth of Clyde. Finer scenery is seldom found than betwen the Island of Arran and Greenock, and as we passed up the Firth the morning sun shone brightly on the hills, mountains, rocks, bays, inlets, towns and villas on each side. Among the towns may be mentioned Ardrossan, Millport, Dunoon, Greenock, Rothsay and Kilcraggan. The Islands of Arran, Bute, Cumbrae, and others of less note were passed. I was much amused by a story, told by an old Scotch gentleman, of the pastor of the church at Cumbrae, who was accustomed to pray for his little parish as follows: "God bless little Cumbrae, big Cumbrae, Bute *and the adjacent Islands of Great Britain and Ireland.*"

A pilot came on board, a staid-looking Scotchman, and was greeted by a hundred voices in chorus, "How's Garfield?" "What's the latest?" "How's the President, is he alive?" etc. He seemed puzzled, but looked calmly on the noisy, gesticulating crowd, and spoke not. Some one seized a newspaper that protruded from his pocket and it proved to be a Glasgow morning paper, but contained no news from the sufferer at Washington. All that could be obtained from the owner of the paper in reply to our eager inquiries was, "I hav'na heerd; he is'na deed that I knaw o';" and with this the anxious but somewhat disgusted crowd of Americans, who had for ten days discussed earnestly and apprehensively the President's condition, were obliged to be content. "We know just as much now as if we had all the morning telegrams in the New York papers to select from," remarked a clergyman of a satirical turn of mind. "Where ignorance is Bliss"—began a young M. D. from Chicago, but the threatening looks of the passengers warned him that punning is out of place on shipboard.

We anchored in the river opposite Greenock, and were soon visited by a tug, evidently on official business. The passengers were requested to place their baggage in line and open it. I suggested to some of the passengers who had but seldom appeared at the abundantly supplied table, that probably the Company was about to reimburse us for the lost meals by sending the steward to place a handsome present in each man's baggage. At this moment a man of bustling importance approached, and pointing to my valise which headed the line, and without being introduced or making any inquiry as to my moral or social status in the United States, remarked in a tone of peremptory inquiry: "Any liquors or tobacco in that bag?" I was so surprised that such a question should be asked *me*, that I presume I hesitated before giving a decided "No." This encouraged him, and seizing my valise he gave the contents a good shaking up. He looked disappointed, and made a chalk-mark on the outside, meaning I suppose "no use," to deter other fellows who were looking for liquors and tobacco from trying the same game. "Passing the customs" this ceremony is called in Scotland.

On stepping ashore at Greenock the first person to accost me was a big barefooted Scotchwoman, with a basket of very large red gooseberries on her arm. She picked out the biggest and ripest berry and handed it to me, saying in the vernacular of the country: "Tak yin sir, thir gude." I was so overcome by her unexpected hospitality that I at once invested in the fruit.

Greenock contains a population of about 60,000, has a fine wharf, and is the seat of a large iron manufacturing and ship building trade. The very largest vessels find it inconvenient, though possible, to navigate the Clyde above Greenock, and many of them stop here. It is twenty-three miles to Glasgow by railroad.

## CHAPTER II.

GLASGOW—BIRTH PLACE OF BURNS.

Glasgow—Cathedral—Necropolis—University—Public Buildings and Parks— Streets — Prices — Rail to Ayr — Burns' Cottage — Kirk Alloway — Tam O'Shanter—Mungo's Well — Bridge of Doon —"Bonny Doon"— Burns' Monument—Museum—Highland Mary—The Kirk-yard—The "Twa Brigs"—Burns—His Writings—Whittier's Estimate.

Glasgow has a population of about half a million, and dates from a Culdee cell built by St. Mungo about the year 560. It is chiefly on the north side of the river Clyde, which runs through the city, and is about three miles in length from East to West, and two miles in width, if we estimate the compact portions. The suburbs, however, stretch much farther in every direction. Its principal business street, Argyle, and its continuation, Trongate street, are well built, as is indeed all the business part of the city. The building material used is a light colored sandstone easily polished and carved, and it has a fine and substantial appearance. St. George's Square, containing the Post-office, Bank of Scotland, and several hotels, was the place I first visited. It contains monuments to Queen Victoria, Prince Albert, Sir Walter Scott, Sir Robert Peel, Sir John Moore, Lord Clyde, James Watt, Robert Burns, and David Livingstone.

In Glasgow, a great deal may be seen by riding on the outside of the "tram cars" (street cars). The intelligent people you ride with are able and very willing to afford any desired information in regard to all matters of local interest.

The cathedral, founded in 1136, is built on the reputed

## THE CATHEDRAL.

site of St. Mungo's cell on the highest ground in the city. It affords one of the finest views of the valley of the Clyde, and I could not help admiring the good taste exhibited by the saint in securing such an eligible location for his cell. Entering the cathedral I was impressed with its great size, the massive style of architecture, and the magnificence of its windows, which are said to contain the most brilliant display of stained glass to be found in Great Britian. There are over eighty of these windows, and at least half of them are thirty feet high, each giving a Bible story in beautiful colored pictures from designs by eminent artists. The cathedral is over three hundred feet long and about sixty feet wide, and owing to its immense size the greater part of it is unoccupied. It was, of course, before the Reformation used for Catholic worship, but is now used by the Established Church of Scotland. The great crypt is one hundred and twenty-five feet long and was formerly used for religious worship and is spoken of as "one of the finest specimens of architecture in Great Britain." I found it difficult however in the "dim religious light" which is permitted to enter through its windows to take in its fine points. It was used for burial purposes, and contained the tombs and monuments of many prelates and high dignitaries of the church, but at the Reformation these, being regarded as "signs of idolatry," were destroyed by the fanatics of the day. The effigy of a single bishop, lacking a head, however, is about all that remains of these works of art.

On a high hill in the rear of the cathedral rises the Necropolis, a cemetery for Glasgow's honored dead. The hill side is terraced in winding walks rising above each other to the summit, and its elegant and costly monuments are so crowded the appearance is rather that of an immense marble factory than a cemetery; indeed from below you see nothing but granite and marble. Among its monuments are those of Dr. Dick, Sheridan Knowles and Motherwell, the poet. There is also near the summit a fine Corinthian shaft and statue to John Knox, and on the shaft is this inscription : "When laid in the ground, the regent said, 'There lieth he who never feared the face of man, who was often threatened with dag and dagger, yet hath ended his days in peace and honor.'" Some of the more imposing and gaudy monuments are of those who merely "made money" in Glasgow, but this defect and misfortune may be observed in cemeteries in all countries.

The university is an immense structure, and though occupied for some time is hardly completed yet. I shall not attempt to describe it. I visited the celebrated Hunterian Museum in a part of the building, filled with objects of interest in science, arts and literature, also the library containing 300,000 volumes. I came away with an overpowering sense of the vast amount of knowledge unattainable, and of the multitude of books that will never be read. One of the finest buildings in Glasgow is the Royal Exchange, costing a quarter of a million dollars, in front of which stands a fine equestrian statue of the Duke of Wellington. The Royal Bank, Mechanics' Institution, some of the hotels and nearly all the churches are fine buildings. The Queen's Park and Kelvin Park are handsomely laid out and well kept. In Kelvin Park I had the great pleasure of hearing an open-air concert by the band of the 71st Highlanders. From three to five thousand persons, mostly of the middle and poorer classes, were in attendance. The music was very fine, especially the Scottish airs. At intervals during the performance, four pipers armed with that instrument of torture, the bag-pipes, with drone, promenaded through the crowd to the great delight of young Scotland.

While the streets of Glasgow during business hours present a busy appearance, being almost as crowded as Chicago or New York, the crowds move much more slowly than in American cities—indeed nobody seems to be in a great hurry about anything. The stores are not open till nine o'clock, and thèn the blinds are removed as if it were more a matter of habit than with any expectation of immediate results. At six o'clock the stores are closed, which in this latitude at this time of the year is full three hours before dark. Great good taste is displayed in the arrangement of goods in the windows. The grocery stores, where one would least expect it, are especially noticeable in this regard. The liquor shops are numerous and do not seem to lack customers. I have been amused in reading the street signs to find "Bread Factory," "Leather Emporium," "Millinery Ware-rooms," etc., but most surprised at finding a "Boot and Shoe repairing *factory*." I find, however, that I am in a land of cheapness. "Black your boots for a penny! "Carry your luggage for a penny!" were some of the street sounds I heard, and when my traveling companion left his measure for a black cloth coat, (ready the next day at the same hour) price two pounds two shillings, about $10.15, I felt as if it would be a good thing to buy a stock of clothing in Scotland. The coat looks well and is as the owner says, "good enough to preach in."

Being in the land of Burns, in company with a Methodist minister from Louisiana, and the chaplain of a New England reform school, I took an early train to visit the poet's birthplace. A finer day could hardly be imagined. The sun's rays were softened by a slight haze, and the air was mild yet bracing. Our destination by rail was the town of Ayr, forty miles distant. In four miles we pass Crookton Castle, now in ruins, once inhabited by Mary Queen of Scots. Three miles farther is the city of Paisley with 50,000 population, and noted for its shawls and cotton thread. A short distance from Paisley is the Oak of

Elderslie, under which William Wallace hid from the English forces. At Kilwinning Junction is seen the ruins of an old Priory, the founders of which are said to have introduced Free-masonry into Scotland. We next reach the town of Irvine, well built, with a population of 8,000. Burns lived here once, and here Robert Bruce surrendered to the English army under Percy. A short distance from Irvine we pass the Castle of Dundonald, and soon reach the village of Troon, a watering place on the lower Clyde. On reaching Ayr, we declined the offer of a good carriage at a moderate price, preferring to make the further pilgrimage of two and a half miles on foot. The road was excellent, and our way lay through verdant fields and well kept grounds.

We soon reached the venerable building where the poet was born. It is a very low one-story stone cottage with thatched roof, and consists simply of a "but and ben," or room and kitchen. The bed stands in an alcove off the kitchen, and a large card suspended over it warns visitors not to "jump into the bed," just as if anybody would think of catching the divine *afflatus* in that way! The kitchen is unaltered; the old fire-place with its internal arrangements, and the griddle on which the "scones" and oat cake were baked, are still preserved. The old clock, made in Ayr, still stands in the kitchen. Burns' candlestick, and a manuscript copy of his poems in the author's hand-writing are also exhibited. The room adjoining is, after the manner of such places, used as a salesroom for mementoes of Burns, made mostly from wood cut on the banks of the Doon. I was very thankful that the kitchen had been spared from such desecration.

Our walk from Ayr,

"Auld Ayr, wham ne'er a town surpasses
For honest men and bonny lasses,"

was on the very road travelled by Tam O'Shanter on "his grey mare Meg," that eventful night, when

> "The wind blew as 'twad blawn its last;
> The rattling showers rose on the blast;
> The speedy gleam the darkness swallow'd;
> Loud, deep, and lang, the thunder bellow'd;
> That night, a child might understand
> The de'il had business on his hand."

About half a mile from Burns' cottage, we reach "Alloway's auld haunted kirk." The building is roofless and fast going to decay. There is a bell cote on the gable, and the old bell yet remains. We looked through the front window as Tam had done, and saw, not a witches dance, but a collection of shovels and an old wheelbarrow almost covered with rank weeds. It required unquestioning faith in the poet to suppose that the little church afforded room for more than one such dancer as "Cutty-sark," and when she "lap and flang," his satanic majesty, who played the bagpipes on that occasion, must have been content to occupy a corner. The fact that he practises on the bagpipes is a significant one, and as such, I commend it to theologians. While quarreling about fire and brimstone, have they ever carefully considered the possibilities of an eternity of bagpipes! In view of such a contingency, might it not be prudent for the "Liberals" to accept, as a compromise, the orthodox arrangement?

Among the places described by Burns, on the road from Ayr to the Doon, is the well

> "Whare Mungo's mither hang'd hersel."

It is within a few rods of Kirk Alloway, and though but mentioned by the poet as one of the places that Tam passed on his midnight ride, is fenced in and exhibited for a small admission fee!—an arrangement worthy of Niagara Falls.

We continued on to the bridge of Doon, about fifty rods from the kirk, and where Tam's ride culminated in the peculiar disaster to his mare. It is a high, narrow, and inconvenient structure, its center being occupied by a row of posts, permitting only travellers on foot to pass. Sitting above its keystone we recited and laughed over the incidents narrated in "Tam O'Shanter," the best known, and most popular of Burns' poems. The Doon is a small stream, and from the loveliness of its scenery, is well entitled to the name given it by Burns, "Bonny Doon." I descended to the water's edge, picked a few pebbles from the bed of the stream, and had a leisurely stroll

"Among the bonny winding banks
Where Doon rins wimplin' clear."

On the banks of the Doon and not far from the bridge is Burns' Monument, erected in 1820 It is a circular structure, in the Grecian style, and about sixty feet high. The grounds cover about two acres, and are finely kept. In a grotto near the monument, are the original and justly celebrated figures of Tam O'Shanter and Souter Johnny, in freestone, by the sculptor Thom. Every detail of garb, even to patches and shoe-strings appears, and the perfect abandon of the pair, as they sit with filled mugs, enjoying their toddy, and pledging each other, cannot be described. In a circular room in the monument is a fine marble bust of the poet by Park, and a number of very interesting relics. —Nanse Tinnock's "quaich," or beer measure; rings containing Burns' hair; the wedding ring of his "bonnie Jean," &c. But that which was to me of most interest was the Bible presented by Burns to his beloved Highland Mary. Their parting was the subject of one of his finest poems.

"Ye banks, and braes, and streams around
    The castle o' Montgomery,
Green be your woods, and fair your flowers,
    Your waters never drumlie !
There simmer first unfauld her robes,
    And there the langest tarry;
For there I took the last fareweel
    O' my sweet Highland Mary.

Mary was a servant in the house of Col. Montgomery, and Burns' attachment for her seems to have been the strongest and purest of his life. He was engaged to be married to her, but previous to their wedding Mary determined to pay a visit to her friends in another part of Scotland. On a May Sunday morning, each standing on a different side of a small stream, they bathed their hands in the water, and, holding a Bible between them, swore eternal constancy They never met again, as Mary was taken ill on her journey and died. It was on the anniversary of her death he wrote what is considered the noblest of all his poems "To Mary in Heaven."

> "Thou ling'ring star with less'ning ray,
> That lovest to greet the early morn,
> Again thou usher'st in the day
> My Mary from my soul was torn.
> O Mary! dear departed shade !
> Where is thy place of blissful rest?
> See'st thou thy lover lowly laid?
> Hear'st thou the groans that rend his breast?"

The Bible I have mentioned as in the museum of the monument, is the one used at parting. On the inside of the cover is, written by Burns and signed with his Masonic mark, "And ye shall not swear by my name falsely—I am the Lord." To the fly leaf has been pinned a long lock of Mary's golden hair.

Returning towards Ayr; we spent an hour in the burial ground of Kirk Alloway. The old tombstones are numerous, and the inscriptions quaint. I reproduce one, that of Miller Goudie, who formerly lived in the Burns cottage.

> "For fórty years it was his lot
> To show the poet's humble cot;
> And, somꝑtimes laughin', somètimes sobbin',
> Told his last interview with Robin:
> A quiet, civil, blythesome body,
> Without a foe, was Miller Goudie."

The enduring fame given to the place by Burns, and the large number of persons who visit it daily, has led many of the wealthy families in the vicinity to use it as a burial place, the old and the new presenting a rather unpleasant contrast. The grave of Burns' father is marked by a plain stone of modern date, the inscription being that written by the poet:

> " O ye whose cheek the tear of pity stains,
> Draw near with pious reverence, and attend!
> Here lie the loving husband's dear remains,
> The tender father and the generous friend;
> The pitying heart that felt for human woe;
> The dauntless heart that fear'd no human pride;
> The friend of man, to vice alone a foe;
> ' For even his failings leaned to virtue's side.' "

We walked back to Ayr. It is a seaport on the lower Clyde, and has 18,000 inhabitants. The weekly auction sale of stock was in progress, and while we looked on, a large number of sheep were sold, mostly ewes of medium size, the price averaging $7 to $8 each. Some of the yards contained the celebrated Ayrshire breed of cattle, but I saw none sold. Being "market day," the streets were full of Scotch farmers and laborers and their families. The streets are paved and wonderfully clean, and quite as much used by those on foot, as the sidewalks, and were largely occupied by gossipers. It seemed as if everybody was out doors and glad to see everybody else, making frequent adjournments to the whiskey shops a matter of course, as drinking seems almost universal in Scotland.

The bridges remain as when Burns wrote his poem of the "Twa Brigs." The old one looks ancient, is narrow, and used for pedestrians only. Its dilapidation reminds one of the contemptuous question, put by the "New Brig:"

> " Will your poor narrow footpath of a street—
> Where twa wheelbarrows tremble when they meet—
> Your ruin'd, formless bulk o' stane and lime,
> Compare wi' bonny brigs o' modern time?"

The new bridge looks substantial, and not at all likely to justify the stinging retort of the "Auld Brig."

> "Conceited gowk! puff'd up wi' windy pride!
> This mony a year I've stood the flood and tide;
> And though wi' crazy eild I'm sair forfairn
> I'll be a brig when ye're a shapeless cairn!"

Recalling some of his poems among the scenes where they were written, one cannot help admiring Burns' wonderful genius as shown in his truthfulness to nature. His muse did not sing of Alpine hills or coral strands, of plumed knights or ladies fair, of gorgeous palaces or kingly pageants. The gently flowing Doon, the ruined mouse's nest, the wounded hare, the daisy uprooted by his plowshare, and the familiar scenes of every-day peasant life, were his themes, and have made his name immortal. The versifier who imagines he could do wonders, if only a subject worthy of his pen presented itself, may study with profit the writings of Burns. The "unco guid" have found it difficult to see any merit in him, and it must be admitted that his failings did not lean to virtue's side. Although a lover of the social glass, he was never a drunkard, indeed no more intemperate than the minister or elder of the period. The immorality of his poems, judged by our modern standards, is undeniable; and yet was not a matter of remark among the religionists of his time. It was his heresy and irreverance they complained of. The Calvinists of his day could ill brook his "Holy Willie's Prayer."

> "O Thou, wha in the heavens dost dwell
> Wha, as it pleases best thysel,
> Sends ane to heaven, and ten to hell,
>     A' for thy glory,
> And no for ony guid or ill
>     They've done afore thee!
>
> \* \* \* \* \* \* \*
>
> When frae my mither's womb I fell,
> Thou mi ht hae plunged me in hell,
> To gnash my gums, to weep and wail,
>     In burnin' lake
> Whare damned devils roar and yell
>     Chain'd to a stake."

Nor did the church at Mauchline care to have "Willie's" morals so pointedly assailed in the same poem, as he was a prominent elder, although he died in the ditch, in a drunken debauch, some years later. The religion of the time consisted largely of a rigid and austere theology, and hair-splitting, and heresy hunting were favorite pursuits. Burns wielded a free lance, and while deprecating his own weakness and inconsistency, struck heavy blows at the formalism and lack of good morals in the church.

"God knows, I'm no the thing I should be,
Nor am I even the thing I could be,
But twenty times I rather would be
An atheist clean,
Than under gospel colors hid be
Just for a screen.

\* \* \* \* \* \*

" All hail, Religion! maid divine!
Pardon a muse sae mean as mine,
Wha in her rough imperfect line,
Thus daurs to name thee;
To stigmatise false friends of thine
Can ne'er defame thee.

Had Burns been better appreciated by his generation, it is possible his course of life might have been different, and English literature enriched with many other products of his wonderful genius. Petted and feted by the Scottish aristocracy as a new wonder, only to be abandoned for the next novelty, a hopeless struggle with poverty crushed his proud spirit, till, at the early age of 37, death released him from the contest. It is but just to the English government to say that they had bestowed on him an office in the excise—with the munificent salary of $350 a year. A noble mausoleum rises above his grave, and expensive monuments have been erected to his memory, the cost of one of which would have relieved the living Burns from many sorrows.

Our own Whittier, purest of men and poets, has I think happily and justly estimated the character and writings of

## WHITTIER'S ESTIMATE OF BURNS. 33

Burns, and I close this record of a day spent at his birthplace and among the scenes he loved, by giving it to the reader.

> " Let those who never erred forget
> His worth, in vain bewailings;
> Sweet soul of song!—I own my debt
> Uncancelled by his failings!

\* \* \* \* \* \* \*

> " But who his human heart has laid
> To nature's bosom nearer?
> Who sweetened toil like him, or paid
> To love a tribute dearer?

> " Through all his tuneful art how strong
> The human feeling gushes!
> The very moonlight of his song
> Is warm with smiles and blushes.

> " Give lettered pomp to teeth of time
> So ' Bonnie Doon ' but tarry;
> Blot out the epic's stately rhyme,
> But spare his ' Highland Mary!' "

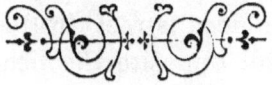

## CHAPTER III.

### EDINBURGH.

Edinburgh—Scott's Monument—The Castle—Regalia of Scotland—Mons Meg—Barracks—St. Giles—Jenny Geddes—Parliament House—Engine—John Knox's House—The Cannongate—Streets and Closes—Holyrood Abbey—Holyrood Palace—Gallery of Portraits—Audience Chamber—Queen's Bedroom—Supper Room—The Grassmarket—Greyfriars' Churchyard—The New Town—Antiquarian Gallery—Calton Hill—The View—Leith—Newhaven Fishwives—Scotch Women—Business Habits.

Edinburgh has a population of over 200,000 and is one of the most interesting and picturesque cities in Europe. It is built on two ridges of hills, the castle and old town being on the highest. It has been called the Modern Athens, but whether for scholastic or topographical reasons I do not know; it is certain, however, that the immense rock on which the castle stands, was admirably fitted by nature for an Acropolis. Formerly a lake or marsh existed between the old and new towns, but it has been drained and laid out in beautiful gardens along the margin of which lies Princes street, the finest modern street in the city. My hotel is on Princes street, and opposite the beautiful monument to Sir Walter Scott, made familiar by prints and engravings to most Americans. This fine monument is erected on a granite platform about thirty feet each way, and is in the form of an open spire, about two hundred feet high. The style is florid gothic, every device which that order will permit of having been used in its ornamentation. But one side of Princes street is built on, and looking from my window across the gardens, the castle, St. Giles' Cathedral and the lofty and antique buildings of the old town rise in picturesque and imposing irregularity.

## EDINBURGH CASTLE.

It is said that a Roman fortification once occupied the site of the present castle. A part of the wall still remaining is ascribed to Edwin, a Northumbrian Prince, who erected here a fortress known as Edwin's "Brugh," or stronghold. The present castle was, however, mainly built in the 15th century. Previous to that time a chapel, which still remains, was built by the pious Queen Margaret, who died in the castle A. D. 1093. This chapel is small, I should say not more than ten by sixteen feet, but is interesting and finely preserved. In olden time, from its isolated position on a high precipitous rock, the castle must have been regarded as a place of great strength.

> "The ponderous wall and massy bar,
> Grim rising o'er the rugged rock,
> Have oft withstood assailing war,
> And oft repelled the invader's shock."

It has furnished many stirring pages for the historian and scenes of romantic interest for the novelist. When in possession of Edward II. it was surprised and captured by thirty young Scotchmen, who at night climbed the almost perpendicular rock, guided by one of their number who had learned to make the ascent to visit his sweetheart. In 1341 it was again captured from the English, this time in broad daylight and by stratagem. The Scotch general caused a cart loaded with wine to be sent to the garrison, which the driver managed to overturn in the gateway so the gate could not be closed. The Scotch soldiers, who were concealed near the castle, rushed in and effected its capture. The old sally port is shown which Dundee climbed to have a conference with the Duke of Gordon, to persuade him to espouse the cause of James I., at a time when a convention was in session at the Parliament house near by, to settle the crown on William and Mary. It was in reference to this exploit of Dundee's that the popular song of "Bonnie Dundee" was written.

"Dundee he is mounted, he rides up the street,
The bells they ring backward, the drums they are beat;
But the Provost, douce man! said, ' Just e'en let him be,
For the town is weel rid o' that deil o' Dundee.' "

Over the portcullis gate is the old state prison where have pined many of Scotland's bravest nobles and chiefs. The grated window of the small room occupied by the Marquis of Argyle the night previous to his execution, is pointed out.

For a long series of years the castle was used as a palace as well as stronghold. It was here that Mary, Queen of Scots, resided when her son, afterwards James I. of England, was born. The room where the event occurred is shown to visitors, also the window through which the infant prince, when eight days old, was let down two hundred and fifty feet to the pavement below, to be secretly conveyed to Stirling Castle. The old oak ceiling remains, also an interesting inscription on the wall, placed there by James I. on his first visit to Scotland after his accession to the British throne. Like everything pertaining to the unfortunate Mary, it possesses interest, and is said to have been composed by her on the birth of her son.

"Lord Jesu Chryst that crownit was with Thornse
Preserve the birth quhais Badyie heir is borne,
And send hir Sonne successive to reigne stille
Lang in this Realme, if that it be Thy will
Als grant O Lord quhatever of Hir proseed
Be to Thy Glorie, Hone and Prais sobied."

The room is now used for the sale of trinkets, as mementoes of the queen and castle, and as the almost sacred associations of the place are supposed to attach to them, about four times the usual price is asked.

In the upper part of the same wing of the building is the crown room where the ancient regalia of Scotland are kept. They were discovered in an old oak chest, exhibited in the room, in 1818, having been concealed for over one hundred years. The crown is that of Robert Bruce, made in the 14th century, and used by the kings and queens of Scotland since that time. The sword of state was presented to James IV. by Pope Julius II. The sceptre is supposed to belong to the reign of James V. The gold collar and badge of the Order of the Garter were presented by Queen Elizabeth to James VI. of Scotland. The coronation ring of Charles I. is also among the crown jewels.

Near St. Margaret's Chapel stands the famous gun known as "Mons Meg," supposed to have been used at the siege of Mons in France, in 1476. It was injured in 1682 in firing a salute to the Duke of York ; was removed in 1684 to the Tower of London, and restored to the castle in 1820 by George IV. The bore is twenty inches in diameter.

The modern barracks and officers' quarters were built in 1796, during the heat of the French war, and detract very much from the appearance of the castle as viewed from the outside. Sir Walter Scott compared them to a cotton mill. By the articles of the Union between England and Scotland, the castle must be kept fortified. It now contains about 600 soldiers, of a Scotch regiment, here known as "Kilties," from their wearing the Highland kilt and going bare-kneed. I saw about 500 of them on parade to-day, each man exhibiting ten to twelve inches—extending above and below the knee—bare! The weather is such that I have on my warmest underclothing and wear an overcoat. Our fashions may be much more ridiculous but hardly so uncomfortable.

From the castle the principal thoroughfare of the old town leads directly to Holyrood Palace and Abbey, distant about a mile. Leaving the esplanade we enter this thoroughfare at the Lawn-market, and passing into High Street reach St. Giles' Cathedral, founded in 854 A. D., but several times rebuilt. St. Giles was born in Greece, but his arm bone—considered a precious treasure—having been presented to the city, he was accepted as Edinburgh's patron saint. The arm has long since disappeared, and at the beginning of the Reformation his cherished image was taken from the church, ignominiously ducked in a pond by a mob, and afterwards burned. St. Giles' is cruciform, and a very large building. After the Reformation it was made to accommodate four congregations, and was used for the meetings of the General Assembly of the Church of Scotland. It was here, in 1643, that the Solemn League and Covenant was sworn to and signed by Parliament and General Assembly. It became the parish church of Edinburgh, and in it John Knox, its pastor, preached those stirring sermons that have become a part of the history of Scotland.

An incident that occurred in St. Giles' has often been told, and had at the time a wonderful influence in arousing popular sentiment against Prelacy, and effecting its overthrow. In 1637 an attempt was made to introduce the liturgy of Laud into Scotland, by authority, and the Bishop of Edinburgh had just asked the Dean to read the "Collect for the day," when a choleric Scotch woman named Jenny Geddes, exclaimed, "Colic, said ye? the De'il colic the wame (belly) o' ye; wud ye say mass at my lug?" Raising her stool, she sent it flying at the Dean's head, who is said to have barely escaped it. The stool I have seen at the Museum. It is a medium-sized camp stool; and is duly venerated as one of the practical arguments used in the overthrow of Prelacy and liturgies in Scotland. In front of the cathedral stands the shaft of the old Edinburgh Cross, recently restored, on what is supposed to be its original site; and on the north-west corner the site of the old Tolbooth, or "Heart of Mid-Lothian," is marked by the figure of a heart on the pavement.

In the rear of St. Giles' is the former Parliament House, used since the Union with England by the Law Courts.

The old Parliament Hall is about fifty by one hundred and twenty feet, and contains many fine pictures and statues The original oak ceiling, with its magnificently carved beams and panels, resting on curiously sculptured corbels, still remains. In Parliament Square is a fine statue of Charles II., erected by the city in 1685. This site had been selected and a model prepared for a statue of Cromwell, but the Reformation changed the plans of the worthy Council. With that lofty fidelity to principle that marked the Vicar of Bray, whose religious creed—during the troublous times when England was alternately Catholic and Protestant— was, to " live and die Vicar of Bray,"they hastened to put away the model of the grim Puritan, and erected this statue of the "Merry Monarch."

As I stepped out of the Parliament House, a machine whose use I did not at first comprehend, accompanied by a half-dozen men in uniform, halted in the square. The presence of a suction hose, and continued efforts to uncover a hole in the street, indicated that it must be a fire-engine. In style and finish it would hardly compare with the ordinary American mowing machine. There was a total absence of shining brass and nickel, and a chimney of about stove-pipe form and dimensions furnished an exit for the smoke. I learned that it was a new machine, to be tried in the presence of some officials who were to decide on its merits. The length of time consumed in preparations made one thankful that it was only an exhibition, and not a fire. Once at work the little machine surprised me by its efficiency. If equal in size to the gorgeous affairs that help to swell American tax-rolls, they would have nothing to boast of except their shine—and cost. The fire-engine, however, is not so prominent an affair here as in the United States. How little ground can be found in our oldest cities that has not been burned over at least once during the last hundred years; and yet in Edinburgh I pass through street after street, two to three hundred years old, with not a single modern building to indicate the occurrence of a fire during that time.

Near St. Giles', on the opposite side of the street, is the house of John Knox. It was built in the year 1490, for a Scotch nobleman, whose coat of arms is carved in the wood work of some of the rooms, and is remarkably well preserved. Over the door is the inscription, "Lufe God abuf all, and ye nychtbour as yiself." On the south front is the place of most interest to visitors, his small study—I should say about 8x12 feet. Here were the purposes formed and the plans laid which more than all else revolutionized Scotland. The rooms contain many pictures of Knox, Archbishop Beton's pastoral staff, ancient thumb-screws, the martyr's iron girdle by which they were confined to the stake, and the famous gag applied to scolding women. A careful examination convinced me that this last would effectually answer the purpose for which it was constructed, *while in use*. In one of the front rooms is shown the preaching window from which, when no longer able to go to his church, Knox addressed his parishioners who stood in the street. Notwithstanding his reported severity of character, Knox is said to have been of an exceedingly social disposition, and like ministers of that period, fond of what were called the "good things of this life." A few days before his death, he ordered his attendant to broach a cask of wine which he had received as a present, that he might share it with some friends, saying he was "not like to tarry till it be finished." He died in the principal room of the house in 1572, and was buried in the churchyard of St. Giles'. A stone in the pavement in front of the Parliament House, with the initials "I. K." marks the spot, and is the only public memorial of Knox I have found in the city!

Continuing down High Street we reach Cannongate, a street formerly occupied by the wealthy and aristocratic canons of Holyrood. The houses present, if possible, a more antique appearance than those of High Street, and their peculiar architecture indicates that at one period this was the court end of the city. Every house has a history, and over the doors the old armorial bearings are yet visible; indeed, Cannongate has been called "Scottish history fossilized." The Cannongate Tolbooth is claimed as a specimen of Scottish architecture, and must have once been considered an imposing building. In front of it, at the east end, is an old stone pillar to which slanderers and scolds were fastened by iron collars.

The streets between the castle and Holyrood are very narrow, and the buildings generally quite high. Though now dilapidated and mean, they were formerly the residences of the proudest of Scotland's nobles and chivalry, and many a kingly and knightly pageant has passed through these narrow streets. They are now mostly used for small stores, cheap boarding houses and tenements, whose swarming occupants protrude through the windows to gaze listlessly at the passers-by. On each side of the principal thoroughfare are entry-ways, leading into what are known as closes, in the rear of the buildings that front on the street. These old closes are historic ground, and associated with them are many important incidents in Scottish history. The White Horse Close is mentioned in "Waverley" as the head-quarters of the Pretender's officers. Strichen's Close is noted as the residence of the "Bluidy Mackenzie," King's advocate under Charles II. Lady Stair's Close, in which occurred some strange incidents told by Scott in "My Aunt Margaret's Mirror." Dunbar's Close, head-quarters of Cromwell after the battle of Dunbar. But a history of these old places would involve a history of the city, if not of Scotland. Prominent literary men have had their quarters in these closes. In St. James' Court, Boswell entertained Dr. Johnson, before making the tour of the Hebrides; in Riddle's Close, Hume wrote most of his "History of England;" in Baxter's Close, Burns had his lodgings, and in Panmure Close Adam Smith resided.

These closes are now mostly mere rookeries, and contain the very dregs of the lower classes of society. Dirty and barefooted women, and half-clothed children, passed me in the entry-ways or scowled at me from doors, and windows. Squalor and wretchedness reign supreme in dwellings once the abodes of valor, of learning, and of genius. A subsequent visit in the evening, in company of a traveling friend, disclosed an amount of drunkenness and disorderly carousing that I was not prepared to find in a Presbyterian "Modern Athens."

Holyrood Abbey was founded by David I., in 1128, to commemorate his deliverance from a stag brought to bay in the hunting grounds, near the castle. Tradition says the king was saved by a mysterious cross, interposed between the royal person and the infuriated animal. All that now remains of the ancient abbey is the roofless walls of the chapel, containing the tombs of some of Scotland's kings and nobles. The floor is a mosaic of grass and tombstones. In this chapel, Charles I. was crowned King of Scotland, James II. married to Mary of Gueldres, James III. to Margaret of Denmark, and Mary, Queen of Scots, to Darnley. The stone on which she knelt before the ancient altar is pointed out, and the susceptible visitor who has become interested in the sad history of

"The beauteous Queen
Upon whose heart, like canker in the leaf
The worm of many sorrows revelled."

may possibly find himself on bended knee on the well worn

stone. The last time this chapel was used for worship, was by order of James VII., when mass was said here, in the king's presence. In the Reformation which followed, this fact induced the mob to desecrate the tombs of the kings, and almost destroy the building.

Holyrood Palace is a large quadrangular stone building, and surrounds an open court about a hundred feet square. At each of the outside corners is a castellated tower, of what is known as the "pepper box" pattern. It was founded by James IV. in 1500 and used by him as a residence till his death at Flodden in 1513. The oldest part of the palace is the north-west tower, containing Queen Mary's apartments. The south wing is more modern and is fitted up for the use of the royal family of England, the Queen stopping here on her way to and from Balmoral, her summer residence in the Highlands. She is expected here in about two weeks, on which occasion there is to be a grand review of volunteer militia, and the popular mind is wonderfully stirred in regard to the anticipated event. The newspapers are full of it and one hears little else talked of; indeed the small boys of a country village could hardly exhibit more interest and excitement over the expected advent of a circus, than do those usually level-headed Scotch people over the review by the Queen.

The old State apartments are exhibited to the public, and on entering the visitor is shown into an ancient hall about thirty by one hundred and fifty feet, used as a picture gallery. It contains portraits of all the Scottish kings, over one hundred in number, from Fergus, B. C. 300 (!) to James VII. They are of course nearly all fancy sketches, if the term fancy may be applied to such daubs, and are said to be the work of a single Dutch artist, who took the job by contract. He seems to have had a definite idea of about how a Scotch king should look, and has carried it out in every instance. The result is a sameness which has led an observing Scotchman to express his surprise that *all* the kings of Scotland should have "a nose resembling the knocker of a door."

The Queen's Audience Chamber has a finely carved oak ceiling, and the walls are covered with faded tapestry. It contains a state bed with embossed velvet curtains and embroidered pillow, used by Charles I. when he visited Edinburg to be crowned King of Scotland. It was also used by the Pretender previous to the battle of Culloden, and afterwards by his conqueror, "proud Cumberland." The furniture is of the time of Charles I., finely carved, and has the peculiar gloss given by age. Near the entrance to this room is the spot where Rizzio is said to have been dragged after his murder by the conspirators. Standing by the place just thirty-five years ago, the blood stains seemed distinct, and wonderfully impressed my youthful imagination. That blood, shed by violence nearly 300 years before, should still mark the old oak floor, would naturally appear to a boy, who had indulged his love of the marvelous by reading all of the Scottish border tales within his reach, as a veritable miracle. I must confess, however, that a diligent search to-day failed to discover any stains or signs of blood, from which it is fair to conclude that my eyesight (or imagination?) must be failing. The fireplace contains an old grate said to be the first used in Scotland, and it looks very much like the first grate. The shovel, poker and fender are no better, and would be considered bad jobs by any modern blacksmith.

From the audience room we enter Queen Mary's bedroom. It is about twenty feet square, has the usual carved oak ceiling, and the walls are covered with fine old tapestry representing scenes in heathen mythology. The hangings of the queen's bed are of crimson damask, with

green fringe and tassels, changed by the silent hand of time
to almost rags. Indeed it seems as if a breath of air through
an open window would reduce to shreds the hangings of
the royal bed. The linen sheets, as seen through the
threadbare counterpane, are much better preserved. Among
the antique furniture in the room is the queen's work-
box, containing a piece of embroidery worked by her
hand. The subject of this fancy needle-work is claimed
to be "Jacob wrestling with the Angel." I failed to become interested in the contest through my inability to
make out which was Jacob, and for a wonder the guide
could afford me no information. He was evidently taken
by surprise, and will no doubt have a ready answer for the
next enquirer. One of the most suggestive relics in the
room is the mirror of Queen Mary, whose great beauty
would seem to have been a chief cause of her misfor-
tunes.

From here we enter the small apartment, a mere closet,
known as the queen's supper room. Here Mary, her
sister the Duchess of Argyle, and Rizzio were sitting when
the six conspirators, who had been preceded by Darnley,
entered by a private stairway, brandishing their daggers
before the queen, one of them holding a pistol to her
breast. The wretched Rizzio was stabbed clinging to her
dress and pleading piteously for mercy. The queen, in
three months to become a mother, was forced into a chair
by her husband and held by him till the conspirators had
accomplished their purpose, leaving the dead Rizzio, with
over fifty dagger wounds, in the Audience Chamber. One
can hardly see how so many persons could find even
standing room in the little apartment where this tragedy, so often told in history and in fiction, occurred.
The surroundings have not been changed in the least and
imagination recalled the scene so vividly that it was a re-

lief to leave the dimly lighted room, and pass out, by the door to which Rizzio had clung in his death agony, into the clear sunlight.

The vicinity of the Abbey of Holyrood is said to be the only remaining *sanctuary* in Scotland, affording protection to debtors where the bankruptcy is not charged as fraudulent. Protections are issued at the Abbey Court House. Curious stories are told of the hair breadth escapes of debtors who claimed the protection of the law. On Sunday they could go where they pleased, but woe be to the luckless debtor who failed to return to the privileged ground before Monday arrived. It is said on one occasion a fugitive closely pursued fell just as he was crossing the line. His body was on the safe side but his legs were captured; and now arose a tremendous question which troubled the big wigs awfully. It was finally decided, however, that as the bailiff could do nothing with the man's legs unless he had the body attached thereto, the debtor must be allowed to take his legs along with him.

In the old town are very many other places of interest, among them the Grassmarket, an ancient place of execution where so many of the "Scots Worthies" suffered for their religion. In the Cowgate is an interesting old church where the General Assembly met in 1578, when it "was concludid that Bischopes sould be callit be their awin names, or be the names of *Breither* in all time coming, and that lordlie name and authoritie be banissed from the Kirk of God, quhilk hes bot ae Lord, Chryst Jesus."

Not far from the Grassmarket is Greyfriars churchyard, formerly the site of a monastery, but since 1566 used as a cemetery. An old flat tombstone is shown where in 1638 the congregation headed by the Earl of Sutherland, signed the Solemn League and Covenant, some of them writing their names with their own blood. Many notable men are buried here, but the most interesting monument is known as the "Martyr's Monument," and the inscription tells a sad story of persecution. "From May 27, 1661, that the most noble Marquis of Argyle was beheaded, to the 17th of February, 1688, that Mr. James Renwick suffered, were one way or other murdered and destroyed for the same cause, about eighteen thousand, of whom were executed at Edinburgh about one hundred of noblemen, gentlemen, ministers and others, noble martyrs for Jesus Christ. The most of them lie here.". After the battle of Bothwell Bridge a corner of this old graveyard was used as a prison—a sort of Andersonville—where, without shelter from the weather, and only four ounces of bread and a mouthful of water daily, the hundreds of Covenanters taken in that battle were so reduced in numbers by disease and starvation, that after five months a small vessel was sufficient to convey the wretched survivors to Barbadoes. The methods employed at Andersonville do not seem to deserve even the poor credit of originality, for history informs us, that if one of these imprisoned Covenanters rose during the night, or passed a certain line during the day, he was shot by the guard.'

The great height of the houses in the old town is ascribed to the desire of the inhabitants to find shelter within the rude walls built in 1450. The highest house I have found is eleven stories, and so irregular is the ground in some places that houses six to nine stories in front are but three to five stories in the rear. From some of the bridges one may look down the chimneys of the tall houses in the streets below.

The new town of Edinburgh is the growth of about a century, and will compare favorably with the modern portion of any city in Europe. Princes street, its principal thoroughfare, is about a mile long and only the north side of the street is built on. To the south, as before described, lie the gardens that separate it from the rocky ridges on which the old city is built. But I cannot afford to describe in detail the new town, its handsome public buildings, numerous and costly monuments, fine churches, beautiful squares, gardens and residences—all these could be duplicated with money. It is the old city that is the Edinburgh of history—

"Edina! Scotia's darling seat"

of the poet.

The Antiquarian Gallery is in the new town and well repays a visit. It contains a large collection of curiosities from all countries, but is especially interesting for its Scottish remains and relics. Here we see John Knox's pulpit from St. Giles' church, and Jenny Geddes' stool, already referred to; the original Solemn League and Covenant signed by Montrose and his associates; a flag of Scotland that waved in the breeze at the battle of Dunbar in 1650, and a banner of the Covenanters captured at Bothwell Bridge; a blue ribbon worn by Prince Charles as Knight of the Garter, and a ring given him by Flora McDonald at parting; some nails from the coffin and a portion of the shroud of Robert Bruce; the pistols of Robert Burns, and a glass from which Prince Charles drank before the disastrous fight at Culloden. There is also a rude guillotine called "The Maiden," made of two upright posts, between which is a loaded axe to be raised by a cord and fall on the devoted neck beneath. By this identical instrument Regent Morton was beheaded in 1581, Sir John Gordon in 1644, the Earl of Argyle in 1685, and at other times many others of lesser note.

Calton Hill is at the east end of Princes street, and not far from Holyrood Palace. It has a monument to Nelson, resembling very much a lighthouse, and about a hundred feet high; a dome supported by pillars, in memory of Dugald Stewart; and the unfinished National Monument, intended to reproduce on this elevated position the Parthenon at Athens. Its erection was to commemorate the Scotch heroes who fell at Waterloo, but after about a dozen immense Doric columns had been placed, at a cost of seventy thousand dollars, popular enthusiasm abated, the funds were lacking, and like a certain monument at Washington, it remains unfinished. The Royal Observatory, a fine Grecian building, is on Calton Hill, and in Calton churchyard is the tomb of David Hume. Not far distant, in St. David street, Hume resided after acquiring fame and money by his writings. The name of this street is supposed to have been intended by the truly orthodox of Edinburgh as a slur on Hume, on account of his well known infidelity. It was viewed in this light by his housekeeper, who appeared one morning in great wrath to inform him that a sign marked "St. David street" had been placed on the house. "Tut, tut, woman," said Hume, with an air of forced resignation, "don't mind it; many a better man than I has been called a saint."

While for picturesque and romantic effects
"Stately Edinburgh, built on crags;"
can hardly be surpassed, Calton Hill seems to be the best point from which to take in the beauty of its scenery and surroundings. When but a youth I spent a whole summer day on Calton Hill, and the scene has lost none of its peculiar and striking interest from the many years that have intervened. Both the old and new towns are seen to advantage. The square, solid looking old palace of Holyrood is at your feet, and as you stand in the line of Princes street its long avenue of buildings, monuments and gardens is in full view. On the opposite rocky and irregular ridge stands the old town, black with age, and terminating at its furthest

and highest point in the castle rock, with its frowning fortifications. Beyond the old city, and forming an appropriate background, lie the Pentland hills. On the south, and quite near, rise Salisbury Crags and Arthurs seat, and flanking them, in the distance are seen the Hills of Lammermoor. West and north the whole Firth of Forth is in sight till it joins the German ocean, and in the foreground, between the Edinburgh and Fife shores, is the Island of Inchkeith. In the far west may be seen the top of Ben-lomond, and "Ben-ledi's distant hill." A gentleman, who had kindly called my attention to some of these places, pointed out in the far distance the identical "Grampian Hills" where "my father fed his flocks." How often have I pointed to these hills, (always over the right shoulder, and looking steadily in front,) when I was a small boy, and my name "Norval."

Leith, the port of Edinburgh, is nearly two miles distant from the east end of Princes street, but fine residences line the way between the two cities. Formerly a bitter rivalry existed between them, so intense that if a merchant of Edinburgh should take into partnership an inhabitant of Leith, he was heavily fined and deprived of the freedom of the city for a year. Commercial interests have forced the cities into close union, and, though separate municipalities, the growth of both has made them geographically one. On my walk to Leith I passed quite a number of the Newhaven fishwives in picturesque costume, carrying on their backs, supported by a strap across the top of the forehead, heavy baskets of fish for the Edinburgh market. They are wonderfully muscular, quite comely in appearance, and, in their way, neatly dressed. Their habits are singular, the men attending to the boats and fishing while the women do the marketing and carry the purse, allowing their husbands such sums as they deem proper for pocket money. An arrangement of this kind would suit an American woman admirably—

## SCOTCH WOMEN.

provided she could hire a German or Irish girl to carry the basket.

The better class of Scotch women seem much more healthy and robust than the same class in America. Contrasting the poorer classes of the two countries, the difference is not so marked, probably caused by the hardships and lack of the good things of this life which the Scotch women of the lower classes are compelled to endure. Among this class both in Glasgow and Edinburgh I should say a majority go barefoot.

In Edinburgh there would seem to be no anxiety to do business, everybody appears to be taking it easy, willing to go slow and sure, rather than worry or take risks in order to get suddenly rich. The Scotch are shrewd and thrifty and said to be the only people among whom the Jews cannot get a foot-hold. The "canny Scot" is more than a match for the son of Abraham in a close bargain, and can economise wonderfully in his methods of doing business. In the rural districts even the dwellings of the very poor have an air of neatness and thrift, as if the occupants had seen better days, or been born for a higher station.

## CHAPTER IV.

### MELROSE ABBEY—ABBOTSFORD.

To Melrose—The Abbey—Scott's Stone—The Wizard's Grave—Tombs—Chapel—Sculptures—The Monks—Village of Melrose—To Abbotsford—House and Grounds—The Entrance—Hall—Rooms—Armory—Library—Study—Museum—Suggested Memories.

Melrose, 37 miles from Edinburgh, is reached by rail, the road passing through a most beautiful and interesting part of Scotland. Our route lay along the Esk and Gala rivers, the hills of Lammermoor to the east and the hills of Moorfort to the west. The way seemed to be lined with the ruins of old castles; the more important being Craigmillar, Borthwick, Crichton, Newbyres, Ewe, Gunzion and Torsonce. We pass at Dalkeith the magnificent palace and grounds of the Duke of Buccleuch, and near Dalhousie the Marquis of Lothian's castle, Newbattle Abbey. The only town of importance is Galashiels, noted for the manufacture of tweeds and tartans.

But a few minutes walk from the station is the Abbey Hotel, a comfortable Scotch inn, of about the third class as to size and appearance, and where no extortions are practised on guests or visitors. The proprietor is governed by a fixed scale of prices, and they are certainly moderate; for instance, a stylish two-horse carriage, with driver, to Abbotsford and return, using up a half day, cost me less than two dollars. In a little house opposite the hotel resides the keeper of the abbey, and for a small fee the rusty iron gate leading to the grounds was opened, and I was in the presence of "fair Melrose." The lady keeper had thoughtfully locked me in, saying she would return and give me any desired information after I had examined the building by myself. I walked around the ruined and roofless walls, and seating myself by the great east window, awaited the coming of the guide. A convention of noisy rooks were discussing some subject of more than ordinary importance overhead, and it would be difficult to imagine anything more weird than my surroundings.

Melrose Abbey was founded by David I. in 1136, and consecrated in 1146. The English forces under Edward II., retreating from Scotland in 1322, did much injury to the building, to repair which King Robert made a grant of two thousand pounds; equal in purchasing power to a quarter of a million dollars at the present time. The restoration of the abbey, probably a rude building at first, took place at a time when Gothic architecture had reached its full development. It was destroyed by the Earl of Hertford in 1545. Tradition says that the English on their way back had passed Melrose, when the bells of the abbey were rung to express the joy of the inmates. Hearing the sound, the English returned, and made of Melrose Abbey the finest ruin in Great Britain. A considerable part of its outer walls have been carried away at different periods to erect buildings in the neighborhood; but it is now well cared for by its present owner, the Duke of Buccleuch.

"If thou wouldst view fair Melrose aright,
 Go visit it by the pale moonlight;"

said the poet, and deprecatingly adds:

"For the gay beams of lightsome day
 Gild, but to flout, the ruins gray."

The necessities of travel, however, obliged me to visit Melrose on a bright summer day. Indeed, my youthful fancy had been so wrought upon by the weird and terrible things which occurred in these aisles, as told in Scott's "Lay of the last Minstrel," that a moonlight visit to the haunted spot would have tested my courage severely. I had in Edinburgh provided myself with a copy of the poem, and found the second canto good reading in the abbey.

Scott's home was but three miles from Melrose, and he is said to have been accustomed to linger among the ruins. Inside and near the east end is "Scott's stone," where he was accustomed to sit. From it is obtained a fine view of the great east window, sixteen feet wide and thirty-seven feet high. It is the most beautiful thing connected with the abbey, and what can be finer than Scott's description :

> "The moon on the east oriel shone,
> Through slender shafts of shapely stone,
>   By foliaged tracery combined;
> Thou wouldst have thought some fairy's hand,
> 'Twixt poplars straight the osier wand,
>   In many a freakish knot had twined;
> Then framed a spell, when the work was done,
> And changed the willow-wreaths to stone."

Not far from "Scott's stone" lies an old-fashioned slab which covers the remains of the "mighty wizard, Michael Scott." I read again the story of his burial, as told by the monk :

> "I buried him on St. Michael's night,
> When the bell tolled one and the moon was bright;
> And I dug his chamber among the dead,
> When the floor of the chancel was stained with red.
>
> "It was a night of woe and dread,
> When Michael in the tomb I laid !
> Strange sounds along the chancel passed,
> The banners waved without a blast—

Also the re-opening of the grave by the monk and William of Deloraine, disentombing the "Mighty Book :"

> "With beating heart to the task he went;
>   His sinewy frame o'er the grave-stone bent;
>   With bar of iron heaved amain,
>   Till the toil drops fell from his brows, like rain.
>   It was by dint of passing strength.
>   That he moved the massy stone at length.

## THE CHAPEL. 55

" Pefore their eyes the Wizard lay,
   As if he had not been dead a day;

" His left hand held his Book of Might.
   A silver cross was in his right;

" Then Deloraine in terror took
   From the cold hand the Mighty Book;
   With iron clasped and with iron bound;—
   He thought, as he took it, the dead man frowned;

" And, as the Knight and Priest withdrew,
   With wavering steps and dizzy brain,
   They hardly might the postern gain.
   'Tis said as through the aisles they passed,
   They heard strange noises on the last;
   And through the cloister-galleries small,
   Which at mid-height thread the chancel wall,
   Loud sobs, and laughter louder ran,
   And voices unlike the voice of man;
   As if the fiends kept holiday,
   Because these spells were brought to day."

Many historic names appear among the tombs. Douglas, the dark Knight of Liddesdale, Alexander II., James, Earl of Douglas, killed by Hotspur (Earl of Percy), at the battle of Otterburn, in 1388. Here also is deposited the heart of Robert Bruce. Bruce requested that his heart might be carried to Palestine and buried near the holy sepulchre. Sir James Douglas, with a picked body of soldiers attempted the task, but was repulsed by the Saracens. The heart was returned to Scotland, and buried in Melrose Abbey.

The chapel is in the form of a Latin cross. The west end of the nave is gone. A square tower had risen in the center to the height of about eighty feet, and one of its sides is still standing, the two pillars which sustain it being among the finest specimens of carved work in the building. Around the walls are the remains of sixteen small chapels, with their broken altars and mutilated carvings of sacred scenes, most of them entirely occupied by the tombs of noblemen, ecclesiastics, and noted persons who have died in the neighborhood of Melrose. The choir and transepts are well preserved ; also the roof of the high altar, which has a figure of Christ on the cross, and contains some finely carved tracery. A window in the north transept has been sculptured so as to resemble a crown of thorns. The profusion and delicacy of the carvings is really wonderful. My attention was called to the likeness of a hand grasping a bunch of flowers, on one of the pillars. I do not know that it was finer than many of the other carvings ; but a close inspection revealed a delicacy, beauty and finish such as I do not remember to have seen, and the lines were as perfect as if cut yesterday. The arches over the seats in the cloister and the corners of the windows, are adorned with the finest carvings of flowers, fruit, leaves, plants, vegetables and shells. The Scotch "kail," a species of cabbage, has a prominent place in the finest carvings, in all parts of the building. There are numerous queer carvings, showing the *freedom* of the times. Some of them seem to reflect severely on the morals of the monks, as they represent members of the brotherhood in situations—to say the least, questionable. They would seem to have led an easy life, and at the reformation were the subject of many satires. Scott gives us an extract from one of them :

"The Monks of Melrose made fat kail
On Fridays when they fasted;
And neither wanted beer nor ale,
As long as their neighbors' lasted."

The ornamental carvings would repay weeks of study, so profuse and varied are they. An historian says, "there are the finest lessons and the greatest variety of Gothic ornaments that the island affords, take all the other religious structures together."

Reading Scott's description of the ruin, I had supposed it made up largely of the poet's fancies. And yet nothing written by the poet is more fanciful than the things which he describes.

> "Spreading herbs, and flowerets bright,
> Glistened with the dew of night;
> Nor herb, nor floweret, glistened there,
> But was carved in the cloister arches as fair.
>
> \* \* \* \* \* \* \* \*
>
> "The darkened roof rose high aloof
> On pillars, lofty, and light, and small;
> The key-stone that locked each ribbed aisle,
> Was a fleur-de-lys, or a quatre-feuille;
> The corbels were carved grotesque and grim
> And the pillars, with clustered shafts so trim,
> With base and with capital flourished around,
> Seemed bundles of lances which garlands had bound."

After examining the ruins in detail, and taking in their grand proportions from the burial ground in which they stand, one is led to wonder what the abbey must have been in its perfection of beauty, when through the windows of gorgeously stained glass the sun lighted up nave and transept, while monkish voices chanting in monotone, echoed through the lofty arches. And all this wealth of beauty and of splendor to be enjoyed by its inmates alone; for Melrose was not yet a village, and Edinburgh but a small town, nearly forty miles distant. The pious zeal of the middle ages which prompted such expenditures, I cannot understand.

The village of Melrose possesses little of interest. The curious stones and devices, and the letters I. H. S. on the older buildings, do not indicate that Presbyterianism is waning in Scotland, but only that the stones of which most of these houses are built have been pillaged from time to time from the abbey.

From Melrose to Abbotsford is three miles, over a smooth graveled road. The day was fine, the scenery charming, and I was glad to observe that here as elsewhere in Scotland there is little of abject poverty or even of shiftlessness apparent. Leaving Melrose the driver called my attention to the three-topped Eildon hills, which he gravely assured me were one till split by the wizard Michael Scott. The country is rolling, indeed, hilly; there are many fine residences in sight, and I caught occasional glimpses of the River Tweed. Abbotsford is not seen from a distance in this direction, and when we approached it I was surprised that Sir Walter should have chosen so low a spot, almost surrounded by hills, for his residence. It was formerly a low moorland farm, and before it received the euphonious name of Abbotsford, was known in the neighborhood by the more descriptive one of "Clarty Hole." Sir Walter is said to have purchased the farm to indulge his antiquarian fancies, as containing the whole of the battle-field of Melrose, the last great border clan fight in which the Scotts took a part; also Thomas the Rhymer's glen, a celebrated spot, where Thomas of Ercildoune was wont to meet his spouse the elfin Fairy Queen. The house is a wonderful combination or aggregation, apparently without design—as if built piecemeal as the needs or fancies of the owner suggested, and yet, taken as a whole, its appearance is quite satisfactory. By an admirer of the poet it has been called "a poem in lime and mortar." The grounds are admirably kept, and as nearly as possible in the same condition as when Sir Walter died. There is a profusion of trees, shrubbery, gravel walks, rustic seats, etc. Into the walls of the house and garden have been introduced many interesting fragments and relics from ancient castles and abbeys. Sir Walter is said to have spent over a quarter of a million dollars on the house and grounds.

The principal entrance is on the east side, and is adorned with petrified stags horns, while over it is a lintel taken from the old Tolbooth of Edinburgh with the inscription:

"The Lord of armies is my Protector,
Blessit are they that trust in the Lord 1575."

On one side of the hall are stained glass windows with pieces of ancient armor between. The ceiling and cornice are of oak and finely carved. The cornice contains the arms of the border clans painted on small shields with an inscription stating that, "These be the coat armoires of the Clanns and chief men of name wha keepit the marchys of Scotland in the auld tyme for the Kynge. Trewe men were they in their defence. God them defendyt." On each side of the door at the end of the hall is a figure in armor; one holds a large two-handed sword, the other a spear. The floor is marble of different colors.

The great hall or armory is ceiled with curious carvings, partly from the ancient palace of Dumfermline. It is well lighted, and the walls are covered with instruments of border warfare, axes, targets, broadswords, daggers, muskets, knives, pistols, hunting horns, etc. There are several full suits of armor once worn by historic characters, and a number of swords and cuirasses picked up on the field of Waterloo. The drawing room is spacious and richly furnished in carved cedar and ebony. The chairs, tables, cabinets, writing desk and piano were presented to the poet by George IV. There is also a fine ebony writing desk, the gift of George III. The dining room has some fine family portraits, among them two sons and two daughters of the poet. There is also a portrait of Sir Walter's great-grandfather, known as "Beardie." After the execution of Charles I, regarded by him as a "holy martyr," he permitted his hair and beard to grow as a token of mourning and remembrance. There are portraits of Cromwell, Charles II. Claverhouse; also Camrood's picture of the head of Mary, Queen of Scots, taken a few hours after her execution—fine as a work of art but a strange subject for a dining room. It was in this room

"The weary wheel of life at length stood still."

and Sir Walter passed away Sept. 21, 1832.

The library is a large room, I should say forty-five by sixty feet. The ceiling, like that of most of the other rooms, is of oak and finely carved. The walls are covered with book cases containing over 20,000 volumes, many of them rare and valuable gifts to the poet. On the north side is a projecting window where the poet loved to sit, affording a fine view of the River Tweed, which runs within a few rods of the house. The custodian informed me that in the library, as in the other principal rooms, no changes have been permitted since the death of Sir Walter. The private study, where his literary work was done, is a small room entered from the library and lighted by a single window. It is now arranged as when used by Sir Walter. The writing table, an arm-chair covered with black leather, and another chair constitute the movable furniture. There are shelves on three sides holding books of reference, and all within reach from the arm-chair. In an adjoining closet is a case containing the last clothes worn by Sir Walter. Blue coat with brass buttons, striped vest, plaid pantaloons, gaiters, heavy shoes and wide brimmed white hat, also his walking cane.

To show the taste of Sir Walter in such matters I give some of the more interesting articles in his museum of curiosities: Napoleon's pistols, pen case, portfolio, and a partly used stick of sealing wax found in the Emperor's carriage after the battle of Waterloo, with an autograph letter of the Duke of Wellington presenting them to Sir Walter; spurs of Oliver Cromwell, armor of James VI., Rob Roy's gun, shield and purse; Claverhouse's pistol, sword of Montrose, presented to him by Charles I., double-barreled gun of Balfour, Prince Charles' sword and knife, war horn from Hermitage Castle; clock of Marie Antoinette, Bruce's candlestick, Helen McGregor's brooch, Tam O'Shanter's snuff box, Burns' tumbler; lock of Selkirk jail, keys of Loch Leven Castle and of Edinburgh Tolbooth; hair of Prince Charles, Duke of Wellington and Lord Nelson; thumb-screws, gags and other instruments of torture; the iron mask worn by

Wishart at the stake to prevent him from addressing the people. But by far the most interesting relic to me was a pearl cross worn by the beautiful and unfortunate Mary, Queen af Scots. As she ascended the scaffold wearing this cross, the Earl of Kent rudely said, "Take away that trumpery, we should wear Christ in our hearts;" to which she quickly replied, "And wherefore should I have Christ in my hand if he were not in my heart?"

Abbotsford is wonderfully suggestive of its gifted founder. Nearly every tree was planted by his hand or under his direction. The large sums received from the sale of his most popular works were expended on the building and grounds. Abbotsford is indeed as much the product of his mind and genius as Waverly or Marmion. Here he surrounded himself, without regard to expense, with the works of art and historical and antiquarian relics which his fancy craved, and here for years practiced an almost princely hospitality. Abbotsford became a kind of show and hostelry, visited by the famous men of Europe.

Abbotsford also recalls those sad days when, advanced in years, and weighed down with bankruptcy, the brave heart drove the failing hand in an honest but strained effort to pay his accumulated debts. He accomplished his heart's desire, his debts were paid—*by his executors*. It also recalls those sadder days when, after in vain seeking health on foreign shores, he returned home to Abbotsford to die, his welcome by his favorite dogs, the childlike delight with which he recognized familiar objects as he moved from room to room, the wish to be again seated by the familiar desk in the old arm-chair—and the silent tears as the pen fell from his paralyzed fingers. All these, and the final good bye, "God bless you all," with which he went to rest, were uppermost in my thoughts and left a saddened feeling as I bade farewell to Abbotsford.

## CHAPTER V.
### LONDON.

Melrose to London—A Station Dining-room—London—The Old City—Modern London—The Albert Memorial—The American Exchange—Charing Cross —Trafalgar Square—The National Gallery—Whitehall—Parliament House —Victoria Tower—Hall, Chambers, Galleries,etc —House of Lords—House of Commons—Clock Tower—Great Tom of Westminster—Westminster Hall—St. Margaret's Church.

From Melrose to London is about 350 miles, through a country thickly settled, and for the most part fertile and well cultivated. In Westmoreland are some barren moors, and as we pass through mining districts, we occasionally find land of a poor quality. I shall not attempt to describe the towns we passed; the principal being Harwich, Skipton, the manufacturing city of Leeds, Chesterfield, Trent, Leicester, Bedford (the home of John Bunyan), and St. Albans. For most of the way I had as fellow passengers a Catholic priest and two commercial travelers, well informed as to the objects of interest on the way, and disposed to afford all desired information.

We stopped thirty minutes for dinner at a station dining-room. There was a fine display of china, glassware and cutlery. The table was set for dinner, and looked well, with plenty to eat, but a great lack of variety; potatoes, cabbage, bread and roast beef being not only the staples, but pretty much all that it afforded. About the time when at such a table in America the waiter rapidly enumerates half-a-dozen kinds of pies and puddings from which one may choose, or hands you a bill of fare in which the dessert figures quite conspicuously, a waiter pronounced quickly in my ear something which sounded like "Chishaw, Chiddaw, Stitton." The English gentleman next to me had said, "Chishaw;" so I followed suit, and in a short time the waiter supplied us with liberal slices of Cheshire cheese. I inquired of my neighbor as to what the result would have been if I had said "Chiddaw or Stitton," and was informed that in that case the cheese would have been Cheddar or Stilton—for dessert I had my choice of three kinds of cheese. The charge for dinner was sixty-two cents. One of the commercial travelers, who had visited the United States, informed me that the great variety of food kept prepared in our hotels, and of which small portions are served as ordered, is unknown in Great Britain. He amused me by a story of an American just landed in England, who, desiring a square meal, made a liberal order for breakfast. After long waiting a procession of waiters entered the room, one bearing a boiled ham, another a boiled tongue, a third a broiled chicken, a fourth a large cooked fish, etc., etc. The wonderful variety ordered had astonished the landlord—the bill astonished the American.

We arrived in St. Pancras' station, London, about nine o'clock at night, in a severe rain storm. This immense depot is the largest I have seen; the train-shed alone is 700 feet long by 240 wide, and is spanned by a single arch 140 feet high. I got into a cab with a fellow traveler and our baggage, and was driven to the Waverley hotel, over two miles distant. On alighting and inquiring the fare, the driver carefully replied, "the *legal* fare is two shillings." The peculiar accent on the word *legal* indicated clearly enough that something more than legal fare would be acceptable, and an extra sixpence—in all sixty-two cents—caused his face to assume a satisfied expression. The same service in New York would have cost from two to three dollars. Purposing to spend some time in London, I started early next morning to find quarters in what is known as a "private hotel," and found just the place I desired, on Charterhouse Square. My room fronts on the square, covered with grass and liberally supplied with trees, yet in the heart of the great city. I am within five minutes walk of the General Post Office or of St. Paul's.

One thing that surprises a stranger at English or Scotch hotels, is the absence of that wonderful genius and encyclopedia of general information—guide book, time table, directory, gazetteer and price list—usually bound in broadcloth, and known in America as the hotel clerk. How often have I applied to him for all kinds of information, and how seldom have I failed to receive prompt and correct answers. On entering the British hotel you usually see several young ladies; approach the one who stands nearest the writing materials, and she can generally tell you if there is a room vacant, but that is about the extent of her information. On no other subject, general or local, does she seem to have an opinion.

Having secured a hotel, I devoted the day to a general survey of the city, and largely as seen from the tops of omnibuses. In this way I made myself familiar with the principal streets, public buildings and parks, my fellow passengers adding considerably to my stock of information on local subjects. For six months before leaving home I had frequently studied a large ordnance map of London, and endeavored to familiarize myself with the location of the streets and places of interest. I find myself quite at home as to the direction of places and of streets, and must say that the city is more like what I expected to see than any strange place I ever visited.

The *city*, or that part of modern London over which the Lord Mayor presides, and known as the *corporate* city of London, is of small extent, and almost entirely occupied for business purposes. It extends from Temple Bar on the west to the Tower on the east. Its southern boundary is the Thames, and it has an area of about a square mile, or to be exact, 632 acres. Its population is about 60,000, a decrease of nearly one-half in twenty years. During the hours of business it is said to contain 500,000 people. This small territory is the commercial center of the world. It contains the Bank of England, Royal Exchange, Mansion House, Custom House, General Post Office, St. Paul's Church and the Tower. It was formerly divided into over 100 parishes; how small some of them were, may be judged by the fact that the open space in front of the Exchange was formerly a parish, and the erection of the post office building used up the whole of another. The value of land may be estimated from a recent sale, where, in Lombard street, it sold at the rate of $10,000,000 per acre. There was a town here before the Romans, but the city walls and forts were built and the gates fixed by them. After 500 years occupation they abandoned it to the Anglo-Saxons, who suffered it to go to decay. William, the Norman conqueror, built the white tower, and granted a charter to the first city of London.

Modern London contains about 140 square miles, with a population estimated at 4,500,000. At the present rate of increase the population will, A. D. 2,000, number over 8,000,000. Within this territory it is said there are more Roman Catholics than in Rome, more Jews than in all Palestine, more Welsh than in Cardiff, more Scotch than in Aberdeen, and more Irish than in Belfast. There is in active operation over 300 miles of railway. The London customs dues equal those of all other places in the kingdom. During the past ten years 70,000 houses have been built, the total number of residences being over 500,000. Its 7,600 streets, placed end to end, would reach nearly 3,000 miles, or from New York to Queenstown. Its 1,100 churches will not seat one-tenth of its inhabitants. There are over 40 theaters, and 400 concert saloons, 7,500 public houses, 1,700 coffee houses, and 500 hotels and inns. There is sold in London annually 3,000,000 quarters of wheat, 250,000 oxen, 1,500,000 sheep, 130,000 calves, 200,000 pigs, 8,000,000 head of poultry and game, 400,000,000 pounds of fish, 180,000,000 quarts of malt liquor, 31,000,000 quarts of wine, 18,000,000 quarts of spirits, and 6,500,000 tons of coal. The daily water supply is 150,000,000 gallons. There are 10,000 cabmen, and 11,000 policemen. In 1879 there were 3,872 street accidents, to 3,961 persons, of whom 237 were killed, the others injured. There were last year 8,483 lost children, of whom 23 were not found. Of the size of the modern city, figures convey but a faint idea. It has already swallowed up 60 villages; and after riding a whole day on omnibuses and tram-cars, I was obliged to hire a cab and drive a long distance to find the country, or rather, to reach a place where the houses began to get scarce.

While riding in the vicinity of Hyde Park, my attention was called to the Albert Memorial, the most imposing and expensive monument of modern times, having cost nearly $900,000. It consists of a gothic cross and canopy, surmounted by a spire reaching to the height of 175 feet. Under the canopy is a gilded statue of the prince, 15 feet in height. The platform on which it stands is approached by four flights of steps, each 130 feet wide. At each angle is a group of statues, representing Europe, Asia, Africa, and America, and around the base are 200 life-size figures and reliefs of the distinguished men of all ages and countries. As the name of each is carved in the stone there is no guide book necessary to understand the grouping of the figures. But this splendid monument is far too elaborate for description in detail. An accurate idea of its general appearance

THE ALBERT MEMORIAL.

may be obtained from the fine engraving. This is but one of the many memorials erected to the memory of the prince consort; they may be found in nearly all the principal cities of the kingdom.

That a plain man, of simple tastes and habits, whose chief distinction—as distinctions are reckoned—would seem to be that he had been husband of the queen, should receive the consideration usually reserved for successful statesmen and soldiers, has excited the ire of Mr. Richard Grant White, to a remarkable degree. He calls it, in a Boston periodical, "the most obtrusively offensive monument in London;" and speaks of the statue of its subject as "the gilded, enthroned, enshrined and canopied effigy of the demi-god of the commonplace." I look at the matter from a different standpoint, and probably not the Bostonian. The successful statesman may be merely the "boss liar." The successful general may owe his fame largely to blind luck, or to a recklessness of life and stolid indifference to suffering that would be invaluable to a thug or butcher, but not calculated to adorn private life. Where military success elevates to high position such a man—it may be of dissolute habits and inherent meanness of character—the contemplation of the original is sufficiently disagreeable, and does not suggest any pressing necessity for a monument. No, no, Mr. White; the widow's cap, the nun's hood, the nurse's apron, the threadbare frock of the factory girl, or the faded calico of the uncomplaining wife of the drunkard may point you to sublimer exhibitions of heroism than can be found in cabinets, or wearing shoulder-straps and gilt buttons. Prince Albert was a man of refined tastes; a poet, a musician, interested in art, and earnestly devoted to the elevation of the working classes. But I am inclined to attribute the veneration in which his memory is held by the English people to other reasons, and that do them honor—their thorough appreciation of the fact that he was a pure and upright man, and an exemplary husband and father. While England is famous for just such men, in an humbler sphere, they have been sufficiently rare in the very highest station, to warrant the pleased and generous recognition of the nation.

One of the first places I visited in London is the American Exchange, on the Strand, near Charing Cross. By paying one dollar and a quarter I am entitled to the privileges of the Exchange for one month. Here I receive my letters, and if absent they will be forwarded to my address. The reading room contains files of the principal American dailies, (among them the Detroit *Free Press*), and here one meets daily with persons from almost every State in the Union. A register is kept of Americans in London, and where they reside, money is exchanged, drafts cashed, etc., etc. It is a most useful institution, and its employes are well informed and ready to afford just such information as the stranger in London is most likely to want. After a day of sight-seeing it is a pleasant place of resort, each evening bringing its list of new arrivals. I find it interesting to listen to the "travelers' stories" of those who have just crossed the ocean, or returned from a tour on the continent. Remarking on the American disposition to "draw the long bow," one of the clerks told us a good story of some passengers just landed from different vessels, and comparing their ocean experiences. One of them told how on the tenth of the month, they had encountered in mid-ocean immense swarms of locusts, so large and so voracious that they "carried off every shred of canvas on the ship." A sedate looking man, who had listened to this monstrous lie, drew a long breath, and proceeded at once to "catch up," by remarking thoughtfully, and with a sigh of relief, "That explains it; yes, that explains all. It was next day—yes, the eleventh—that we met that swarm of locusts, and every one of them wore a pair of canvas pants!" "How did the man who told the first story take it?" inquired some one. There came a "far away look" in the honest clerk's eyes as he replied, "He got right up and went out, looking so despondent that we followed him, afraid he would make for the river, but found him just around the corner in the Strand, kicking himself!"

Charing Cross is regarded as the geographical center, and on that account is the vicinity in which Americans usually prefer to find hotels or boarding houses. It derives its name from the fact that Edward I. erected a cross here, in the village of Charing, in memory of his wife Eleanor. The historian says: "Wherever Eleanor's corpse rested on its transit from Grantham to Westminster Abbey, Edward erected a cross in memory of her." The original cross was of wood, replaced by stone and destroyed by order of the "Long Parliament." The site was for some time used as a place of execution, and a pillory erected. On it now stands a statue of Charles I., erected in 1674. This statue had been cast in 1633, but not erected when the civil war broke out, and was sold by the parliament to a brazier with the singularly appropriate name of John Rivet, who pretended to sell parts of it both to the friends and foes of the Stuarts in the form of charms, etc. At the restoration, however, Rivet produced the statue entire. Being a good royalist, he had buried it in his garden, and in 1674 it was erected on its present site. A *fac simile* of the original cross stands in an enclosure in front of the Charing Cross railway station. It is seventy feet high, quite elaborate, and said to have cost $10,000.

Charing Cross forms a part of what is known as Trafalgar Square. This famous square has for its chief attraction the Nelson Column, 145 feet high and said to be the exact proportions of a Corinthian column of the Temple of Mars at Rome.  There is a granite statue of Nelson on the top, seventeen feet in height.  The pedestal has remarkably fine bronze reliefs, which, like the other ornamentations are made of captured French cannon.  They represent the battle of the Nile, battle of Copenhagen, battle of St. Vincent and the death of Nelson at Trafalgar.  Around the base of the column are four large lions, in bronze, designed by Sir Edwin Landseer assisted by Baron Marochetti.  Near the column are two very fine fountains, discharging 150 gallons per minute to a height of about forty feet.  There are also in Trafalgar Square, statues of Sir Henry Havelock, Sir Charles Napier and George IV.  The west side of the square is occupied by the Union Club building, and adjoining it is the Royal College of Surgeons.  At the north-east corner is the beautiful church of St. Martin's-in-the-Fields. In its burial ground are the graves of Jack Shepard and Nell Gwynne.

The National Gallery is on the north side of Trafalgar Square and has a front of 500 feet.  The building has a Corinthian portico and a dome, but has a singular, squatty, one-story appearance, and is not such a building as one would expect to see used as the great National Picture Gallery of England.  It dates only from 1832.  There are eighteen rooms containing over 1,000 pictures, about half of them by English artists.  The largest contributors in the English department are Lawrence, Reynolds, Gainsborough and Landseer.  Rosa Bonheur's celebrate picture, "The Horse Fair" is in this department.  Over 100 foreign artists are represented.  Some of the more celebrated artists have several pictures, and the great value of the collection may be judged of by the number of such—Rembrandt fifteen, Rubens fourteen, Raphael six, Murillo three, Salvator Rosa three, Titian nine, Teniers ten, Guido seven, Paul Veronese six, Vandyck six.  Among the more celebrated paintings are Raphael's "St. Catharine of Alexandria," costing $25,000; Corregio's "Holy Family," "Ecce Homo," and "Mercy Instructing Cupid," the three costing $50,000; Rubens' "Judgment of Paris," and "Rape of the Sabines," Murillo's "Vision of a Knight" and "Holy Family," Paul Veronese's "Family of Darius," and Da Vinci's "Christ Disputing in the Temple."

Whitehall, and its continuation, Parliament street, lead from Charing Cross to the Houses of Parliament and Westminster Abbey. But a short distance from Charing Cross, on the east side of the street, is Scotland Yard the head quarters of the Metropolitan Police. Passing the Admiralty office and pay department, we reach the barracks known as the Horse Guards. Nearly opposite to it formerly stood the ancient Palace of Whitehall, the home of Wolsey as Archbishop, and afterward the residence of Henry VIII., who was married to Anne Boleyn in a room of the palace. Whitehall was from this time a favorite residence of the reigning monarchs. Cromwell also resided here, and is said to have preached sermons three hours long to the people assembled in the palace hall. But few places are more intimately identified with the history of England than the palace of Whitehall. Now only the banqueting house converted into a Chapel Royal by George IV. remains, the rest of the palace having been destroyed by fire. It was in front of the banqueting house and nearly opposite the Horse Guards that Charles I. was beheaded. The scaffold was erected in the street and a door broken through the wall, through which the king passed to execution.

Passing the Treasury and Colonial buildings we reach Parliament Square. On the east side are the new Houses of Parliament, by far the most extensive buildings in London, covering an area of eight acres, and being four times as large as St. Paul's Church. They occupy the site of the ancient palace of Westminster, used as a residence by the sovereigns of England from the early Anglo-Saxon times till York Place, the residence of Wolsey, was confiscated by Henry VIII., and became his royal palace of Whitehall. In the old palace of Westminster was the original "Star Chamber," so called from the gilt stars upon its ceiling. Here sat in secret session a court, whose judges were not subject to the ordinary forms of legal procedure, who sentenced the accused without a hearing, inflicting torture, mutilation, branding, etc., at their pleasure. After an existence of two centuries it was abolished in 1640. The palace of Westminster was used by the lords and commons as a parliament house, from 1547 till 1834 when it was burned, excepting the famous Westminster Hall which remains. The New Parliament Houses were commenced in 1840 and occupied in 1859. The east front faces the river, from which really the best view is obtained, and is 940 feet, or, say fifty-seven rods long. There are eleven quadrangular courts and 500 apartments, with eighteen official residences, some of them quite large, for the officers of the lords and commons. There is also a convenient chapel for the use of the inmates. The style of the building is Gothic, and I was surprised at its fine appearance and eligible location. I had read that there was "neither symmetry nor beauty about the building as a whole," which, allowing me to be the judge, is very far from true. It is built of a dark red sandstone, blackened, of course, by the London smoke. Its outer walls are everywhere ornamented with statues and elaborate carving. It has two large towers, and a richly decorated belfry spire, rising to the height of 320 feet.

At the chamberlain's office, near the Victoria Tower, I received, by merely asking for it, a ticket of admission to the state apartments and houses of lords and commons. The Victoria Tower is the largest and highest square tower in

## THE ROYAL GALLERY.

the world, being seventy-five feet square and 336 feet high —or over 400 feet to the top of the flag staff. The royal entrance is at the base of the tower, by a very high archway on the west side. The royal carriage enters the tower, stopping at the royal staircase, which leads from it to the House of Lords. The interior of the tower contains statues of St. George, St. Andrew and St. Patrick, also a very large statue of Queen Victoria, with figures on each side, representing Justice and Mercy. The walls and roof exhibit a great amount of rich emblematical carving, and all this richness is bestowed on a room which only serves as an entrance-way for the sovereign, when visiting, at long intervals, the House of Lords.

Ascending the royal staircase, we pass through the Norman porch, decorated with statues of the Norman kings, to the queen's robing room, fifty-four by twenty-seven feet and twenty-five feet high, lighted from the south by six windows of stained glass. At the east end, on a raised platform, is a chair of state, a most elaborate affair, and the walls are covered with frescoes illustrating scenes in the life of King Arthur. The floor is inlaid with various woods, with an oak border containing many emblematical scenes. The fireplace is of the finest marble, and the furniture is covered with gold. We next pass into the royal gallery, a magnificent room, forty-five by one hundred and ten feet and forty-five feet high. It is to this gallery that the privileged public are admitted to view the royal procession on its passage to the House of Lords. There are raised seats on each side, the entire length of the room, for the use of the sight seers on these occasions. The walls above these seats are decorated with frescoes, among which are fine paintings of "The Meeting of Wellington and Blucher after the Battle of Waterloo," and "The Death of Nelson at Trafalgar." The windows are of stained glass and below them is a belt of shields with the arms of royalty in different forms and devices. The ceiling is dark blue with a very large amount of gilding. There are gilded statues of King Alfred, William I.. Richard I., Edward III., Henry V., Elizabeth, William III., and Anne.

The Prince's chamber comes next and serves as a kind of ante-room to the House of Lords, and it is here the queen is received by the principal nobility, before entering the house. This room has a very large statue of Queen Victoria, supported by figures representing Justice and Mercy. The walls are covered with full-length portraits of the kings and queens of England from 1485 to 1603. Henry VIII. and all his wives appear. There is also a fine full-length portrait of Mary, Queen of Scots. The ceiling is beautiful; a dark blue, with the arms of the three Kingdoms and floral and other designs in gold.

We now enter the House of Lords, and are in what the guide book says is "The finest specimen of Gothic civil architecture in Europe.", The chamber is ninety by forty-five feet, but the great height of the ceiling (forty-five feet) makes it appear much smaller. The throne is at the south end, next to the prince's chamber, and with the platform and space surrounding it, occupies about one-third of the room. The light comes through twelve lofty windows of stained glass, six on each side. The stained glass is remarkably brilliant, representing all the kings and queens, both regnant and consort, from William the Conqueror to Queen Victoria. There are more female figures than male, and as the artists were not hampered by those ideas of sanctity and its supposed appropriate paleness of color which affect the robes of saints and martyrs in cathedral windows, but were allowed to revel in all gorgeousness of color in the rich draperies of the queens, the effect is rich and brilliant beyond description. A narrow railed gallery surrounds the House, that at the end opposite the throne being the reporter's gallery, and in a recess back of it is the stranger's gallery. The House is divided into three parts, at the south end the throne with its appendages, and at the other end a small enclosure known as the bar, is railed off. The bar would probably accommodate, conveniently, a dozen people, and is supposed to contain the members of the house of commons when her majesty reads her message to both houses. It is also used by counsel when judicial proceedings are in progress before the house. On one side of the bar is the quarters of the usher of the black rod, and at the other seats for the sons of peers.

The space between the platform of the House and the bar is seated for the use of the members. It is a space, I should judge, not exceeding forty-five by fifty-five feet and has seats or rather benches, said to accommodate 250 members. The "Woolsack" is a large ottoman, so heavily cushioned with crimson cloth as to somewhat resemble in form its namesake, and is the seat of the lord chancellor. There are, in the center, a number of desks for the clerks, and on the sides, rows of benches rising above each other, circus fashion, for the use of the members. The benches are broad and the backs look comfortable, being covered with purple morocco and stuffed. The lords have no desks or tables, but sit like the boys in a country schoolhouse before desks were invented. One would suppose the position must be uncomfortable. The coat tails of the noble lords in front must be respected, the seats cannot be "tilted," and there is no chance to get the heels up on anything. No American legislative body would endure such an invasion of personal liberty and individual rights for a single day. To be honest about it, and jesting aside, it seems to me it would be difficult to devise a place more

4

inconveniently arranged for the purposes of legislation, than the House of Lords.

The throne, although used but seldom, as her majesty's visits are few and far between, occupies, as I have said, about one-third of the room. It is elevated three steps from the floor, the platform being covered with the richest scarlet velvet; the figures are lions and roses worked in gold, with a heavy gold fringe by way of border. At each side of the throne, and a step lower, is a chair of state. One was intended for the Prince Consort, the other for the Prince of Wales. There is a canopy over each, that over the throne being much higher and the decorations much finer than over the chairs of state. The beauty and richness of the carvings, gildings and colorings of the canopy, and the recess back of the throne, it is impossible to describe. The throne is a high, gabled arm chair, elaborately carved, and entirely covered with gold. It rests on four small gilt lions. The footstool is about eighteen inches long, covered with the richest crimson velvet, embroidered with gold.

The frescoing is a marvel of art, the entire walls being covered with historical paintings by the best artists England affords. There are numerous small gilded statues in the niches, among them the effigies of the eighteen barons deputed to obtain Magna Charta of King John. I have noted the subjects of most of the paintings but shall not inflict them on my readers. Indeed, it is impossible to convey any idea of the beauty and magnificence of this room. All that the highest art, stimulated by money without limit, could do, has been done to make the House of Lords the most royally magnificent room in the world.

The Peers' lobby is the principal entrance to the House of Lords. It is thirty-eight feet square and thirty feet high. It is decorated in the most elaborate style, and has a peculiarly elegant appearance. The walls, ceiling and floor might be described at great length but I forbear. The most novel thing in this room is the massive brass gates of the south door, weighing one and a half tons. The workmanship is wonderfully intricate and beautiful.

The central hall is sixty feet in diameter and octagonal in form, vaulted over with stone. The enormous stones which form the ribs of the roof, are inlaid with Venetian glass mosaic in numerous devices. Each of the eight sides has archways with six niches, beautifully designed; in each, and filled with statues of kings and queens.

The House of Commons is seventy by forty-five feet and forty-five feet high, and is much plainer in its decorations and furnishings than the House of Lords. The speaker's chair is at the north end and beneath it is the clerk's table, on which lies the mace, made after the restoration to replace the "fool's bauble" which Cromwell ordered his soldiers to take away. Over the speaker's chair is the visitors' gallery. The benches to the right of the speaker are occupied by the party of the government for the time being, the leaders occupying the front seats. The opposition occupy the benches on the other side. There is sitting room for 476 members, and there are no desks except for the clerks. Now, there are 658 members of the house of commons, so that 182 members are not provided with seats. Of course, members can vote by proxy, and yet it seems strange to me that in a building covering eight acres there should not have been provision made for seating all the members of the popular branch of the government.

The metropolitan police are in charge of the building, and although watchful, are very polite and willing to give information. One of them, evidently proposing to do me a favor, took pains to conduct me to an ante-room, where was an extensive system of hat-racks, each peg bearing the card of a member of the house of lords. He solemnly pointed to a card bearing the name of "Beaconsfield." I gazed at the peg where was wont to rest the tile of the deceased Jew with as interested an expression as under the circumstances I could assume—the kindly intention of my guide was evident.

The clock tower is 320 feet high and said to contain the finest tower clock in the world. The dial is the largest yet made, being twenty-three and a half feet in diameter. This tower occupies the site of the clock tower of Edward I., where the "Great Tom of Westminster" sounded the hours for the judges of England who held court in the adjoining buildings. The expense of erecting the tower had been defrayed by a fine on Hingham, Chief Justice of England. An old chronicle says, " It's intent was, by the clock striking continually, to remind the judges in the neighboring courts to administer true justice, they calling thereby to mind the occasion and means of its building."

In the reign of William and Mary a curious circumstance occurred in connection with this clock. One of the guards at Windsor Castle, twenty miles distant, was accused of having fallen asleep at his post, was tried, and condemned to death. He however asserted his innocence, claiming as a proof of his being awake that at midnight he had heard Great Tom of Westminster strike thirteen. This was doubted, both on account of the great distance and its improbability, but before the time fixed for the execution, the evidence of this little eccentricity on the part of the clock was so conclusive that the condemned man received the royal pardon.

Adjoining the parliament houses on the west, and now used as a vestibule, is Westminster Hall, built by William Rufus, who held court here in 1099. It has witnessed more tragic scenes in English history than any other building in England except the Tower of London. It is 290 feet long,

70 feet wide, 90 feet high, and its large square towers and high gable front on New Palace Yard. Parliament assembled in Westminster as early as 1248, and in it the highest court in England has been held for over seven centuries. Here Sir Wm. Wallace and Sir John Oldcastle were condemned to death, and it was here the Duke of Buckingham, on being condemned to the scaffold in 1522, made the touching speech familiar in the words of Shakespeare. Sir Thomas More, Bishop Fisher, Protector Somerset, Duke of Norfolk, Earl of Essex, Duke and Duchess of Somerset are a few names of the many who have been tried and received their death sentence in Westminster. Here in 1640 Charles I and his queen listened to the eighteen days' trial of the Earl of Strafford, the king being compelled to abandon his favorite to the vengeance of the growing puritanical sentiment in parliament. Nine years later the king himself sat in Westminster Hall a prisoner, with the banners captured at Naseby hanging over his head, and was condemned, as a "tyrant, traitor, and murderer," to be executed in front of his palace of Whitehall. The last great trial in Westminster Hall was that of Warren Hastings, so eloquently described by Macauley. Many other scenes and pageants occur to me as I gaze on its carved oak ceiling and bare walls; the only thing it now contains is about a dozen statues of English kings and queens. All the coronation banquets from Wm. Rufus to George IV. have been held in Westminster Hall.

On the opposite side of Parliament street is Parliament Square, an open space containing a beautiful Gothic fountain and a number of bronze statues of modern statesmen. Adjoining this square, on the south, is St. Margaret's Church, a place of much interest. During the commonwealth St. Margaret's was the church of the house of commons, and its pulpit was occupied by the leading

Puritan divines, among them Calamy, Owen, Baxter and Lightfoot. The preaching of that day was wonderfully personal in its character, and the minister did not "beat about the bush" in making the application. In St. Margaret's the leading men of the day, even Cromwell himself, were freely denounced on account of their supposed shortcomings. One of these fiery Puritans, preaching before General Monk, cried out : "There are some who will betray three kingdoms for filthy lucre's sake," and threw his handkerchief in the General's pew ! " I wish we had such a preacher in Washington," said an American lady, as the story was told us by a reverend divine, evidently posted on the history of St. Margaret's. "Where in the world would the poor man find a supply of handkerchiefs" was the quick response of another lady, evidently posted in regard to Washington.

A beautiful window, presented by Ferdinand and Isabella of Spain to Henry VII., is much admired. It represents the crucifixion with attendant horrors in truly Catholic style, but with a beauty and delicacy of coloring that is rarely seen. The monuments and inscriptions are numerous, and many of them of much historical interest. Beneath the altar rest the remains of Sir Walter Raleigh, beheaded in Palace Yard in 1618.

## CHAPTER VI.

### LONDON.

Westminster Abbey—Anticipations—First Impressions—History—A City of the Dead—Poet's Corner—Monuments and Memorials—Henry VII's Chapel —Chapel of Edward the Confessor—Coronation Chair—Musings and Recollections—Outside Surroundings.

Next to St. Margaret's Church, on the south, is Westminster Abbey. For a quarter of a century I had indulged the hope of one day visiting this historic building—"the silent meeting-place of the great dead of eight centuries;" a spot sacred to all who inherit the English tongue. It had been a sort of day-dream,

> "Through the aisles of Westminster to roam,
> Where bubbles burst, and folly's dancing foam
> Melts, if it cross the threshold."

It was therefore with feelings of no ordinary interest that, approaching it from the west, I first beheld its lofty and pinnacled towers. The deeply recessed Gothic doorway below, and huge Gothic window above, seemed familiar, so often had I seen them illustrated in books and engravings. The exterior has much Gothic decoration, and, darkened by the breath of centuries, would be interesting and imposing on merely architectural grounds, were it not for the wonderful attractiveness of the interior, and its wealth of noble dust.

There is a great deal in first impressions; and I am glad that my first visit to this, the most interesting of the historical places in London, or, indeed, in England, was made on a beautiful Sunday morning, to attend Divine service, and not with the week-day visitors, to be shown around at so much per head. Phrenologists say my bump of reverence is not largely developed, and I was surprised to find myself so moved and impressed by my surroundings. As I walked down the aisle to a seat in that part of the nave railed off for church service, my eyes took in the profusion of monuments and statues which encircle the walls and aisles of the building. The solemn notes of the organ were echoing through the lofty columns and arches, and as the fine choir joined in an anthem of praise, I felt as if I was indeed on holy ground. An English writer has said "In St. Peter's at Rome, one is convinced that it was built by great princes. In Westminster Abbey, one thinks not of the builder; the religion of the place makes the first impression, and though stripped of its shrine and altars, it is nearer converting one to popery that all the regular pageantry of Roman domes." Sweeter music I never heard and the acoustic qualities of the building must be excellent as every word of the anthems and hymns could be distinctly heard. The responses in monochord by the choir, were simply perfect. An American, sitting beside me, must have been impressed as I was. He whispered, "Did you ever hear so much music in an Amen," and I confessed that I never had. The service was read by Canon Duckworth, the clergyman that, according to the newspapers, the Princess Louise wanted to marry, and the very excellent sermon was by Canon Pierson.

I visited the abbey next as a sight-seer, note book in hand, but with a reverence for the place and its surroundings already established. Like many of the English churches, Westminster Abbey is said to occupy the site of a heathen temple. The first Christian church was erected by Sebert, king of the East Saxons, A. D. 610. It was destroyed by the Danes, but rebuilt by Edward the Confessor, A. D. 1050, who made it an abbey, and ordained that all the English monarchs should be crowned here. The coronation of every English sovereign since that time has taken place in Westminster Abbey. Here too are buried many of England's kings and queens. The poet has happily expressed it :

> " That antique pile behold,
> Where royal heads receive the sacred gold;
> It gives them crowns, and does their ashes keep;
> There made like Gods, like mortals there they sleep,
> Making the circle of their reign complete—
> These suns of empire, where they rise they set."

Here also are buried so many of the distinguished men of Great Britain, as to almost make it a national temple of fame. Indeed the highest honor that can be bestowed on a deceased Englishman, is burial here. "Victory or Westminster Abbey" was the electric cry, understood and appreciated by his men, with which Nelson entered the battle of Cape St. Vincent. This venerable edifice has seen England successively Saxon, Norman, and English. Within its walls the Catholic mass has been chanted, and the Anglican service read ; and under its roof the Westminster Assembly's Confession of Faith was formulated and from thence was published. It has seen England an absolute monarchy, a republic and a constitutional monarchy. Indeed the memories and histories which are associated with this place, are calculated to excite and interest in a wonderful degree one familiar with English history.

The abbey is in the form of a cross, about 400 feet long, and 200 wide at the transepts. To this may be added Henry VII's Chapel, built on the east end, 115 feet long and 80 feet in width. There are various styles of architecture employed in the interior, especially in the chapels and cloisters, but the interesting memorials they contain make one neglect or forget the fine points of the noble building; and yet, as my eye followed the curves of the massive and finely wrought arches till they met one hundred feet above me, I could not help feeling that

> "They dreamed not of a perishable home
> Who thus could build "

Indeed there is a great pleasure in contemplating the arched and ornamented ceilings of lofty cathedrals. The upturned eye does not call back the aspiring soul to count cracks or cobwebs, but one enjoys to the full the

> "Arch'd and ponderous roof,
> By its own weight made steadfast and immovable,
> Looking tranquility!"

One is not impressed at any point in the interior with the great size of the building. It is so broken up by partitions, and screens, and railings, and columns, and arches, that it must be seen and studied in detail. There is but little sameness ; scarcely a chapel or tomb or memorial resembles any other. The impression soon takes possession of one that he is in a great city of the dead. Every inch of space has its tomb or memorial, and

> "Speaking marbles show
> What worthies form the hallowed mould below;
> Proud names, who once the reins of empire held;
> In arms who triumph'd, or in arts excelled;
> Chiefs, graced with scars, and prodigal of blood;
> Stern patriots, who for sacred freedom stood;
> Just men, by whom impartial laws were given;
> And saints, who taught and led the way to heaven."

Hardly a noted family in England but is represented here by some of its members.

Entering the south transept we are in what is known as Poet's Corner, a name first mentioned by Goldsmith. Geoffry Chaucer, "the father of English poetry," was buried here in 1400, and near him lie Spencer, Drayton, Dryden, Cowley, Gay, Prior,—" enough almost to make passengers' feet to move rythmically, who go over the place where so much poetical dust is interred." There are monuments or memorials to those I have mentioned and also to Milton, Goldsmith, Thompson, Campbell, Gray, Butler, Southey, and others, whose names and works are not so familiar. Indeed one is surprised to find so many of the great poets unrepresented, and led to accept the statement of Addison, that "There are many poets who have no monuments, and many monuments which have no poets." There is a fine statue of Addison and near it rest the remains of Macauley and Charles Dickens. There are also monuments to Garrick, Sheridan, Beaumont, Thackeray, Grote and "rare Ben Johnson." There is a fine monument to Shakespeare, the figure of the poet representing an elegant and refined gentleman in an easy attitude. The heads on the pedestal represent Henry V., Richard III., and Queen Elizabeth. On a scroll appears the well known lines of the poet:

> "The cloud-capp'd towers, the gorgeous palaces,
> The solemn temples, the great globe itself,
> Yea, all which it inherit, shall dissolve;
> And, like this insubstantial pageant faded—
> Leave not a rack behind."

I greatly admired a fine monument to Handel by the sculptor Roubiliac. The left arm of the composer is resting on a group of musical instruments, and he is represented as listening interestedly to the music of an angel, playing a harp in the clouds over his head. Before him lies the score of the Messiah, with the page open containing the well known air, "I know that my Redeemer liveth."

The nave contains a wonderful variety of tombs and memorials, very many of them being designed to perpetuate the memories of persons long since forgotten. Indeed, the number of almost unknown persons who have secured recognition, in all parts of the building, is surprising. Buried in a country churchyard they might, by a costly monument, have acquired a local fame, but in Westminster Abbey none will pause to read their vulgarly obtrusive epitaphs. I can give but a very few of the more important names which appear in nave and transepts.

A fine monument to Sir Isaac Newton, shows a reclining figure of the philosopher, his right arm leaning on four of his books.  Over him is a large globe, on which is a figure of Astronomy sitting, with her book closed.  Underneath is a bas-relief showing the principal discoveries of the deceased, the most striking of which to me was a representation of Sir Isaac weighing the globe with a steelyard!  Near by rest the remains of Sir John Herschel.  Near a new and magnificent memorial window, and under a life size statue of brass lie the remains, of Robert Stephenson, and near by Lord Clyde and David Livingstone.  In the pavement is a memorial stone to "Rare Ben Johnson," who is buried beneath it.  Near each other rest the great rival orators, Charles James Fox and the younger Pitt, who both died in the same year, 1806, recalling the words of Sir Walter Scott:

> "The mighty chiefs lie side by side;
> Drop upon Fox's grave the tear,
> 'Twill trickle to his rival's bier;
> O'er Pitt's the mournful requiem sound,
> And Fox's shall the notes rebound."

In the choir are the Tombs of King Sebert, who first built a church on this site, and died in 616, and Athelgoda his queen, who died in 615.  Also of Edward Crouchback, son of Edward III., and of Anne of Cleves, wife of Henry VIII.

In the north aisle and transept are fine statues of Sir Robert Peel, George Canning, William Pitt, first Earl of Chatham, Lord Palmerston, Lord Mansfield, Jonas Hanway, Richard Cobden, and Lord Halifax.  There is a fine new monument to Fowell Buxton, the abolitionist; also one to the memory of Wilberforce, the philanthropist, with a very long inscription giving an accounpt of his life and labors.  There are also memorials to Hunter the anatomist, and Brunel the engineer.  The eminent musicians and composers, Dr. Croft, Dr. Arnold, Dr. Blow, Henry Purcell, William Sterndale Bennet, and Dr. Charles Burney, author of a valuable history of music, are buried here.  On Purcell's tomb is the decidedly extravagant inscription: "Here lies Henry Purcell, who left this life and is gone to that blessed place, where only his harmony can be excelled."

In the south aisle are busts of Charles Kingsley and Frederic D. Maurice; also a very fine statue of the poet Wordsworth and memorials to Keble, author of the "Christian Year," to Dr. Watts, and to John and Charles Wesley. There is a fine monument to Lord Viscount Howe, containing a figure said to be "the Genius of the Province of Massachusetts Bay," whatever that may mean. The tomb according to the inscription, in remarkably large letters, was erected by an order of the "Great and General Court of the Province of Massachusetts Bay, bearing date February 1, 1759." On a moulded and paneled base stands a sarcophagus, with an inscription to the memory of Major Andre, who is buried near by, erected by order of George III. There are bas-reliefs containing figures of General Washington and others. Washington is represented as receiving the bearer of a letter written by Major Andre the night before his execution, pleading for a soldier's death, and not to "die on the gibbet." Washington is now wearing his third head, two having been knocked off and carried away, either by the relic hunters or by sympathizers with the unfortunate Andre.

There are twelve chapels in the abbey, affording resting places for departed greatness, and mostly for members of the royal families of England. All are interesting, and there is a wonderful variety, both in the character of the designs and in their execution. The changes in architecture and in the arts during eight centuries are represented, both in the chapels and the memorials which they contain. I can afford space for but a brief description of two of these chapels, from which some idea of the general character of the others may be obtained.

Passing up a flight of steps, through a magnificent archway and great gates of brass, we enter Henry VII.'s chapel. I recalled the words of Irving, which had seemed to me fanciful and extravagant, but now, in view of the scene described, tame and commonplace: "On entering, the eye is astonished by the pomp of architecture, and the elaborate beauty of sculptured detail. The very walls are wrought into universal ornament, incrusted with tracery, and scooped into niches, crowded with statues of saints and martyrs. Stone seems, by the cunning labor of the chisel, to have been robbed of its weight and density, suspended aloft, as if by magic, and the fretted roof achieved with the wonderful minuteness and airy security of a cobweb."

This chapel is 115 by 80 feet and the ceiling about 70 feet high. Its interior has been more freqently illustrated by pictures and engravings than any other part of the abbey, and is wonderfully beautiful. The stalls of the knights of the bath surround the chapel, the end stall being decorated by a figure of Henry VII. About a hundred statues of patriarchs, saints, and martyrs surround the walls, placed in niches supported by figures of angels. Not far from the center of the chapel is the tomb of Henry VII., and his wife, Elizabeth of York. It is enclosed in a chantry of brass, ornamented by brass statues of saints and angels, and of the Virgin and Child. Within, on a tomb of black marble, are effigies of the royal pair wrapped in mantles descending to their feet. The crowns they once wore have been stolen. This tomb was pronounced by Lord Bacon "One of the stateliest and daintiest tombs in Europe." Near to it is the tomb of George II. and his queen.

A restored altar marks the burial place of Edward VI. The ancient altar was destroyed in the civil wars, but a part of it was found in the grave of the king, and has been inserted in the new altar, which also contains a piece of an Abyssianian altar brought from Magdala, a fragment of a Greek altar, and a piece of the high altar of Canterbury, destroyed in 1174. This restored altar was first used in 1870, when Dean Stanley administered the sacrament to the revisers of the New Testament, composed of representatives of almost all the protestant denominations, an exhibition of christian love and brotherhood, severely criticised in certain quarters.

In the south aisle is the old royal vault, containing the remains of Charles II., William III., and Mary his queen, Prince George of Denmark and Queen Anne. Near by is the tomb of Edward VI., and also of a large number of the members of the royal family. In the north aisle are buried Edward V. and his brother the Duke of York, the young Princes murdered in the Tower by their treacherous uncle Richard III. They were privately buried near the scene of their murder in the Tower, but their remains were, by order of Charles II., removed to Westminster Abbey. Here is the magnificent tomb of Queen Elizabeth, erected by her successor, James I., and in the same tomb is buried her half sister Queen Mary, the last Catholic sovereign of England interred here. It required all Elizabeth's wonderful sagacity and cunning to keep her head on her shoulders during Mary's troubled reign, and her Protestantism kept England in a ferment as to her succession to the throne, and now, Catholic and Protestant, they rest in one tomb. And as if to illustrate more fully the folly of human enmities and rivalries, but a few feet from the tomb of Elizabeth stands the magnificent tomb of her victim, the unfortunate Mary, Queen of Scots,—and both tombs were erected by James I., son of the beheaded Mary!

Taking advantage of a neighboring stairway I had a good view of the features of Elizabeth, as shown in her effigy, reclining on a rather high tomb. She is represented as old, and with a decidedly haggish and ghoul-like expression, just the sort of face one would like to forget as soon as possible. It occurred to me that if the spirit of Elizabeth could occupy that marble form, how the unceasing sigh of pity over the grave of her victim, the "unfortunate" Mary, would echo as an everlasting torment to the soul of the "illustrious" Elizabeth. In all parts of this chapel may be found elaborate monuments to persons illustrious in English history. The last interment is that of Dean Stanley, his wife had been buried here in 1870.

The chapel of Edward the Confessor is usually considered the center of interest in the abbey. Near its center is the ancient shrine of the confessor, who died in 1066, and was canonized in 1161. It was once most beautiful, but has been sadly defaced, and robbed of its loveliness by devotees and relic hunters, bound to have a piece of the tomb of this most pious man. His shrine was before the Reformation a place of pilgrimage, and is still so regarded by Roman Catholics. Beside him rest the remains of his wife Editha, who died in 1073, and many of his relatives. Near by is the grave of Matilda, daughter of Malcolm, King of Scots, and wife of Henry I., who died in 1118. On the north side of the chapel is a tomb of fine material and workmanship, to the memory of Henry III., who died in 1272. It has a fine gilt effigy of the king and is one of the richest looking works of art in the chapel. The tomb of Henry V., "Henry of Monmouth" and hero of Agincourt, is next, and contains a marble slab on which lies a headless figure of the king. The body was carved of English oak, but the head was cast of silver, and has been stolen on account of its intrinsic value. In the chantry above the tomb are some interesting relics—the saddle, shield and helmet used by the king at the battle of Agincourt. It was on this saddle he

"Vaulted with such ease into his seat,
As if an angel dropp'd down from the clouds.

And the helmet is "that very casque that did affright the air at Agincourt," and shows plainly the marks of the sword of the Duke of Alencon. The king refused to have this battered helmet carried before him on his triumphal entry into London, "for that he would have the praise chiefly given to God." The king ordained that masses for his soul should be "forever" offered in the chantry. The last mass said in the abbey was at the funeral of Mary in 1558.

The tomb of Edward III. and his queen is covered with a Gothic canopy, and is, like most of the others, surrounded with statues of the family and friends of the deceased monarch, numbering about thirty in all. This feature of these ancient tombs is of great interest, as they are probably correct likenesses of the persons they are intended to represent. Richard II. and his queen have a joint tomb, on which lie the royal pair in effigy. The king had ordered that they should be represented with hands joined in loving clasp, but their arms have been ruthlessly stolen; indeed almost every tomb in the chapel has been despoiled of some of its parts or ornamentation. One of the plainest tombs is that of the famous crusader, Edward I., greatest of the Plantaganet kings. Near by is the tomb of his queen, "Eleanor of good memory," her effigy shows a face of great beauty.

In this chapel is the coronation chair, in which all the sovereigns of England from Edward I., or for nearly seven centuries, have been crowned. It is a high-backed and gabled arm chair. The seat is split and it looks rickety. It has been much whittled and sadly marred by relic seekers who desired a piece of the chair, and the name and initial cutting fiends have at some period had it all their own way.

What could be more disgusting than to see J. Smith, in capitals, carved on the seat. Securely fastened under the seat by iron bands is a stone, fifteen by twenty-six inches and eleven inches thick, known as the Stone of Scone. According to tradition, this stone is the pillow on which Jacob rested his head, when he dreamed of the angels ascending and descending the ladder which reached to heaven. The stone was carried by his descendants into Egypt, and after many migrations it found its way to Ireland, where it served the useful purpose of testing the claims of rival aspirants for the throne. If when the new claimant was placed upon it, it remained silent, it proved him to be the true successor; if it groaned aloud, it showed him to be a pretender. From Ireland it was captured and carried to Scotland where, in 840, it was enclosed in a chair of wood and placed in the chapel of the abbey at Scone. It was now used as the coronation seat of the kings of Scotland. One cannot but regret its removal from Ireland, for although the stone, so far as we know, has remained silent, that unhappy country has not been quiet since. After the battle of Dunbar in 1296, Edward I. had himself crowned king of Scotland, at Scone, seated upon the "Sacred Stone." Returning to England, he carried the stone with him, and had it placed in the coronation chair of England, where it has since remained. Only once, since that time, has it been outside of Westminster Abbey. When Cromwell was installed as Lord Protector in Westminster Hall, the famous chair and stone were brought from the abbey for the occasion. Probably no other incident in its history so fully illustrates the importance attached to it. Cromwell could afford to ignore Westminster Abbey, the coronation place of kings, but did not care to be installed ruler of England except as seated on the Stone of Scone. There is another coronation chair, very similar in appearance to the ancient one, made about 200 years since, for the coronation of Mary, wife of William III., who reigned jointly with her husband.

I spent some time in the various chapels, re-reading the history of England, in the presence of tombs erected by kings and queens whose names I had been accustomed to associate with the remote ages of the past. Occasionally, through an open door, the solemn notes of the organ, accompanying the fresh and musical voices of the boy choir could be heard, and

> "The fretted aisles prolong
> The distant notes of holy song,
> As if some angel spoke again
> All peace on earth, good will to men."

To put in fitting words the thoughts that oppress one amid such surroundings is impossible. Jeremy Taylor has well said, "A man may read a sermon, the best and most passionate that man ever preached, if he shall but enter into the sepulcher of kings."

> "Think how many royal bones
> Sleep within these heaps of stones!
> Here they lie—had realms and lands,
> Who now want strength to lift their hands,
> Where, from their pulpit, sealed with dust,
> They preach, 'In greatness is no trust,'
> Here's an acre, sown, indeed,
> With the richest royal seed
> That the earth did e'er suck in
> Since the first man died for sin."

I was much impressed by the deeply religious character of the old tombs in the chapels, with their profusion of saints and angels, martyrs and confessors, as compared with the semi-paganism of the modern monuments in the nave and transepts. Indeed some of these modern memorials seem out of place, in a building consecrated to Christian worship. While figures representing Britain, history, fame, liberty, death, etc., may be permissable; Neptune, Apollo, Minerva and Hercules seem out of place. Another thing that attracted my attention was the peculiar dress of the modern statesmen, as seen in the nave and transepts. Why a deceased Englishman should be represented in a Roman toga, any more than in a Highland kilt, I cannot imagine. Nor can I admire the taste, which, on their monuments, strips almost naked men of respectability, who had the decency to wear clothes during their lifetime. It is a small matter, to be sure, but I could not help speculating on how the brave British sailor, Sir Cloudsley Shovel, came by his Roman helmet and sandals!

Tired, almost bewildered with what my eyes had seen, and the historical incidents which they had recalled, I sat down in a seat near the center of the nave. The sun's rays, passing through the richly painted memorial windows, fell directly upon me. Monuments, tablets, statues, busts, historical inscriptions, and emblematical groups and figures seemed to entirely surround me. I rested my head on the seat before me, and soon, by some occult chain of thought, my mind was directed to a far different scene. I remembered that this 17th of August is my birthday, that this afternoon hour is noon in a far off home, that in a familiar room mother, wife and children are enjoying the mid-day meal. Do they think of me? Are there any delicacies on the table to remind the children that this is papa's birthday? Can the baby talk plainer, and will he know me when I return? A feeling of home-sickness, a moistness of the eyes—when the sharp bang of a door aroused me to my surroundings, and warned me that the hour for closing the abbey had arrived. The attendant seemed surprised, as he saw a visitor hastily arise and wipe his eyes before leaving the abbey. He did not know how far from Westminster, and all that makes it interesting and glorious, was the stranger's heart and thoughts; or that the recollection of his Michigan home and loved ones had obliterated for the time being, and in its

## VICINITY OF WESTMINSTER.

sacred presence, the venerable pile and all that it contained.

On leaving Westminster Abbey, I selected the corner of King and St. George's streets as affording the finest view of the abbey and its surroundings. South of the abbey is the Dean's Yard and in front of it a fine memorial column to the Scholars of Westminster School who died in the Crimean war. On the east are the Parliament Houses, Westminster Hall and the Law Courts. On the west the Royal Aquarium. On the north St. Margaret's Church, Parliament Square, and the Session House—sometimes called Westminster Guildhall. Following the line of St. George's street east, is Westminster Bridge leading to Lambeth. It is seldom that the eye is permitted to take in such a scene. When the abbey was founded its site was on an island, outside the walls of the city, surrounded by almost impenetrable woods and extensive marshes, and known as the Isle of Thorns. Now London has so enlarged its borders that I stand near the abbey and not far from the heart of the largest, most populous and busiest commercial center in the world.

## CHAPTER VII.

### LONDON.

The Strand—Somerset House—Law Courts—Temple Bar—Fleet Street—Temple Gardens—Ludgate Hill—St. Paul's Church—Sabath Services—Monuments—Crypt—Tombs of Wellington and Nelson—Whispering Gallery—In the Ball—Paternoster Row—Newgate—St. Sulpice's—London Stone—The Monument—Billingsgate—Tower of London—St. Thomas' Tower—White Tower—Chapel of St. John—Horse Armory—Crown Jewels—Tower Palace—Prisoners of the Tower—Beauchamp Tower—Inscriptions—Chapel of St. Peter—Ancient Scaffold—Anna Boleyn, Lady Jane Grey, etc.—By the Traitor's Gate.

Returning from Westminster to my starting point at Charing Cross, I will proceed by the ancient highway of the Strand, Fleet street, and Ludgate Hill to St. Paul's Church. The Strand is a street near the river and running nearly parallel with it ; indeed it derives its name, Strand, from this fact. It is now a very plain and substantial business street, modern in appearance, and with but little taste observable, either in the stores or in the arrangement of goods in the windows.  It was formerly a street of palatial residences, and the great highway between the royal palace at Westminster and the royal palace on the Fleet, as well as between the Tower and Westminster Abbey.

One familiar with English history will recall many a coronation procession, royal wedding party, and knightly pageant that has passed through the Strand; and how many royal and noble funerals has it witnessed, on their way to Westminster, since the coffin of good Queen Eleanor rested at Charing Cross !  It was here, Charles Lamb said, he "often shed tears of joy at such multitude of life ;" and a poet of the seventeenth century speaks of

## THE STRAND.

> "The Strand, that goodly throw-fare betweene
> The Court and City: and where I have seen
> Well-nigh a million passing in one day."

We pass Charing Cross station and hotel, one of the largest in London, and soon reach on our right, Somerset House, on the site of an old palace erected by Lord Protector Somerset. The present building is about a hundred years old and is quadrangular in form, with an inner court in which is a very ugly statue, said to represent Father Thames. "Why did you make so frightful a figure?" said Queen Charlotte to the sculptor. "Art cannot always effect what is ever within the reach of nature—the union of beauty and majesty;" was the cunning reply of the artist. There is another bronze statue in this court, to which my attention was called as that of the "last king of America." To my surprise, it was neither Roscoe Conkling nor Jay Gould—only George III. The river front of Somerset House is about eight hundred feet in length. It is in the Italian style, enriched with much ornamentation, and is one of the finest works of the kind in London. The building is now used principally for government offices.

Nearly opposite Somerset House is the church of St. Mary's Le Strand, occupying the site of the old Maypole. The church is in the street, narrowing the Strand to about half its usual width. St. Clement's Danes Church comes next, and like St. Mary's, occupies part of the street. Harold Harefoote, a son of Canute, and other Danes are buried here. Dr. Johnson was for twenty years a worshiper at this church, and there is a tablet to his memory in the pew which he occupied in one of the galleries. At the termination of the Strand is the new Courts of Law. They are immense buildings, partly occupied and not quite completed. The Strand front is about thirty rods long and is partly in Fleet street, so that part of the buildings, including the great Campanile or Bell Tower, are in the city, the remainder being in the "shire." These buildings are intended to accommodate all the higher law courts in the city. Instead of a description I will give a few facts as to their cost; etc. They cover seven acres, and contain 1,100 apartments. Parliament paid seven and a quarter million dollars for the land on which they are built, and which was occupied by some of the poorest tenement buildings in the city, containing however some places of much historic interest. The contract price for the buildings is three and a half million dollars. I would say here in regard to all modern buildings in London, that I am told they can be built for about half what it would cost to erect similar buildings in the United States. The 50 to 100 per cent. steal on some of our public buildings is not reckoned in this estimate.

Temple Bar, was a gate crossing the street where Strand ends and Fleet street begins, and served to indicate where the jurisdiction of the city of London ended. The city proper terminated at Ludgate, but the "liberty," or "freedom" of the city extended to Temple Bar. The pictures of the old Bar represent quite an imposing structure, with Corinthian pilasters and statues of kings. It was on spikes, over this Bar, that the head and limbs of persons executed for treason were exhibited. Formerly when the sovereign visited the city from the palaces of Whitehall or Westminster, it was customary to keep the gates at Temple Bar closed till admission was demanded, when the gates were opened and the Lord Mayor surrendered his official sword, which was graciously returned by the sovereign. The old Bar greatly obstructed travel on so important a thoroughfare, and was recently removed and a memorial erected on its site. The memorial is about six by eight feet and about thirty feet high. Its position, in the center of the street, furnishes a refuge for persons crossing the road. As a work of art it is very fine. There are on the sides, marble life-size statues of the Queen and Prince of Wales, and medallions and bas-reliefs containing views of the old Bar and scenes in the life of the present queen.

Having passed Temple Bar, we are in Fleet Street. It derives its name from the Fleet, a small stream which used to run between it and Ludgate Hill, emptying into the Thames at Blackfriars. On our right is the Temple; so named from the Knights Templar, who occupied the place from 1184 until their estates were forfeited by the pope. It afterward became the property of the crown, and is now held in trust by an association of lawyers, for the purpose of lodging and educating members of that profession. The gateway on Fleet Street was built by Sir Christopher Wren. The Middle Temple Hall was built in the sixteenth century. Temple Church consists of two parts—the round and the choir. The round is the ancient church, and was built by the Knights Templar in 1185, after their return from the second crusade. The whole edifice has been restored, at great expense, during the present century, and is now in excellent repair. Back of the Temple, and between it and the Thames, are the Temple gardens. One is surprised to find gardens in so thickly settled a locality, but these are of historic interest. It was here, according to Shakespeare, that the War of the Roses originated:

PLANTAGANET—
"Let him that is a true born gentleman,
And stands upon the honor of his birth,
If he supposes that I have pleaded truth
From off this briar pluck a white rose with me."

SOMERSET—
"Let him that is no coward nor no flatterer,
But dare maintain the party of the truth,
Pluck a red rose from off this thorn with me.
 \*   \*   \*   \*   \*   \*   \*

WARWICK—
"This brawl to-day
Grown to this faction in the Temple Gardens
Shall send, between the red rose and the white,
A thousand souls to death and deadly night."

We now pass Chancery Lane, the great legal thoroughfare of London, running from Fleet Street past Lincoln's Inn, to Gray's Inn. The Church of St. Dunstan's-in-the-west is on our left,—a new church, erected on the site of a very old one. We pass Fetter Lane, a place of many historic associations. In the Moravian chapel in this lane, Richard Baxter once preached. We reach Farringdon Street, where stood the Fleet Prison, and through which ran the Fleet River. On part of the prison site a Memorial Building has been erected, in memory of the victims of religious persecution incarcerated here—among them Bishop Hooper, and others, who were burned at the stake for opinion's sake. After the abolition of the Star Chamber the Fleet became a debtor's prison, and was not abolished until 1846, having existed for eight centuries. Fleet Street is known as the center of the newspaper business. Here are the offices of the *Daily Telegraph, Daily News, Standard, Morning Advertiser, Daily Chronicle, London Punch* and a very large number of other papers and periodicals.

Fleet Street ends at Farringdon Street, and is continued to St. Paul's Church as Ludgate Hill. The crossing at Farringdon Street is called Ludgate Circus, the corners of the buildings being cut off so as to form a circle. This, by the way, is quite common in all parts of the city, and explains the frequent use of the word Circus. The name of the ancient gate which stood here—Ludgate—is said to be derived from King Lud, 66 B. C. From Farringdon Street to St. Paul's the ascent is somewhat steep. On our left is the Old Bailey, a criminal court; on the right an archway leads by a narrow lane to Printing House Square, where the king's printing house stood in the days of the Stuarts, but where now the London *Times* is printed from a roll of paper 300 miles long, at the rate of 100 papers per minute. On the left is St. Martin's Church, and Stationers'

Hall, where books are registered to preserve the copyright; "Entered at Stationers' Hall," being the English copyright mark. We are now enjoying the grandest view of St. Paul's which can be obtained, near to it; the Campanile towers in front, and the great dome being in full view as we ascend Ludgate Hill. St. Paul's stands at the head of the street, and on the highest ground in the old city. The streets which circle around it on each side, are known as St. Paul's Churchyard, and, like all the streets we have passed since leaving Charing Cross, are used for business purposes.

We have now walked together from Westminster Abbey to St. Paul's, passing through Parliament Street, Whitehall, Strand, Fleet Street and Ludgate Hill. From the Abbey to Charing Cross is about three-quarters of a mile; Charing Cross to Temple Bar about three-quarters of a mile; Temple Bar to St. Paul's a little over half a mile. Our course has been near, and almost parallel with the Thames, on the outside of the circle here made by the river. Near our course are very many places of historic interest. The streets through which we have passed are crowded with omnibuses, carts, wagons and pedestrians. Carriages can now make the distance in half the time by avoiding the crowded thoroughfare, and taking the way by the Thames embankment on the river-side, or the Holborn Viaduct on the other.

The west front of St. Paul's Cathedral, as seen from Ludgate Hill, is the best view, except the more distant one from the river, or Blackfriar's Bridge. The first St. Paul's on this site was built in the seventh century, and burned in the tenth. The second church, known as "Old St. Paul's," was a very large building, being 690 by 130 feet, with a spire 520 feet high. It is famous in history for its splendid and costly shrine, and its valuable plate and jewels. Its wealth tempted the cupidity of the lustful and unscrupulous Henry VIII., who swept the accumulated wealth of the cathedral into his treasury, probably in his assumed role of reformer. During the commonwealth, old St. Paul's was used as a stable, and for other base uses, by the soldiers of Cromwell. It was burned down in the great fire of 1666. A few relics of the old church are shown in the crypt of the present building, mostly statues of great men, exhumed from its ashes. Among them is a well preserved statue of the father of Lord Chancellor Bacon.

The present church was commenced in 1675, and completed in 1710. Its length from east to west is 500 feet, the west front, with the campanile towers on each side, being 180 feet wide. The width of the transept is 250 feet, and the walls are about 100 feet high. The entire circumference of the church is 2295 feet. On a pedestal at the west front, is a marble statue of Queen Anne. I was surprised to find on the pedestal, not only Britannia with her spear, Gallia with her crown, Hibernia with her harp, but America with her bow. My first visit to St. Paul's was on Sunday afternoon, at Divine service. The first impression on entering the cathedral, is one of vastness and bareness. Everything seems large, and there is a remarkable lack of decoration. I was early enough to secure a seat near the pulpit, and under the vast dome. The organ is of great power as well as sweetness of tone, and Dr. Stainer, well known as a musical composer and writer, is organist. The solo and quartette singing were exquisite, in their way, but I heard not a word that was sung. The delightful harmony echoed through the columns and arches of the lofty building, but the closest attention failed me to catch an intelligible word. An English gentleman who attended service with me, seemed to admire this feature of the music, attributing it to the vast size of the building. I stood up for my country, and honestly and truthfully assured him that almost any quartette in America could render the words just as unintelligibly in a building of the smallest size. The sermon was by the celebrated Canon Liddon, one of the London preachers that I most desired to hear. While the preacher held the rapt attention of those in hearing distance, there was great disorder in other parts of the building, a constant stream of sight-seers passing in and out during most of the service.

Over the north door is a tablet to the memory of the architect who planned the vast structure. Translated from the Latin, it reads as follows :

"Underneath is buried Sir Christopher Wren, the builder of this church and city, who lived about 90 years, not to himself, but to the public good. Reader if thou seek'st his monument look around."

I shall not attempt a description of the monuments in St. Paul's in detail. They are generally very elaborate, and nearly all erected by order of parliament. Those of Wellington, Nelson, Rodney, Howe, Cornwallis and Abercromby, cost over $30,000 each, and there are fifty others that cost from $5,000 to $25.000 each. Here, as well as in Westminster Abbey, there is a wonderful and unaccountable reverence manifested for cobwebs and dirt. Indeed, it would be hard to say which place is worse in this respect. The authority that shall cause a general dusting and cleaning of the monuments, in both places, will earn the regard of all cleanly disposed people. While Westminster abounds in monuments of kings, statesmen, orators and poets, St. Paul's commemorates mostly the deeds of England's military and naval heroes. Wellington, Moore, Napier, Abercromby, Cornwallis, Picton, Hay, Packenham, and others not so well known, represent her soldiers. Nelson, Collingwood, Duncan, Rodney. Napier, St. Vincent, and many others of lesser fame, represent her sailors. There are also monuments to Dr. Johnson, Bishop Heber, Dr. Donne, Dean Milman, Bishop Middleton, Sir Astley Cooper, Sir William Jones, John Howard, Henry Hallam, and others.

The central area under the dome is an octagon, formed by

eight massive columns or piers, about thirty by forty feet each. Looking up, the dome presents a wonderfully light and beautiful appearance. Though so vast, such are its fine proportions and beautiful coloring, that it looks like a huge parasol spread to keep out the sunlight. The woodwork of the entire building is admirably constructed. The carvings on parts of the choir, are said to be the finest on any public building in London.

Descending into the crypt, we find it, like the body of the church, divided into three parts by immense pillars. In the vaults beneath the crypt, and near each other, lie the remains of some of England's most celebrated painters: Reynolds, Barry, Opie, West, Lawrence, Fuseli and Landseer.

Entering the enclosed portion of the crypt, we descend a few steps, and are in the chamber specially prepared as a resting place for the remains of the Duke of Wellington. The sarcophagus is of porphyry, and in two pieces; the lower part containing the coffin, and the upper part forming the lid. Its immense size may be judged of by the fact that it weighs seventeen tons. The walls of this chamber are of polished Scotch granite. In a similar apartment adjoining, rest the remains of Nelson, with those of Collingwood and Northesk on either side. The upper part of the sarcophagus of Nelson is of black marble, and most beautifully wrought and polished. It is said to have been prepared by Cardinal Wolsey for his own tomb. Passing to the west end of the crypt, we find the funeral car on which the remains of Wellington were brought to St. Paul's, drawn by twelve black horses. It is a massive affair, cast from guns taken in actions in which the duke was engaged, which are enumerated on both sides of this magnificent car. The proximity of the tombs of England's most honored heroes, Wellington and Nelson, recalls the lines of the poet, who puts in the mouth of Nelson, buried first, the question :

" Who is he that comes like an honored guest
With banner and with music, with soldier and with priest,
With a Nation weeping and breaking on my rest ?"

And the reply :

" Mighty seaman, this is he
Was great by land as thou by sea ;
Thine Island loves thee well, thou famous man,
The greatest sailor since the world began ;
Now, to the roll of muffled drums,
To thee the greatest soldier comes:
For this is he
Was great by land as thou by sea."

Provided with a ticket authorizing my ascent to the topmost part of the building, I ascend to the library. Strange to say, it is not so famous for its books, which number about 10,000, as for its floor, made of about 2,500 pieces of oak, beautifully inlaid, and said not to contain a single nail or peg. I next reach the great bell, weighing 11,474 pounds. The tone is lower A, and is remarkably fine. The clock hammer weighs 145 pounds, and is raised precisely as in clocks of the present time. The clapper is very heavy, but is only used for tolling the bell on the death of a member of the royal family. The quarters are struck on smaller bells. The clock has two faces, west and south, about twenty feet in diameter. The minute hand is ten feet long, and weighs seventy-five pounds. The pendulum is sixteen feet long, with a weight of over 100 pounds at the bottom, and beats once in two seconds. The figures I give will indicate that the clock must be of large size. I examined it with a good deal of interest, and admired its perfect mechanism. It was made in 1708, and I cannot see that any important novelties have been introduced in the construction of tower clocks, since that time.

The Whispering Gallery runs entirely around the base of the cupola, and has an ornamental iron railing on the inside. Suicides have been committed from this gallery, and the opportunity to make a sure thing of it is excellent,—215 feet to the floor of the cathedral, and solid marble to strike upon. The gallery is 140 yards in circumference, and the faintest whisper against the wall is heard on the opposite side, apparently louder than when it started. From this gallery is seen to best advantage the paintings in the dome, representing scenes in the life of St. Paul. Most readers have heard, from the pulpit or platform, the story of a painter on a high scaffold, stepping backward to admire his work, and saved from falling by the presence of mind of a bystander, who, seeing his danger, seized a brush and daubed his picture, causing him to spring to the rescue. The guide assured me that the incident occurred here, in painting these scenes on the interior of the dome, and that Sir James Thornhill was the artist whose life was saved by the marring of his picture.

I next reach the stone gallery surrounding the dome on the outside. The day is clear, I have a good telescope, and London, with its noble parks, vast buildings and busy river, is at my feet. This is the highest point usually reached by visitors; but being dared to ascend to the ball below the cross, at the top of the dome, I accepted the challenge, and after some hard climbing reached my destination, 350 feet from the pavement below. The ball, which looks small from the street, is said to weigh 6,000 pounds, and will hold half a dozen people. From the inside of the ball nothing is seen, but immediately below there is a good resting place, from which a good view may be obtained. There is not however any advantage gained, so far as the view is concerned, that will compensate for the fatigue incurred in reaching the highest point.

In the vicinity of St. Paul's are many places of interest. When a small boy my Catechism and Child's Magazine bore the imprint of 66 Paternoster Row. For a very long time this quite small and narrow street has been a sort of literary headquarters. It runs parallel with St. Paul's churchyard on the north, with but a single row of buildings between, extending from Cheapside on the east to Stationer's hall on the west. It is still almost entirely devoted to the book publishing trade. The offices and stores have a low, dingy appearance, and contain but few books except those published in the Row. Indeed, I have not seen in London what would pass in America for a first-class retail book store. But the names on the signs in Paternoster Row look familiar —Bagsters, Nelson, Chambers, Blackwood, Longmans Religious Tract Society etc.

Newgate street commences at the east end of Paternoster Row, and following it in a westerly direction, passing three or four streets, we reach Newgate prison on the corner of Old Bailey street. It is a dingy old building, and over the door is tolerably well carved in stone a representation of the shackles that may be found within. In front of this prison was, for a long time, the site of the gallows on which London criminals were hanged. I am told that on such occasions the streets in the vicinity would be crowded over night by the vicious and criminal classes, to secure a good position from which to view the execution in the morning. St. Sulpice's Church, near by, is a very ancient one, and the tolling of its bell during an execution, with the dingy surroundings of the prison, made a fitting background for the scenes of the scaffold. Tyburn was a place of execution before Newgate, and criminals passed St. Sulpice's in the "Tyburn cart," on their way to execution. Some benevolent individual, with a peculiar idea as to the fitness of things, provided in his will for the presentation to such criminals, from the steps of St. Sulpice's, as the cart passed, a bouquet and a pot of beer.

Returning toward Cheapside we pass Panyer Alley, running from Newgate street to Paternoster Row. A stone is built into the wall of one of the houses, representing a pannier or basket with a boy on the top ; beneath, and near the level of the sidewalk is the inscription :

> "When you have sought the city round,
> Yet still this is the highest ground."

The stone bears date August 27, 1688. At the junction of Newgate street with Cheapside, on the corner of St. Martin's Le Grand, is the general post office, but two narrow blocks from St. Paul's. It is a very large and fine building, and on the corner opposite is the general telegraph office. In 1870 the government purchased all the telegraph lines in the kingdom for thirty million dollars, and they have since been operated in connection with the post office department.

At the east corner of St. Paul's Churchyard we enter Cannon street and proceed in an easterly direction toward the Tower, about a mile distant. We reach St. Swithin's Church in the south end of which, and near to the ground, is built in the wall the celebrated London Stone. This is an interesting relic of the Roman period. It was the central milestone from which all others marked distances, like the millarium in the Forum at Rome, the centre from which all Roman roads radiated. This stone is frequently mentioned by historians and antiquarians, and Shakespeare describes Jack Cade as entering Cannon street in triumph and " striking his staff on London Stone," saying, " Now is Mortimer Lord of the city. And here, sitting on London Stone, I charge and command, that of the city's cost the conduit run nothing but claret wine the first year of our reign."

Passing a fine statue of William IV., we turn down Fish street on the right and are at the monument, designed by Sir Christopher Wren, and built to commemorate the fire of 1666. It was erected by order of parliament, is 202 feet high and stands just 202 feet west of the spot in Pudding Lane where the fire originated. I reached the top by a circular stairway on the inside and had a fine view of the city. The monument becoming a fashionable place for suicides, the gallery at the top is covered with strong iron bars. The great fire broke out on Sunday morning, September 3d, 1666, and burned for three days, destroying eighty-nine churches, many public buildings, 400 streets—in all 13,200 buildings. The ruins covered 436 acres, leaving in the city but seventy-five acres of buildings unharmed, and the loss was estimated at sixty million dollars, a sum then equal in purchasing power to more than five times that amount at the present time. All the church spires in the burned district, including the dome of St. Paul's, are painted black, so that from the top of the monument one can trace the course of the fire.

We proceed to Lower Thames street, near the river, and now follow the course of the Thames. We soon reach Billingsgate, the famous fish market, said to derive its name from Belin, king of the Britons, who A. D. 400, built a gate here. This place is famous for having given to the English language the word Billingsgate—meaning abusive or foul language. I heard not a word objectionable on moral grounds, but plenty of cockney English. Harper's guide book had informed me that the proper thing for visitors is to eat a fish dinner at the Three Tuns Tavern, a respectable hotel close to the market. After picking my steps for a short time through the market, taking in its many sights, and, in as limited quantities as possible, its many smells, I declined to dine at the Three Tuns, cured of all hankering for fish during the remainder of my stay in London. Passing the custom house, a very large and plain building, we reach the entrance to the Thames sub-way, a tunnel under the river for foot travel, about a quarter of a mile long, and well lighted with gas. I made the trip at a cost of one cent, and, emerging into daylight on the other side, was surprised to find by a corner street sign that I was in "Tooley street," celebrated as the residence of the "three tailors," who passed some high sounding resolves. For six cents a boatman rowed me back across the river, landing me at the steps leading to the Tower.

Procuring the necessary tickets I crossed the drawbridge leading over the moat to the Tower of London. It is said that a fortification existed here under the Romans, but the oldest of the present buildings was built by William the Conqueror in 1078. Over twelve acres are enclosed by the moat and outer walls, and there are nineteen separate towers, besides barracks, officers' quarters, chapels, offices, armory, etc. We enter under the Middle Tower, and pass the Byward Tower defending the entrance by the drawbridge. Next on the left is the Bell Tower on which was formerly mounted the alarm bell of the garrison. Queen Elizabeth, before her accession to the throne, is said to have been imprisoned in this tower. On the right and on the river's bank is St. Thomas' Tower, and under it the Traitor's Gate, which the poet Rogers calls

"That gate misnamed, through which before,
Went Sidney, Russel, Raleigh, Cranmer, More."

It was the place of entrance or exit for prisoners brought here or removed by water. Opposite St. Thomas' Tower is the Bloody Tower, through which is the principal entrance to the inner ward. The archway by which we enter is thirty feet long and fifteen feet wide, and was erected in 1327 by Edward III. The portcullis and gate show the marks of great age. It was in the Bloody Tower that the young princes, Edward V., and the Duke of York were murdered by their uncle, the Duke of Gloucester.

The White Tower was built in 1078, and is a splendid specimen of Norman architecture. It is quadrangular in form, 116 by 96 feet on the ground and 92 feet high, with turret watch towers on each corner. The outside walls are fifteen feet thick, the partition walls seven feet thick. The rooms on the first floor are said to have been the prison of Sir Walter Raleigh, in which he wrote the history of the world. Above is St. John's Chapel, the finest specimen of Norman architecture in England. "This is consecrated ground, please remove your hats," said the attendant as we entered the chapel "consecrated eight centuries ago, and unchanged in form or in substance since." The stones are well dressed, the tool marks as distinct as when laid in the wall, and are laid in regular courses with a thick mortar joint, the mortar being as hard as the stone. There are three windows of fine stained glass, added by Henry III, in 1240. For centuries, and during all the periods when the Tower was used as a palace, this was the court chapel. In this tower is a large room, used as a council chamber when kings held court here, and in which Richard II. abdicated in favor of Henry of Bolingbroke, and from which Lord Hastings was ordered to instant execution in front of St. Peter's Chapel, by Protector Richard, Duke of Gloucester. There is also a large banqueting hall, in which the successors of William the Norman entertained their guests. Both council chamber and banqueting hall are now used for the storage of small arms, the arrangement of which shows great ingenuity. Imagine the Prince of Wales' wedding cake, roses, passion flowers, and various other devices worked out by an ingenious arrangement of muskets, cutlasses, bayonets, daggers, pistols, etc. But it is not all mere display, for tier upon tier and closely packed in wooden racks, are 70,000 of the latest pattern of Henry-Martini breech-loading rifles.

Attached to the White Tower is a new building completed in 1827, known as the Horse Armory. It is about 150 feet long and 35 feet wide. For many centuries the Tower has been used as a storehouse for arms and accoutrements, and in this building may be found specimens of war material, from the period of the Norman conquest to the present time. In the days of the first Norman king of England, defensive armor consisted of small pieces of leather, overlapped like fish scales and sewed stoutly together. About 200 years ago, in the reign of William III., defensive armor was discarded entirely. By means of over twenty effigies, mostly equestrian, clad in the armor of the different periods, and arranged according to date, we are enabled to study the various changes in armor and weapons, for a period of eight centuries. The Norman shield was kite-shaped, a long cutting sword, and a lance with small flag or streamer being the weapons in common use. Chain mail was introduced in the reign of Henry III., about 1240, and consisted of small rings interlacing one another and forming a connected garment. In the reign of Edward II., besides the chain armor, plates of metal were worn on the arms and legs. In Edward III.'s time the armor became splendid and costly, so that knights that might have been made prisoners were slain for the sake of their armor. In the reign of Mary we are told, the armor was so heavy that knights unhorsed could not rise again. The history of defensive armor bears some likeness to that of defensive armor on ships, which is likely soon to reach the point when the heaviness of the iron or steel plating will be the greatest peril of the vessel, and suggests the query, may not defensive armor on ships be abandoned as was the heavy armor of knights?

Certain suits of armor are exhibited which possess especial interest on account of their former owners. Among them is an effigy of Henry VIII. on horseback, in armor worn by that king. Also a suit of armor for both man and horse, said to be the most curious and costly known, made in Germany, and presented to Henry VIII. on his marriage with

Katharine of Aragon, by the Emperor Maximillian. There is also a matchlock harquebuss and fowling piece, both breech-loaders, belonging to the king. There is a boy's suit of very fine armor worn by Edward VI., and a figure on horseback wearing the armor of Dudley, Earl of Leicester, 1560. There are also equestrian figures wearing the splendid armor of Charles I. and James II., both suits being remarkable for their fine workmanship. To describe the many suits of fine armor here, marking their many peculiarities, from the thick leather garment of the Norman period to the heavy armor of metal, covering the entire person, in later times, would require a knowledge of technical terms which I do not possess. The variety of weapons exhibited is wonderful. Among them are two-handed swords, sabres, pikes, maces, glaves, bills, partizans, pavices, arbalests, military flails, cross bows with winding apparatus, battle axes, pole axes, tilting lances, spears, daggers, halberds, harquebusses, pistols, etc. Multiply this very defective list by the average number of varieties of each, and you have material for weeks of study.

A large collection of fire-arms, arranged chronologically, and showing the progress of invention in England since the time of James II. is very interesting. It contains ancient breech-loaders, also revolving barrels and revolving cylinders, leading one to wonder what was left for American inventors, who seem to have carried off all the glory, to discover. There are thumb-screws, bilboas, and other instruments of torture used in the Tower, among them an iron frame for confining and compressing the whole person, and known as "The Devil's Masterpiece." Here also is the famous "heading block" and axe, used last at the execution of Lord Lovat in 1747, the last criminal beheaded in England. There are numerous interesting trophies, captured by the armies of England in every quarter of the globe, and very many relics of much historical interest which I omit.

The crown jewels of England have been kept in the Tower for over six centuries. At present they are in the Wakefield Tower. Ascending a narrow stairs one is at once ushered from a dark passage way into a well lighted room, in the centre of which, enclosed in a very large glass case and surrounded by stout iron bars, is a display of gold and jewels, such as I never expected to behold. Fifteen million dollars is the modest estimate put upon this show case. The crown of Queen Victoria is a cap of purple velvet enclosed in hoops of silver and surmounted by a ball and cross. It fairly glows with precious stones. In the centre of the cross is the "inestimable sapphire," and in the centre of the crown is a heart-shaped ruby worn by the Black Prince and which shone in the helmet of Henry V. at the battle of Agincourt. The cost of this crown is known to have been about $600,000. St. Edward's crown is of the well-known form represented on the coins of the realm. It is made of gold, and is ornamented with precious stones. The Prince of Wales' crown is formed of pure gold, unadorned with jewels. The ancient queen's crown was worn at coronations by the queen consort. The queen's diadem was made for the consort of James II. St. Edward's staff is of beaten gold about five feet long; the orb at top is said to contain a portion of the true cross. It is carried before the sovereign at coronations. The attendant assured me that while the sceptres are hollow and comparatively light, this staff is solid and weighs over seventy pounds. There are two royal sceptres of gold ornamented with precious stones. At the top of one is a cross, on the other a dove, and both are held by the sovereign at coronations. The queen's sceptre is quite small, but contains many precious stones. There is a richly wrought golden sceptre supposed to have been made for the queen of William III. There are three swords borne before sovereigns at coronation, also the bracelets, spurs, and annointing vessel and spoon used on such occasions. The golden salt cellar is a model of the White Tower and of beautiful workmanship. A baptismal font used at the christening of royal children, dishes, spoons, and a service of sacramental plate all of gold, form the remainder of the crown jewels. In a separate case are the insignia of the orders of the Garter, Bath, Thistle, Star of India. St. Michaels, and the Victoria cross, all of beautiful workmanship.

But the Tower has been not only a fortress, an armory, a treasure house—but a palace, a prison and place of execution as well. It was for several centuries used as a residence and court by the English kings. The Tower palace with its halls and galleries occupied the south-east part of the grounds, fronting on the river, and connected with the central White Tower, which contained the council room, banqueting hall and St. John's chapel. The civil wars and commotions for several centuries after the building of the Tower made it a desirable residence as affording security and protection to the sovereign. Extensive additions and repairs were made by Henry III., who gave to it much of its grandeur and importance. The chapel of St. John's was especially cared for, and was the scene of many a pompous religious ceremonial during his reign. The festivities of the court by the custom of the times included tournaments, and on such occasions the chivalry of Europe were sometimes invited to participate. The splendid gilt armor and huge tilting lances, exhibited in the armory, have shone in the lists when the Tower grounds was filled with the beauty and chivalry of England. Here, Henry VIII. gave a royal reception to each of his queens on their marriage. The custom of royal coronation processions through the streets of London from the Tower to Westminster Abbey was kept up till the time of Charles II., and the reader of English history will recall many interesting descriptions of the pomp and show incident to such occasions.

During the wars of Edward I., Edward II. and the Black Prince, the Tower afforded quarters for the kings and knights taken prisoners in war. Baliol and David Bruce, kings of Scotland, Prince James, William Wallace, and King John of France, with many of his nobles, were prisoners here. The Tower was for centuries used as a prison for persons charged with treason, an offense easily charged and under the custom of the times as easily proved. The proceedings were ordered by the king, and were in secret. The accused was not permitted to confront his accusers, or hear the witnesses testify against him. The witnesses, if unwilling to give the desired testimony, were taken to a dungeon of the Tower, stretched on the rack and statements wrung from them under torture written down, and produced in court as evidence against the accused. The many quarrels as to the succession caused the spilling of royal blood, sometimes without even the color of law, while the adherents of such royal victims were shown no mercy. In 1418, under Henry V., a different class of persons began to be imprisoned in the Tower. In that year Lord Cobham was arrested on a charge of "heresy," an epithet which it is as easy for error to apply to truth, as truth to error, for his supposed acceptance of the doctrines of Wycliffe. He was condemned, and burned at Smithfield as a heretic, and for nearly two centuries capital punishment for opinions sake was not uncommon in England. Many suffered for the so-called heresy of refusing to reject the Pope and accept the brutal and profligate Henry VIII. as head of the English church, or for refusing to comply with the conditions of an act passed during his reign, and frankly entitled,

"An act abolishing diversities of opinion!" Others were victims of the terrible persecution under Mary when the prisons of the Tower and the fires of Smithfield were relied on, to prevent the spread of the doctrines of the Reformation.

Near to the north-west angle of the fortifications is the Devereux Tower named for Robert Devereux, Earl of Essex, a courtier and "favorite" of Queen Elizabeth, condemned to death on a charge of plotting against the queen's life. Readers of English history will remember the long struggle on the part of the queen, "between resentment and affection," before she signed his death warrant. It is a pretty theme for the historian and novelist, and they have made the most of it; and yet the ordinary man, to this day, fails to perceive that it was the correct thing for this *maiden* queen to be always having an affection for some good looking "favorite" of the male persuasion. Essex was beheaded on the green in front of St. Peter's church. The Bowyer Tower was formerly the residence of the Master Provider of the King's Bows. It was in this tower that the Duke of Clarence, brother of Edward IV., was drowned in a butt of Malmsey wine in 1474. The Brick Tower is said to have been the prison of Lady Jane Grey. My previous reading had assigned this noble prisoner to the Beauchamp Tower, but I am assured that no ladies were ever imprisoned in that tower, and that the most careful search has failed to find any mementoes that would certainly indicate what room she occupied while a prisoner. Fox, in his Book of Martrys, says she traced with a pin on the walls of her prison these words:

> "To mortals' common fate thy mind resign,
> My lot to-day to morrow may be thine."

The most dilligent search has failed to discover this interesting inscription. The Beauchamp Tower is about the center of the western line of the inner ward, and derives its name from Robert Beauchamp, Earl of Warwick, imprisoned in this tower in the reign of Richard II., A. D. 1397. It is two stories and on each floor is a room about twenty feet square, with smaller rooms or cells adjoining. The walls are about fifteen feet thick and the cells are arched over with heavy stone work, giving it a wonderfully strong and prison like appearance. Near to the cells on the first floor is cut in the wall the name of "Marmaduke Nevile" a prisoner here for supporting the claim of Mary, Queen of Scots, to the English throne. Near to this is a large carving of the crucifix, a bleeding heart, a skeleton and the word "Peverel." Over the fireplace is an interesting autograph of Philip Howard, Earl of Arundel, condemned to death, but who died here before sentence was executed. On the right side of the fire-place is a large sculpture executed by John Dudley, Earl of Warwick. With his father and two brothers he was imprisoned on a charge of treason, for attempting to make Lady Jane Grey, wife of his youngest brother, Queen. The names of "Arthur Poole" and "Edmund Poole," occur frequently on the walls. They were convicted of treason for conspiring to place Mary, Queen of Scots, on the throne, but were not executed, they died in prison; these inscriptions are all of a religious character. Near one of the cells is the word IANE, the royal name of Lady Jane Grey, cut by the hand of her husband, Lord Guilford Dudley. There is also the autograph of "Thomas Fitzgerald," executed in 1539 for treason, on account of a rebellion in Ireland. Of course I give but a few of the many inscriptions on these prison walls, and they possess a wonderful interest as the last mementoes of noble and accomplished men, many of whom knelt before the headsman centuries ago.

## THE CHAPEL OF ST. PETER.

The chapel of St. Peter stands near the north-west corner of the fortifications, and was built in 1272 by Edward I. It is sixty-six by fifty-four feet, and was the chapel of the prisoners, as St. John's was the chapel of the court. Macauley says of it: "There is no sadder spot on the earth than this little cemetery.. Hither have been carried, through successive ages, by the rude hand of jailors, without one mourner following, the bleeding relics of men who have been the captains of armies, the leaders of parties, the oracles of senates, and the ornaments of courts." A memorial tablet at the entrance gives the names of thirty-four persons of historic note buried here. Among them are John Fisher, beheaded in 1535, by Henry VIII., for refusing to take the oath of supremacy, and Sir Thomas More, beheaded a month later for the same offense. Queen Anne Boleyn and her brother, George Boleyn, beheaded in 1536, Cromwell, Earl of Essex, Margaret Plantaganet, Queen Catharine Howard, Lord Thomas Seymour, Lord Protector Somerset, Dukes of Northumberland, Suffolk and Norfolk, Lady Jane Grey, Earl of Eessex, Duke of Monmouth, and Lords. Kilmarnock, Balmerino and Lovat. All these were beheaded, and their dissevered bodies lie in the church and cemetery of St. Peter's. Others rest here who pined away and died in prison, or were tortured to death in the dungeons of the Tower.

In the open square, and near to St. Peter's, is the site of the ancient scaffold. This open space was formerly covered with grass, and known as Tower Green. The spot is marked by an iron railing enclosing a stone, with this inscription: "Site of the Ancient Scaffold. On this spot Queen Anne Boleyn was beheaded, May 19th, 1536." It is a beautiful day, and I sit down by the iron railing. I am surrounded by high walls and gray Norman towers. My explorations of the towers and dungeons, armories and treasure house, aided me in recalling vividly the scenes that had transpired in this old fortress. The inscription on the stone reads, "May 19th, 1536." Three years before, on a beautiful May day, Anne had arrived at the Tower from Greenwich, escorted by the Lord Mayor of London and his civic train, and landed "amidst the great melody of trumpets and divers instruments, and a mighty peal of guns." Next day her gay marriage procession passed from the Tower to Westminster Abbey, Anne, "arrayed in silver tissue, and a mantle of the same arrayed in ermine, her dark tresses flowing down her shoulders and her head encircled with precious rubies." On the spot enclosed by the little railing by which I sit, three years later, Anne with her own hand took the coifs from her head, putting on a linen cap, and saying: "Alas, poor head, in a very brief space thou wilt roll in the dust of the scaffold." Kneeling down, one of the ladies covered her eyes with a bandage; "and then they withdrew themselves a little space and knelt down over against the scaffold, bewailing bitterly and shedding many tears, and thus, without more to say or do, was her head stricken off; she making no confession of her fault, and only saying: 'O God have pity upon my soul,' and one of the ladies then took up her head, and the others the body, and covering them with a sheet, did put them into a chest which then stood ready, and carried them to the church which is within the Tower." One cannot help admiring the devotion of her women, which nerved them to stay with her to the last, and care for her dishonored remains. A gunner stood by a loaded cannon on the wall near by, lint-stock in hand, and as the sword of the executioner fell the report of the cannon informed listening London that a royal head—the head of a woman—had fallen on the scaffold. The king, arrayed in a hunting suit, impatiently awaited the signal gun, and as the booming cannon announced the murder accomplished, jumped into the saddle and rode with all haste to the residence of Jane Seymour, to whom he was married the next day.

And still another queen of England, wife of the same monarch, was executed here,—Catherine Howard, with her attendant, Lady Rochford. Later still, the aged Margaret Plantagenet, Countess of Salisbury, was found guilty of treason, and beheaded on the same spot. Refusing to stoop or place her head on the block, "as traitors do," she was seized by her gray hair and forcibly held over the block till executed.

Lady Jane Grey was executed here during the reign of Mary, on a charge of treason. Her husband, Lord Guilford Dudley, had been executed outside the walls, on Tower Hill, the same day. From her window she saw him walk to the scaffold, and afterwards saw his body taken out of a cart— his head in a cloth. Gardner had begged of Mary that the lives of two persons so young and so innocent, might be spared. But she was not likely in that reign to be pardoned who could say, a few days before her death : "I ground my faith upon God's word and not upon the church. For if the church be a good church the faith of the church must be tried by God's word, and not God's word by the church." And so the historian says she went forth to die, "her countenance nothing abashed, neither her eyes anything moistened with tears." For over three centuries the fate of this victim of the ambition of others has stirred the sympathy of all true hearts, and nothing could be added that would better the simple narrative of the times : "She tied the kerchief about her eyes; then, feeling for the block, said : 'What shall I do? Where is it?' One of the standers by guided her thereto, she laid her head down upon the block, and stretched forth her body, and said : 'Lord, into thy hands I commend my spirit,' and so she ended." The only other execution on Tower Green, was that of the Earl of Essex, in the reign of Elizabeth, already noticed; the ordinary place of execution was on Tower Hill, outside the walls.

Before leaving the Tower I visited again the Traitors' Gate, by the river's side, and read the long list of persons who had passed through it accused of crime, or as condemned criminals. The long array of royal and knightly names did not particularly impress me, but that more noble and kingly band, condemned for obeying the dictates of conscience—how they stand before me! I see Cobham and Cranmer, and Latimer and Ridley, passing—erect, yet conscious of their impending doom. And the venerable John Fisher, and Sir Thomas More, and Archbishop Laud, too, just as conscientious in adhering to the supremacy of the pope. Many incidents occur to me; the willfulness of the Princess Elizabeth, afterwards queen, and her sulky stubbornness when compelled to pass the gate; the willing haste of the infamous Judge Jeffries, glad to escape the mob that would have torn him to pieces; and, most impressive of all, the parting scene between Sir Thomas More and his daughter, so often described in history, and so frequently illustrated, the old Traitors' Gate invariably serving as the background for the picture. I cross the drawbridge, stepping again into the world of the nineteenth century, and try to realize that I am within a mile of the busiest business centre of the commercial world of to-day; and brushing away my dreams of the dim and shadowy past, thank God that during all these centuries the world has been growing better.

## CHAPTER VIII.

### PARIS.

A Channel Steamer—Dieppe—Normandy—Arrival in Paris—An Election—Place de la Concorde—Dinner—A Traveler's French—Sunday Night in Paris—The New Opera House—Grand Foyer—The Madelaine—Hotel des Invalides—Arc de Triumphe—Buttes Chaumont—Pere la Chaise—Cathedral of Notre Dame—The Pantheon—Parisian Churches—The Music—In the Streets—An American Girl.

The inducement of pleasant company led me to join an excursion party to Paris, leaving many very interesting places in London to be visited on my return from the continent. We left London on Saturday evening, by railroad, for Newhaven, where the steamer is taken for Dieppe. The accomodations furnished on the Channel steamer were of the most limited kind. There was probably about comfortable standing room in the cabin for the first-class passengers. Three cushioned shelves on the sides furnished a resting place for the first comers, who rushed in and took possession; the remainder occupied the tables and floor. As soon as it was daylight I escaped on deck, finding hardly room for my feet as I stepped over the sleepers. The sea was quite smooth and I observed no sea-sickness; had it been otherwise the consequences would have been disagreeable in the crowded condition of the cabin.

The French coast in the vicinity of Dieppe is rocky and bare, and has a white, chalky appearance. We landed on a quay by the railroad station. The formality of passing the customs was gone through with by the owners of trunks, but I walked through the customs office, satchel in hand, unquestioned. There was some hitch in the railroad arrangements affording me a couple of hours to see the ancient town of Dieppe. It was formerly the principal port of France, now it is a fishing town with a population of about 18,000. It is resorted to as a watering place, and the new part of the city consists largely of hotels, boarding houses and bathing establishments. The old city is the dirtiest and worst smelling I have ever been in. The gutters are in the center of the streets, and seem to be the receptacle of everything that can smell bad about a house. The first group that attracted my attention was seven women and four men towing a vessel out of dock; the women took the lead on the rope and seemed to do pretty much all the pulling. They all wore heavy shoes and kept time with their feet, taking short, quick steps, and making quite a noise. Although Sunday morning, all the places of business were open and all kinds of work going on, just as if it was a week day. I managed to get an inside view of the old cathedral, which was open for worship, and dates from the thirteenth century. A great deal of the work of all kinds seems to be done by the women, who all wear the high Normandy caps. I am told that it is a part of their religion that these caps should be white, clean and stiffly starched. As a class they are the homeliest women I ever set my eyes on.

We leave Dieppe for Paris, two hours behind time, and in about an hour reach the ancient city of Rouen, the fifth largest town in France, having a population of about 150,000. It has a splendid cathedral, containing a tomb in which is buried the heart of Richard Cœur de Lion, and a fine monument to Joan of Arc, erected on the spot where she suffered death by burning. After leaving Rouen the country becomes more hilly and picturesque, and we several times cross the Seine, which must be a very crooked river.

## ARRIVAL IN PARIS.

Small villages are numerous, but look old and generally somewhat dilapidated. Indeed until we pass out of Normandy we see but few new buildings ; the farm houses especially, built of stone, with tile roofs, and nearly all out of repair, look ancient. The principal places we pass are Vernon, Mantes and Poissy. As we near Paris, fine residences in modern style, with well kept grounds and handsome flower gardens, become frequent, and the country generally presents those indications of wealth that denote nearness to a great city. About ten miles from Paris we pass the forest of St. Germain and soon reach St. Lazare station, where carriages are waiting for our party, and into which we are hurried by gesticulating drivers and porters, as if a moment's delay would be dangerous. A detention of half an hour, that certain trunks might pass the customs, sadly tried our patience. We were, however, in a busy street in front of the station, and had an opportunity of observing how Sunday is kept in Paris. At last the trunks appeared, a terrible cracking of whips was the signal for our departure, and we were hurried through the busy streets to the Hotel Perey on the Rue Boissy Anglas, within three minutes walk of the Madelaine, or of the Place de la Concorde. There was more than a dozen in our party and we were received by all the employes of the hotel on the broad stairway leading to the office, where we were rapidly assigned to rooms. My room proved satisfactory in every respect and after a hasty lunch I started out to see Sunday in Paris.

At noon many of the places of business close, but the smaller shops and all places where refreshments or food of any kind is sold, and all the cafes, remain open. It is my first experience in a large city where I do not understand the language. Compared with London, what a contrast. There a clear sky is a rarity, and the buildings, mainly of brick, have been sadly begrimed with smoke. Even the

finer stone buildings have a dingy appearance.  Here is a
beautiful clear sky, and the buildings, mostly of a light
cream colored stone, look fresh and clean.  More taste is
displayed in the arrangement and decoration of a single
show window than in a whole street in London. Everybody
seems smiling and happy, and there is a sort of gayety in the
streets and gardens that seems to be infectious.  It may all
be a sham and a mockery, covering vacuity or rottenness,
but the delusion is a pleasant one, and the stranger is willing to accept it for a week as it seems, and would rather not
be disenchanted.  My first effort was to reach the Madelaine, to catch some strains of its fine music.

 I fell into conversation with an English gentleman on the
steps of the Madelaine, who informed me that an important
election for members of the Corps Legislatif was in progress—all elections here are held on Sunday.  When did an
American citizen fail to become interested in an election?
He kindly gave me instructions by which I found one of
the principal polling places.  On the sidewalk in front of
the building stood five or six sedate looking men, with
broad white bands on their hats, bearing the name of the
candidate whose ballots they distributed.  The voters received their tickets with great calmness and deliberation,
after which they passed into the building.  I looked at
these solemn looking ballot distributors and wondered if
enlightened American methods had found acceptance in
the new republic of France.  Do they really pass out the
men's tickets whose names appear on their hats, or have
they reached that stage of progress which, in the great
Western Republic, enables "workers" at the polls to take
one candidate's money and peddle another candidate's
tickets?  Are they able to practice that refined American
legerdemain which enables a "straight party man" to
deal split tickets *from the bottom of the pack?*  But ques-

tionings were useless; I was in a foreign country, a fact which the ballot distributors seemed to know as well as I did. I passed into the building and followed a French voter up stairs. An officer at the landing seemed disposed to dispute my passage, with forcible gestures and inquiries which I did not understand. I talked back in English, repeating several times with emphasis the word "American." He seemed non-plussed, probably had never encountered so much cheek before, and taking advantage of his hesitation I passed boldly on to the room where the voting was done. Here I was mistaken for a voter and referred to a man with a book. I felt satisfied that my name was not in the book, and did not require him to make any examination. Smiling and repeating again the word "American," I was permitted to watch the voters deposit their ballots. It was a wonderfully tame affair, as compared with a lively contest for street commissioner or some other important office in the first ward.

Returning up the gay and crowded Rue de Rivoli, passing the Palais Royale and the beautiful gardens of the Tuileries, I spent an hour in the Palace de la Concorde, said to be the most magnificent square in the world. It is about forty-five by seventy-five rods, is in the heart of the city, bounded on the north by the Rue de Rivoli, on the south by the Seine, east by the gardens of the Tuileries and west by the Champs Elysees. In the center of the Place, on a granite pedestal, stands the Obelisk of Luxor, a single stone about seven feet square at the base, and seventy-six feet high—said to weigh 500,000 pounds. It is of reddish granite, and covered with hieroglyphics on all sides. It formerly stood in front of a temple at Thebes and was erected by Rameses II., in the fourteenth century before Christ. Its removal from Egypt and erection here occupied three years and cost $400,000. There are two large and very beautiful fountains in the square, throwing a profusion of water in many streams to a height of thirty feet. Around the square are eight statues, of colossal proportions, representing the eight principal cities in France—among them Strasburg. The figure representing Strasburg is adorned with black crape—suggestive of the past, or of the future?

But the Place de la Concorde has an interesting history, and has not always been a place of concord. In the revolution of 1793 more than 2,800 persons suffered death by the guillotine on the place where the obelisk now stands, among them Louis XVI., Marie Antoinette, Duke of Orleans, Charlotte Corday, Danton, Robespierre, Desmoulins and Dumas. In 1814 a solemn service was performed here, in presence of the Emperors of Russia and Austria, the King of Prussia and the Russian and Prussian troops, in honor of Louis XVI., after which Te Deums were sung in honor of their victory over Napoleon. A year later, after Waterloo, the Place was occupied by British troops. In 1871 the German troops bivouacked here. A few months later this square was the scene of a bloody conflict between the National troops and the Communists. The latter had erected a strong barricade across the Rue Royale, their cannon commanding the Place. After a fierce cannonade, in which, fortunately, the obelisk was unharmed, the barricade was carried by storm. Three hundred Communists, who sought shelter in the beautiful church of the Madelaine, were shot down before its altar—not one escaped! Sitting here, this bright summer Sunday afternoon, near to the ancient obelisk and the magnificent fountains, enjoying a view said to be finer than any other city in the world affords, it is painful and indeed difficult to associate the place and its surroundings with the scenes of ten years ago.

Groups of well-dressed children are passing up the Rue Royale, where stood the Communists' barricade. Crowds of pleasure seekers, in holiday attire, for Sunday is a holiday in Paris, surround the beautiful fountains and statues. A few hours ago, in the Church of the Madelaine, where occurred the terrible massacre, I saw a worshiping assembly devoutly kneel, the arches, which had echoed the shrieks of the dying and the shouts of the victors, bearing to my listening ear the solemn notes of the organ, accompanying a penitential hymn.

I returned to my hotel at 6 o'clock, and in company with a dozen other hungry Americans, sat down for the first time to a French table-d'hote dinner. But little dinner could be seen, and yet by the changing of plates seven times, making eight courses, I managed to get a hearty meal. The dinner occupied one hour and seventeen minutes, which is considered fast time in Paris, but Americans will persist in doing everything in a hurry.

In company with a gentleman of our party, who seemed confident of his ability to talk French, I started to find the English Wesleyan Chapel, being told that Bishop Simpson would probably preach there. My friend seemed confident of his French, and I left the name of the street, which we had seen on a card at the hotel, to him. After traveling a short distance he made repeated efforts *in French*, to obtain directions of policemen and others, but failed. We had traveled some distance and it was near the time of service. He remarked, almost out of temper, "Here comes a lady, I'll ask her. The men in this country don't seem to know anything." He tried his French vehemently on the lady. A smile soon lighted up her face, and she seemed with difficulty to suppress her laughter. She interrupted my friend by saying in beautiful English, "I suppose, sir, from your using the word Wesleyan, and from its being Sunday evening, you desire to find the Wesleyan Chapel. If so, it is in the next street to the left, a few doors from the corner." I cruelly said to the lady, "Then you don't understand French?" She replied with a laugh, as she viewed the chopfallen expression of my friend's face : "Bless you, yes, just as well as I understand English." My friend passed on in silence. At length I said in a tone of inquiry, "Strange that the *only* word that you said, which the lady understood, was the English word Wesleyan." He groaned, implored me not to give him away at the hotel, and at once renounced all pretensions to French. I am told that it is a matter of great surprise to young ladies who have graduated in French at American high schools, to find that French is not spoken in Paris.

Returning through the brilliantly lighted streets and boulevards, I had an opportunity of seeing how Sunday night is observed in Paris. A newspaper could be read in the center of the principal streets, while the brilliant jets in front of the cafes almost discounted sunlight. In front of the cafes were chairs and tables, in many places occupying at least half of the very wide sidewalks, where sat their customers, sipping their wine or coffee, or indulging in something bearing a remote resemblance to American icecream. The scenes I witnessed were novel and would be difficult to describe ; no drunkenness, or vulgarity, or boisterous conduct of any kind, and everybody apparently enjoying themselves, with no other restraints than good breeding imposes. I passed into the Place de la Concorde, and wondered how the old obelisk, if it could think, must regard the new-fangled electric lights by which it is surrounded. Looking towards the Champs Elysees, the wide avenue leading to the Arc de Triumphe, a still more brilliant scene was before me. Concert gardens, and saloons, and outdoor entertainments of various kinds occupy the sides of this

## THE OPERA HOUSE.                              131

great thoroughfare and pleasure ground, lighted more brilliantly than anything I had seen in the streets or boulevards. I looked on for a few minutes at half a dozen places, most of them accommodating several thousand persons—admission free, but pay for your refreshments. The performances seemed to be what in America we would call "Variety" entertainments, but the order and decorum observed was remarkable. I strolled around till a late hour, but the streets were as brilliant and crowded as earlier in the evening, the theatres pouring out their thousands to throng the streets and cafes. It will do to look at once, as a sight seer, but I retired, sincerely thankful that Parisian Sundays are unknown in America.

Our arrangements for sight-seeing in Paris were made through Caygill's agency, and included carriages and conductor for all places of interest in Paris, with a day's visit to Versailles. The programme was faithfully carried out, and our conductor, a Frenchman, proved to be intelligent and well informed on matters of history. As a resident of Paris during the siege by the Germans, and its occupation by the Communists, he was able to give us much interesting information in regard to the terrible scenes of 1870–71.

One of the most imposing buildings in Paris is the new opera house, bearing on its front the inscription, "Acadamie Nationale de Musique." It is the largest theatre in the world, covering an area of nearly three acres, but has seating accommodations for only 2,500 persons, being less than several other large theatres. Over 400 houses were removed to make room for the vast building and the square in which it stands, known as the Place de L'Opera. It was commenced by Emperor Napoleon III., in 1861, and intended to be the grand architectural glory of his reign; it has been completed by the government of the republic at a total cost to the nation, including site, of about twelve million dollars.

It is lighted by 9,000 gas jets and has dressing-rooms for 600 performers. The principal front, approached by broad flights of stone steps, is three stories high. The portico has seven arches, the two outer ones forming the principal entrance. The entire front seems to be covered with columns, arches, statues, busts, groups, and medallions, in various colored marbles; there is also a large amount of gilding and bronze work. From the center of the building rises a low dome and behind it a colossal Apollo, with golden lyre, and on each side a Pegasus.

Having admired its beautiful exterior, I purchased a ticket to the opera, costing a dollar and a quarter, to see its splendid interior. The front gates are covered with gold, and passing in we ascend the grand stairway, thirty feet wide, the steps of white marble. The balustrades are of a reddish marble, with a hand-rail of Algerian onyx. Each story has a balcony looking down into the vestibule, from which one can take in the throng pressing into the audience room. The landings are decorated with allegorical designs, and numerous statues of marble and bronze occupy niches in the balconies. The vestibule and balconies are brilliantly lighted, and the effect is wonderfully fine. Entering the audience room one is surprised at its size and beauty. There is the usual parquette, and four tiers of boxes, divided into bays by eight huge columns; there is also above the boxes a gallery forming a fifth story. The boxes are very roomy and seem to be all fitted up alike. The decorations of the ceiling are on plates of copper, and the magnificent lustre overhead with its 400 jets shines like an immense crown of diamonds. The stage is 74 by 178 feet, and 196 feet high—about 50 square rods of stage, nearly a third of an acre! The immense drop curtain is of red and gold and unadorned with paintings or devices of any kind. The parquette is for gentlemen only and there are no re-

FOYER OF THE GRAND OPERA HOUSE, PARIS.

quirements as to dress; in the boxes a full dress suit of black with gloves, etc., is necessary. The occupants of the boxes seemed to be largely French, and finely dressed. The orchestra numbers about 100, the chorus proper about 150, and as the opera of Faust was performed, about 75 soldiers added their voices in the "Soldier's Chorus." The scenery and arrangement of the stage was perfect. I noticed in village scenes and festivals, the full proportion of children and young people one would expect to see in such places were present, and acted their parts as naturally as the older people. The same careful attention to detail characterized the entire performance. At the close of the first act the audience arose and began to leave, a proceeding that puzzled me very much, and no one near me seemed to speak English. I concluded to keep my seat and see what would come of it, when a gentleman passing and probably noticing my perplexity, said to me; "Everybody goes out between the acts to see the other parts of the building." I felt relieved and at once joined the procession.

Following the largest number, I found myself in the room known as the Grand Foyer. It is 180 feet long, about 40 feet wide and 60 feet high, and is lighted by ten large lustres and a number of huge chandeliers, so brilliantly as to almost distress the eyes, and mar somewhat the effect of the coloring. Along the walls are twenty columns, bearing statues emblematical of the qualities an artist should possess. There are two splendid chimney pieces, and immense mirrors at the ends indefinitely prolong the room. The decorations, which look as fresh as if completed yesterday, seem to be of solid gold. The beautiful illustration represents the scene, as perfectly as black ink can portray all the colors of the rainbow, with gold, and crystal, and variegated marbles and mosaic, in a gorgeous profusion which one can hardly imagine, thrown in besides. I have never seen so much or so perfect gilding, or so magnificent mirrors. The ceiling seems to be of mosaic, representing Diana, Orpheus, Mercury, etc. Above the mirrors is represented a procession of children carrying the musical instruments of all nations. On the walls are fine paintings representing the various kinds of music and dancing and their effects, among them David playing before Saul, and Salome dancing before Herod. The many scenes from heathen mythology were beyond my ability to decipher. All that modern art could do has been done to make this room gorgeous, and so far as I could discover, it has no other use than as a grand promenade and show room. Its lavish decorations, as well as those of the entire building, were no doubt intended to hand down to posterity the name of Napoleon III., and yet I failed to find a statue, bust or medallion of the emperor, and doubt if there are any in the grand opera house. Even the "N" which marked the Imperial box in the audience room has been removed. Three times the audience retired between the acts, giving me an opportunity to examine the various parts of the building, but I am afraid my somewhat lengthy description has already proved tedious to my readers.

A short street, the Rue Royale, leads from the Place de la Concorde to the Place de Madelaine. It is a large square, on the sides of which are some fine trees, and in the center, the beautiful "Madelaine," or Church of St. Mary Magdalene. I have referred to it as the scene of the terrible massacre of the Communists who had sought shelter under its altar from the fury of the national troops. Although the immense foundation was laid in 1764, the building was not completed till 1842, at a cost of nearly $3,000,000. It is in the form of a Grecian temple, 350 feet in length, 140 feet wide, and 100 feet high. The entire structure rests on a basement twenty feet high, and is approached by marble steps, extending the entire width of the building. It is surrounded by fifty-two massive Corinthian columns, each fifty feet in height, which support the porticos and roof. There are no windows in the sides of the building, the ceiling inside being finished in three dome-shaped sections, through which the light is introduced. The doors are of bronze, thirty-five feet high and sixteen feet wide, and are ornamented with scenes illustrating the ten commandments. The walls and floor of the interior are of marble, and the fine pictures and statues altogether too numerous for description. The high altar has a fine group in marble, representing Mary Magdalene borne to heaven by angels.

There is an extensive flower market in the square, near the church, and the morning hour seems to bring numerous customers. It is really interesting to watch the motions and gestures of buyer and seller, not understanding a word spoken by either. The fearful rolling of the r's, the peculiar shrugging of the shoulders, the wonderful movements of the eyebrows, and peculiar inflections of the voice, are novel and amusing.

From the Place de la Concorde, looking southerly across the Seine, is a fine building, with magnificent gilded dome, the Hotel des Invalides. Crossing the Seine by the Pont de la Concorde, and passing the Chamber of Deputies and some other public buildings, we reach the Esplanade des Invalides, containing about ten acres, handsomely laid out and bordered with several rows of trees. Arriving at the outer court we find it surrounded on three sides by a dry moat. Here is a battery, used for firing salutes, and a large number of captured cannon, representing almost every country in Europe, and most, if not all, of the continents. Soldiers who have been disabled, or who have seen thirty years' service, are entitled to a home in the hotel, and there are accommodations for over 5,000, though less than 1,000 are here at present. In one wing of the building is a large military museum, containing arms, armor and trophies of great interest, and many fine pictures. Feeling especially interested in one of the historical paintings, I asked the conductor a question, and was about to enter his reply in my note book. He looked at me with an amused expression, and pointing to my book, said: "No use; too many paintings to be seen for that. I will show you seven miles of paintings at Versailles alone!" I inquired if fine paintings were reckoned by the mile in Paris? He replied, "No; but there are a great many miles more of them than you have any idea of, so you may as well save your note book for something else."

The Church of the Invalides, which is the great object of interest, consists of a nave and dome separated from each other by a screen. The nave is about seventy feet wide, and more than 200 feet long, and is adorned with flags taken in Algeria, Russia, Italy, China and Mexico. In 1814, the evening before the allies entered Paris, 1,500 flags taken by Napoleon, were burned in the court of the Invalides, to prevent their capture by the allied troops. That part of the church known as the dome, is square on the outside, and about 200 feet each way. It is surmounted by a magnificent dome, gilded at enormous expense, by Napoleon, and again in 1861, by the process of electro plating. This dome is ninety feet at the base, and its top about 350 feet above the pavement. The interior of the dome is circular, the corners cut off being used as chapels, and it is entirely of marble, of the finest quality and finish. In the center is a circular crypt, about twenty feet deep and forty feet in diameter, surrounded by a marble balustrade. The walls are of polished granite, and decorated with bas-reliefs by the most eminent sculptors of France. In the center of the crypt is a sarcophagus of brown granite, covering the remains of the Emperor Napoleon I. It is a single stone, thirteen feet long, seven feet wide and fifteen high, weighs about seventy tons, and was brought from Finland in the rough at a cost of $30,000. Around the crypt, and facing the tomb, stand twelve colossal statues, representing victories. The pavement of the crypt represents a huge crown of laurels, worked in green marble in a tessellated floor of black and white marble. The light is admitted through windows of purple glass, and, falling on the polished floor and decorations of the crypt, gives it a peculiarly delicate violet hue that is very beautiful. The marbles, sculptures, and decorations of the crypt and dome, preparing it for the tomb of the great Napoleon, cost nearly $2,000,000. I do not think a more simple and appropriate, yet magnificent and beautiful conception for the resting place of a great man, has been carried out since Cheops built the great pyramid.

Near to the Invalides are many other places of interest. among them the Ecole Militaire (military school), a most imposing building. During the revolution it was used as a barracks, and accommodated 5,000 men and 1,500 horses. A better idea of its vast size may be had from the fact that its grand front is a full quarter of a mile long! In the center is a large Corinthian portico, surmounted by a quadrangular dome. Between the Ecole and the Seine is a bare space of about twelve acres, known as the Champs de Mars. It is used for military reviews, and was the site of the exposition buildings of 1867 and 1878.

From the Champs de Mars the Seine is crossed by the Pont d'Jena, built in 1806-1813, to commemorate the victory of Jena. On the opposite side of the river, on high ground, is the beautiful Palace de Trocadero. In front of it is a fine park and grounds, rising gradually from the river, with a small lake and cascades and fountains. The Trocadero was erected for the exhibition of 1878, and as seen from the river, is one of the most attractive buildings in Paris. It is in the Oriental style and in the form of a crescent, with a high circular building, about 200 feet in diameter and surmounted by a dome, in the centre. There are beautiful minarets, 270 feet high, on each side of the dome. The entire front is nearly a quarter of a mile in extent.

Up to this time I have seen but few soldiers in Paris, and these singly or in paires, but in the streets near the Trocadero I saw several regiments pass by. I had supposed French soldiers to be as we sometimes say, "Soldiers all over," and expected to see a martial bearing and fine marching. On the contrary, the marching was heavy and poor, and the ranks seemed to be filled with innocent agriculturists and mechanics, anything but soldierly in appearance. The splendid fighting qualities of the French cannot be questioned, but their appearance in the ranks would not indicate it.

North of the Trocadero, and reached by the Avenue d'Jena, is the Arc de Triumphe, said to be the largest triumphal arch in existence, and from its position one of the most prominent objects in Paris, as viewed from the suburbs or any of the numerous towers. It was commenced in 1806, by Napoleon, to commemorate his victories, but was completed by Louis Philippe, in 1836. It is 146 feet wide, 72 feet deep and 160 feet high, and cost about ten million dollars. Its appearance strikes one as massive rather than elegant. It is adorned with a wonderful amount of sculptures, representing French victories, the names of over one hundred being inscribed on it. On the roof of the transversal arch are the names of nearly seven hundred officers killed in battle. One of the finest sculptures is a colossal group representing the blessings of peace ; it almost seems out of place amid such surroundings. From the top of the Arc is said to be the finest view of Paris, its fortifications and environs. I found an hour, with a good telescope and guide, well spent in making myself familiar with the locations of the various objects of interest in and near the city.

The cemetery of Pere la Chaise is the largest in Paris, containing over two hundred acres. For a long distance before reaching the gates, the street is lined with shops of marble and stone cutters, and the manufacturers of the various devices used here to indicate mourning. Flowers, natural and artificial, mostly the latter ; bugle and bead garlands and wreaths of all colors ; crosses, stars, and anchors ; porcelain and plaster cherubs, lambs and doves ; small framed pictures of weeping widows, sorrowing parents, death bed scenes, empty cradles, and mottoes for all degrees of grief are part of the singular array of merchandise that one sees in windows, doors, and in front of the stores in this melancholy looking street. In an American cemetery we are accustomed to burial lots of some size, the grounds and shrubbery being well cared for, and the graves marked by monuments, usually showing taste and skill—though sometimes only the wealth of the family. Here, there are no graves, it is not a garden, a "God's Acre," but a miniature city of the dead. It is formed of vaults, it may be twenty feet deep, the coffins on shelves one above the other. On the surface are little stone or marble houses, standing close together along the edges of the walks, and usually about six by ten feet on the ground and eight to ten feet high. On the front is the family name, or the name of some very distinguished person buried in the vault beneath. A grated, and sometimes open window, affords a view of the memorials and offerings within. These house-like monuments are frequently ornamented with expensive sculptures, but the general appearance of such a cemetery strikes an American as most singular, and not in accordance with his ideas of the fitness of things. On looking through the small grated or open windows, you see on the back and sides the names of those buried in the vault. There is usually, on a shelf, a crucifix and candles, and on the other shelves memorial offerings to the deceased. Bead work, representing wreaths, crosses, baskets, etc., are common, also imitations of flowers and plants, made of painted metal, mottoes on painted glass, pictures of tombs with weeping relatives, etc. Even in the more expensive tombs, the decorations and memorials would be considered by an American cheap and tawdry. In their sorrow for bereavement the French do not forget their natural habits of economy, or "throw themselves wide open" to be fleeced and robbed, as Americans do on similar occasions.

The grandest tomb is that of the Russian Princess Demidoff; but the center of attraction is the ancient and decayed Gothic chapel, which forms a roof for the sarcophagus containing the remains of Abelard and Heloise. Their statues represent an old man and woman, and their last resting place is the Mecca of despairing lovers. Among the distinguished men buried here are Cherubini, Herold, Bellini, Chopin, Rossini, Mehul, Pleyel, Wely, Thiers, Perrier, Raspail, Marat, Ledru Rollin, De Morny, Kellerman, Saint Cyr, Macdonald, Suchet, Foy, Massena, Ney, Beranger, Balzac, Lafontaine, Moliere, Racine, Michelet, Cousin, etc.

Looking into an open vault, I saw some graves of children, and beside them, preserved in glass cases, their childish toys—dolls, balls, rattles, etc. In an instant a little porcelain dog, and other trinkets, carefully treasured, but nearly 4,000 miles away, flashed before me—and with them, a sweet, pale face. Strangely enough, Pere la Chaise, with ts rough pavements and stone vaults, and beautiful Glenwood with its spreading trees and gravelled paths, seemed to have become common soil, transformed by the sacred touch of a mutual sorrow and bereavement.

The most ancient part of Paris is an island, now near the center of the city, and surrounded by the water of the Seine, known as the Ile de la Cite. At the time of the conquest of Gaul by Julius Cæsar, it was occupied by a tribe known as the Parisii. On this island is the metropolitan church of Paris, the Cathedral of Notre Dame. Its foundations were laid by Pope Alexander III., at the time a refugee in France, in 1160. It was consecrated in 1182, but not completed till 1420. It is 410 by 150 feet, and the vaulted ceiling is supported by seventy-five large columns. The general appearance of the interior is both ancient and grand. There are thirty-seven large windows of stained glass, mostly very old, and through which the sun has shone on scenes that have made their mark on the history of France and of the world. The desecration of the cathedral during the first revolution has become matter of history, and is frequently referred to from the rostrum or pulpit to "point a moral." In 1793 a decree was passed devoting the noble building to destruction, but afterwards rescinded that it might be converted into a "Temple of Reason." The statue of the Virgin was replaced by one of Liberty. In the choir an emblematical "Temple of Philosophy," in the Greek style, was erected, covered with busts of Rousseau, Voltaire, and other liberalists of the day; and inside the temple the "Torch of Truth" was kept burning. The enthroned figure of "Reason" was represented by a ballet-dancer who here, surrounded by damsels of like character dressed in white and bearing torches, received the homage of her votaries. Orgies of the most indecent character were conducted in the side chapels, and the world looked on in wonder while "Reason gloriously freed from religious superstitions" held lascivious riot, and observed rites and ceremonies in honor of the new God, or Goddess, more ridiculous than the worship of savage tribes. That instrument of enlightenment, the guillotine, in front of the Hotel de Ville, kept time with the "march of Reason" at Notre Dame.

Phrenologists have told me that my bump of veneration is not largely developed, and that I am not a very religious person; and yet, standing on the spot where "pure Reason" was once enthroned, I avow my willingness to subscribe to any form of superstitious doctrine or heresy ever promulgated in the name of Christ, Calvinism, the worst of all, not excepted, rather than become a votary of Reason, divorced from religion. The cathedral was closed from 1794 till 1802, when, by order of Napoleon, it was opened for religious worship. The first Napoleon was here crowned Emperor and in one of the aisles I heard an English lady read a description of the grand pageant to a little group that surrounded her—how Napoleon assumed the weight of empire in a mantle so extravagantly gorgeous as to weigh eighty pounds; how Josephine wore a white satin dress embroidered with gold, and crimson velvet mantle lined with ermine, and wore a diadem of diamonds and pearls; how Pope Pius VII. came from Rome for the occasion, and how Napoleon lifted the Imperial crown and placed it on his head and afterwards placed a crown on the head of Josephine, leaving only the prayers and benediction for the pope. The Emperor Napoleon III. was married at Notre Dame, and I was shown the font used at the baptism of the late Prince Imperial, presented by Pope Pius IX.

The Pantheon occupies the site of the tomb of St. Genevieve, the patron saint of Paris, who died in the sixth century. The foundation of the present church was laid in 1764, and when completed it was dedicated to St. Genevieve. During the first revolution it was converted into a memorial temple and named the "Pantheon," and indeed the exterior resembles more a heathen temple than a church. It is in the form of a Greek cross, and surmounted by an imposing dome. The portico is formed of huge Corinthian columns, eighty feet high, and the designs on the tympanum are hardly churchly in character, representing as they do Napoleon, Carnot, Laplace, Voltaire, Rousseau, etc. The entrance to the interior is by three beautiful bronze doors, and on entering one is impressed with the singular majesty and yet simplicity of form and style. It is to be decorated with frescoes of a national and historical character, several of which are completed and others in progress. Mirabeau and Marat were buried here, but their remains were afterward removed, by order of the convention. Voltaire and Rousseau were also buried here, but after the restoration their remains were removed and their resting place is unknown. In the revolution of 1848 the Pantheon was the headquarters of the insurgents, and was also occupied by the Communists, in 1871, who had deposited gunpowder in its vaults to blow it up, but were dislodged before they could accomplish their purpose.

The history of most Parisian churches is about as follows: built thirteenth to eighteenth century ; desecrated and closed during the first revolution ; restored under the empire or monarchy ; used as a stable, hospital or store house, by the Communists, in 1871, who meant to burn it or blow it up, but failed on account of the unexpected entrance of the Versailles troops. They are of various degrees of architectural merit externally, but I found all the interiors both beautiful and interesting. Their ritualistic and showy worship has its charms for all, and is equally within the reach of rich and poor. • To one who has stood in the vestibule of Grace Church, New York, and felt humiliated under the searching look of the late lamented Brown, sexton or proprietor, I never could make up my mind which, and has entered with a loss of self respect, impelled by a desire to hear the finest church music in America, it is a matter of surprise that in cathedrals four times the size and costing twenty times as much, no self important official bars the way. You enter as unmolested as if it were a railway station. There seems to be absolutely no distinction of race, color, wealth or birth ; the market woman, seamstress or mechanic, may have as eligible a seat as anybody. Here "the rich and the poor meet together," and their surroundings are not calculated to give the lie to the idea that the Lord is "maker of them all." A back seat by the door or a free seat in the aisle does not remind the poor man of his poverty, or the annoyed stare of a pew holder make a man feel as if he were a trespasser in what should be his Father's house. A Parisian church, with its wonders of architecture and art, and the perfect equality of its worshipers, is a much more effective sermon than some I have heard from American pulpits on "the Fatherhood of God." Too many of our Protestant churches seem possessed with the idea of the lady whose pastor opposed some of her notions of church management by gently reminding her, that in Heaven there would be no distinctions of wealth or rank, and received the startling reply, " That is just the reason we should keep them up here while we can !"

The music is very fine, but church-like and simple. Indeed, I have not heard operatic squalling in any European church. The organs are especially fine, and are not tormented by constant and sensational changing of the stops, as are many of their diminutive brethren in America. The lack of strain or effort in the music, is positively restful. The ordinary American choir is always after "something new," and, if within their ability to execute well, they don't want it at all. Their great ambition is to wrestle in church with anthems several sizes too big for them. The excuse for inflicting this misery on the congregation usually is, that practicing difficult music increases their musical proficiency, in other words, that thereby they are learning something. The reverse of this is generally true ; there is more musical culture gained by singing simple music finely than by singing *at* the most difficult music in the world. The athlete gains muscle by practicing with a club he can handle easily and gracefully. Suppose he had commenced physical culture by trying to lift a locomotive ; it would have been as sensible as for choirs of very limited ability and culture to undertake the music to which many of such choirs in America aspire.

In the streets of Paris but few finely dressed women are met, and my guide assures me that, "when you meet a finely dressed lady in the street, she is either a foreigner or a prostitute." I was shocked at this coupling of foreigners with the disreputable class named, but the statement no doubt has much of truth in it. French women keep their fine dresses for home, the ball, the opera, but not the street. What an amount of self denial it would require of the beautiful women who parade the streets of our large cities, gay as butterflies, to adopt the French style,—which after all seems more sensible.

Pedestrians seem to have no rights that a driver is bound to respect. French drivers will shout and swear, but it is all they will do ; the idea of turning out never occurs to them, and the endangered pedestrian must look out for himself. "What do your courts do when a man gets run over?" I asked. "Fine the man that gets run over," was the prompt reply. A Parisian driver would be at once arrested in Michigan for cruelty. They crack their whips with a noise resembling the firing of musketry, and as if cutting the horses to pieces. I was indignant at this, till I found that the horses were untouched during the entire performance ; and as it seemed to do the driver a vast amount of good, and not hurt the horses, I got used to it.

I have been accustomed to regard the French as a wonderfully active and energetic people. Their gesticulations, and the force displayed in even ordinary conversation, had deceived me in this regard. I have looked in vain for an active or busy mechanic, or laborer working on the streets, or buildings, or public gardens. A slower class of people I have never seen, and I am inclined to think they must work off their surplus energy in conversation. I watched a gang of hands this morning repairing a street, and it induced a sort of home feeling. I almost imagined myself in Michigan, looking at a gang of hands "soldiering," under the fostering care of a street commissioner.

Desiring to see the streets of Paris as they appear on a week night, I started out early in the evening, and alone, to take notes. In most large cities a majority of the stores close early in the evening, and the streets, after the lamps are lighted, present a deserted appearance. But here, the lighting of the lamps or electric lights, and of the places of business, is the signal for a general stampede of carriages and pedestrians, to the more attractive streets. The Boulevards des Italiens and Capucines, and Avenue de l'Opera, seem especially brilliant and thronged. Those great thoroughfares, like most of the other fifty boulevards, are very wide; I should estimate the sidewalks at thirty-five feet each, and the carriage-way, which is of asphaltum, about ninety feet wide. There is a continuous stream of carriages going in each direction, and all carrying two bright lights, so that looking down one of these grand avenues it seems like a gorgeous torchlight procession. The sidewalks are full of pedestrians, and the chairs in front of the cafes are all occupied; but for a few centimes I rent a chair by the curbstone, and sit down to rest and gaze at the gay procession which occupies the carriage-way and sidewalks. The only difference I can see between Sunday night and Tuesday night is that a wealthier class seem to be out. The middle and poorer classes, who have their holiday on Sunday, are not seen in such numbers, but there are more people on the boulevards. Passing down the Avenue de l'Opera, brilliant as gas and electricity can make it, to the Jardin du Palais Royal, I walk around the arcades and shops which surround it. Here are about 200 small jewelry and diamond stores, close as they can be packed together in arcades. Each of the small outer arches has its brilliant gas jets, and the little shops are blazing with gold and silver and gilt, and precious and other stones. How 200 of these jewelry and fancy stores can flourish side by side I do not know; but their windows are a marvel of neatness and taste, and the proprietors look comfortable and happy. Returning to my hotel at eleven o'clock, I observed no diminution of numbers in the streets or cafes.

Our party from London included an American girl from Missouri, nineteen years old, and traveling alone. Stopping at the same hotel for a couple of days, I learned from some ladies of our party who became interested in her, that she had but little money, and had started for Paris "on her own hook," to complete her studies in French and music. At the end of the two days she had secured a cheap boarding place at six dollars per month, and made arrangements as to lessons. A more striking example of female foolishness I never saw. Her English education was evidently only begun. She talked and acted like the ordinary country girl, who has had only the advantages of a district school. I heard her at the piano, with a book of Gospel Hymns before her. Her voice had most of the bad qualities, and she had about reached the "Hold the Fort!" stage in musical progress, with a fair prospect of reaching "Grandfather's Clock," or possibly "The Maiden's Prayer." And yet she had come from the far distant west, friendless and alone, to "complete her education!" She excited the sympathy and pity of our party. As she left the hotel for her boarding house, a Methodist minister, who had become interested in her on account of her unprotected loneliness, startled me by ejaculating with true Methodist fervor, "Thank God, she's homely!" and the wag of our party surprised me by an equally fervent and serious "Amen!"

## CHAPTER IX.

PARIS.

Champs Elysees—Bois de Boulogne—Palace of St. Cloud—Versailles—Grand Trianon—State Carriages—Dejeuner—The Grand Palace—Grand Apartments—Paintings—Theater and Church—Sevres and its Museum—Hotel de Ville—Halles Centrales—The Tuileries—Place du Carrousel—The Luxembourg—The Louvre—Galleries — Egyptian Department—Museum of Curiosities—Place de la Bastille—Porte St. Martin—Column Vendome—Gobelins—Jottings—Taxation—Future of Paris.

Versailles is twelve miles from Paris, and in company with a number of Americans, I devoted a day to visiting its palaces, parks and gardens. A convenient and quite showy vehicle, a sort of tourists' van, drawn by four horses, made quite an imposing turn-out and accommodated our entire party. We drive through the Place de la Concorde and enter the Champs Elysees, a noble avenue and pleasure ground, about eighty rods wide. We proceed quite slowly, to take in the various objects of interest, and enjoy the fine view of central Paris, its palaces and pleasure grounds. We pass on the south side the Palais de l'Industrie, erected in 1855, by a company, for the first exhibition, and now owned by the government. It contains at present an exhibition of electrical apparatus and inventions, from all nations, in which America is said to be well represented. Nearly opposite is the Palais de l' Elysee, originally the residence of Madame Pompadour, and after its purchase by the government known as the Elysee Bourbon. It is now the official residence of the French president. Theaters, cafes, concert gardens and other places of amusements have found a place on either side of the wide carriage-ways, till we reach Rond-Point, where the avenue becomes narrower and ends at the Arc de Triumphe, about a mile from the Place de la Concorde.

On passing the Arc we enter the Avenue du Bois de Boulogne, about twenty-five rods wide, with a carriage-way in the centre, a riding course on one side, and alley for pedestrians on the other. Once outside of the fortifications we have a fine view of the great fortress of Mont Valerien, and enter the magnificent park and pleasure ground known as the Bois de Boulogne, containing 2,250 acres. It was formerly a dense forest, and had a bad reputation as a hiding place for criminals. In 1814–15, during its occupation by the allied armies, much of its wood was cut down or destroyed. The Emperor Napoleon III. did much to restore and beautify it, and in 1852 presented it to the City of Paris, on condition that $500,000 should be expended on it, and that it should be thereafter maintained by the city. During the siege of 1870–1 it was much injured and many of the trees cut down. It has since been restored and improved, and is now the favorite park and pleasure ground of Paris. There are a number of lakes, and several cascades—some of them of considerable height, well supplied with water, and arranged so as to produce the best possible effect. Winding paths through shady groves, with an abundance of comfortable benches, furnish retreats for weary pedestrians, while the fine broad carriage-ways, are occupied during all hours of the day by the gay equipages of the rich, and plainer vehicles of the poor. A number of Swiss cottages furnish, at a moderate cost, refreshments for hungry or thirsty pleasure seekers. At the head of one of the beautiful lakes is the great race-course of Longchamps, containing about 150 acres, and fitted up in the most costly manner, where during the season, races are held every Sunday afternoon!

Passing through Boulogne, a place of 20,000 inhabitants, we cross the Seine and are in St. Cloud, with a population of about 5,000. The Palace of St. Cloud was a favorite residence of the Bonapartes. During the siege of Paris it was occupied as a military post by the Germans, and was set on fire by shells thrown by the French fortress of Mont Valerien ; only its blackened walls remain. Its ruins indicate that it must have been a beautiful and imposing building. It was here that the Council of Five Hundred met, in 1799, to be dispersed by General Bonaparte and his grenadiers. In 1815 it was the headquarters of Blucher and in it the second capitulation of Paris was signed. It was the favorite summer residence of Napoleon III., who entertained Queen Victoria at St. Cloud, on her visit to Paris, in 1855. The town seems to have suffered more severely than any other of the suburbs of Paris during the siege, especially from the guns of Mont Valerien. The spacious barracks in the vicinity, and many houses, indeed whole squares, were destroyed by the French in their attempts to silence the batteries erected by the Germans at St. Cloud.

Approaching Versailles by a very wide street, we pass through a noble avenue of lime trees of large and uniform size, and tastefully trimmed to represent arches. The place has a wonderfully quiet and sleepy appearance, and I am told subsists on the recollections of its dead past, being largely supported by sight seers, and by the people of Paris, who delight to visit its palaces and pleasure grounds. Louis XIV. seems to have selected the site of Versailles without any reference to fitness. To create a palace and park that would command the admiration of Europe, he expended the enormous sum of two hundred million dollars ! The expense of constructing and maintaining the vast establishment is said to have been the principal cause of the first revolution. Louis XVI. saw the palace sacked by a Parisian mob, and was compelled with his family to abandon Versailles and accept a residence at the Tuileries. In the revolution which followed the Palace of Versailles would have been sold had it been possible to find a purchaser. Since that time it has not been used as a permanent residence of royalty. Napoleon neglected it, owing, it is said, to the vast expense its repair and furnishing would have entailed. Louis Philippe repaired it, converting the greater part of it into an historical art gallery. During the siege of Paris it was the headquarters of the King of Prussia, and it was here that by unanimous vote of the German States he was saluted Emperor of Germany. After the departure of the German troops Versailles became the seat of Government, and it was from here that McMahon directed the attack on the city of Paris, then in the hands of the Communists.

We first visited one of the minor palaces, known as Le Grand Trianon. It is about half a mile north-west of the Grand Palace, and is an exceedingly handsome villa of one story, originally in the form of a horse-shoe, to which wings have been added. It was built by Louis XIV. for his mistress, Madame de Maintenon, and is principally interesting as a favorite residence of Napoleon and Josephine. There are numerous valuable paintings and choice pieces of sculpture, which I shall not describe. The decorations are exceedingly rich and to my mind exhibit rare good taste. Among the older rooms are Louis XIVs'. reception room, breakfast room, and smoking room, with the original furniture. Coming down to Napoleon I. we have his reception room, sitting room, work room, billiard room, bath room, and bed room with the original furniture and decorations as when used by him. In the council room is a table, covered with faded velvet, on which was signed the fatal divorce which broke the heart of Josephine and dimmed forever the star of Napoleon. The bed room of the Empress Josephine, with the original bed and furniture, as when occupied by her, excited more interest in our party than all else the Trianon contained. That the memory of the divorced and degraded wife should possess more interest, and be regarded with a more kindly feeling, than that of her Imperial husband, or of the Austrian Princess who succeeded her as Empress of France, may have a moral for husbands who contemplate a divorce, or for women willing to accept a man mean enough to discard a faithful wife merely to make room for her successor.

Near the Grand Trianon is a building known as the Musee des Voitures, being a collection of state carriages, from the time of the first empire. They are fine specimens of gilding, carving and upholstery. There is the carriage of Napoleon as First Consul, used by Josephine after her divorce. The grand coronation carriage of Napoleon I., used also at the marriage of Napoleon and Josephine. The carriage of Napoleon and Maria Louisa. A beautiful carriage for the young King of Rome, son of Napoleon I., and used at the marriage of Napoleon and Eugenie. The carriage of Count de Chambourd, used by Queen Victoria and Prince Albert on their visit to Paris. And most gorgeous of all, the carriage of Charles X., which cost $200,000, restored and regilded for the baptism of the Prince Imperial, son of Napoleon III. There is a very large collection of harnesses from the time of Louis XIV., exhibited in show cases; three curious looking things called sledges, owned by Louis XIV.; and probably the most interesting relic of all—the sedan chair of Marie Antoinette, adorned with gold and embroidery. Many hundreds of thousands of dollars are represented in this grand carriage house, and crowds of French people, who seem to regard with wonderful veneration these relics of the past, fill the building. And yet no living French statesman or soldier dare ride in such a carriage to-day, so jealous are the mob of everything that betokens royalty. I am told that in deference to public opinion the president of the republic uses a plain carriage, with but two horses, while some of the state carriages I have described were drawn by ten. The hour for dejeuner, regarded as a sort of second breakfast, having arrived, our party with the exception of myself and another, were driven to a restaurant. We had a disagreeable remembrance of the dejeuner of the day before, and had provided ourselves with a substantial lunch, with the ingredients of which we considered ourselves reasonably familiar—assorted biscuits, cake, and gingerbread, Swiss cheese, and delicious French plums. We wended our way to the small lake and large fountains in the garden, fronting the Grand Palace, and seated ourselves near the colossal Neptunes, Tritons, and Nymphs. There were groves and orangeries on either side, and we had a fine view of the palace, its gardens and terraces. I enjoyed my out-door lunch exceedingly, wondering what Louis XIV., XV., or XVI., would think, if from the windows of the king's room, near to which we were sitting, they could look on us, irreverent Americans, eating our lunch in the most prominent spot in their flower garden.

We rejoined our party and all proceeded to the Grand Palace of Versailles. I confess to a feeling of weariness as I surveyed the front of the vast edifice, over a quarter of a mile long, with its 375 windows. It is three stories high, and has in the center a projection of 300 feet front. Our guide had already informed us that seven miles of pictures were exhibited here, and I felt discouraged at the prospect. The palace was first converted into an

VERSAILLES: THE GARDEN FRONT.

historical museum by Louis Philippe, who placed here choice historical paintings, taken from the Louvre and other palaces, and purchased fine paintings from living artists. He is said to have expended over three million dollars, and since that time subsequent governments have expended large sums in the same way. A few paragraphs describing a short visit will be quite as unsatisfactory to myself as to my readers, but it is all that is possible under the circumstances.

On the ground floor are about twenty rooms, containing portraits of the marshals, generals and admirals of France. These rooms, like all others in the palace, have their ceilings decorated with paintings of an historical or allegorical character. The room of the kings contains portraits of sixty-seven of the monarchs of France, from Clovis I. to Napoleon III., and has a fine bronze statue of Napoleon I. The gallery of Louis XIII. contains mostly battle scenes, and has statues of Louis XIII. and his queen. The gallery of the empire has thirteen rooms devoted to pictures illustrating the campaigns of Napoleon I. The gallery of the history of France contains eleven rooms with historical paintings from Charlemagne to Louis XVI. The gallery of the Crusades has five rooms devoted to battles of the crusaders, in which the taking of Jerusalem is several times illustrated. In one of the rooms is a mortar from Rhodes, and the gates of the hospital of St. John, of that place, presented by the Sultan of Turkey. There are several extensive galleries of sculpture, besides busts and statues in rooms not devoted to sculpture. They consist mainly of statues and busts of distinguished Frenchmen, with a few historical groups.

What are known as the grand apartments occupy the whole of the first floor of the central projection, to which we now ascend, and are nearly all ornamented with paintings illustrating the life of Louis XIV. We pass through more than a dozen rooms, containing choice paintings and statuary, among them a ball-room, state bedroom and throne room, into one of the finest rooms in the world, the Grande Galerie of Louis XIV. This magnificent room is 230 feet long, 35 feet wide and 25 feet high. The ceiling is richly decorated by the painter LeBrun, with about twenty large pictures, illustrating the victories of Louis XIV. This long room fronts on the garden and has seventeen high arched windows; opposite each window is a mirror with a gilded frame. Between the mirrors, which are of immense size, almost covering the entire wall, are Corinthian pilasters of red marble, with niches containing statues. To walk through this room, mirrors, gilding, and marble on one side, the choicest paintings overhead, and the gardens, lakes, fountains, statues, terraces, orangeries, and park of Versailles, as seen through the seventeen large windows on the other side, is to have enlarged ideas of beauty and grandeur. It was in this magnificent room the King of Prussia was proclaimed Emperor of Germany in 1871. I wonder if the old soldier did not glance upward and smile at some of the scenes overhead illustrating French victories over the Germans.

The bed chamber of Louis XIV. has been called the "Gem of the Palace." Its decorations may well be called gorgeous, and it contains the richly adorned bed on which the king died, its drapery embroidered by Mme. de Maintenon. The furniture is largely in tortoise-shell and gold. It was from a balcony off this room that, on September 1, 1715, as the last sigh quivered on the lips of the dying king, the eager chamberlain broke his official wand, saying, "The King is dead," and in the same breath, seizing another wand, exclaimed to the crowd below, "Live the King." The plaudits of the assembled courtiers showed that their only feeling in regard to the king's death, was to transfer their allegiance and enjoy the favor of his successor. The story, though often told, has still its moral, and not for kings only.

The bedroom of Marie Antoinette, in which she was asleep, and from which she narrowly escaped, when, in 1789, a Parisian mob burst into the palace, is both beautiful and interesting. An extra fee introduced me to the private apartments of Marie Antoinette, mostly quite small and finely furnished, among them the maids of honor room, boudoir, red and blue library room, bath room, and saloon of the queen, also the salle des valets, where the queen's guards were butchered by the mob. On this floor is the Galerie des Batailles, 400 feet long, containing large pictures illustrating the battles of France, from the fifth to the nineteenth century; also busts of about a hundred celebrated generals who have fallen in battle. The gallery of Constantine has seven rooms, containing many fine pictures, especially a series of battle scenes by Vernet—subjects modern, mostly in the Crimea, Algiers, Italy and Mexico. The second historical gallery contain ten rooms, with scenes from 1800 to 1835. Eight rooms, formerly known as the queen's apartments, contain fine pictures, some of them very valuable, as for instance the coronation of Napoleon I. by David, costing $20,000. And yet there is another floor to which I ascended, and through the almost interminable rooms of which I dragged myself, but shall not drag my readers—pictures, pictures as before, till the eyes can hardly discern colors, and the tired mind fails to receive a distinct impression of any kind.

Of the outside attractions of Versailles it is difficult to speak. Language can convey but a faint idea of its magnificent parks, gardens and terraces; its groves, orangeries, flowers and green-sward; its lakes, grottoes and fountains and the splendid works of art by which they are adorned.

Indeed, it is sometimes difficult to tell where nature ends and art begins. The extravagant and luxurious style on which the great palace was planned, may I think be well illustrated by the fact that it contains both a church and theater. The latter is a splendid affair, capable of seating 2,000 persons. The church is 114 by 60 feet, has one of the finest organs in France, and as to decorations can hardly be surpassed. To be able to attend church or theater without stepping outdoors seemed just the thing to the old French king, and he built on so vast a scale that neither church nor theater are more prominent than a billiard room or study in a modern residence of the first-class.

We returned from Versailles by way of Sevres, a town over 1,300 years old and containing about 5,000 inhabitants. It is celebrated for its porcelain manufacture, owned and operated by the government since 1759. It is in a large and handsome new building, employs 180 hands, and has a large and most interesting museum. The legend over the door, "Musee Ceramique," had a chilling effect, as I never took any stock in old cups and saucers, and wash-bowls; my particular insanity runs in the direction of old coins. Most of the things looked bright and new, but more gorgeous and expensive than anything I had ever seen. Tea sets, $3,000 to $4,000; copies of the paintings of Raphael, Michael Angelo, Titian and other great painters, on Sevres ware, and durable and unfading as the porcelain, $5,000 to $10,000 each. There are also specimens from all countries of clay, earthenware and china, showing the progress of invention and forming a complete history of the art. The establishment has never paid expenses, being devoted largely to experiments of which private manufacturers have the benefit.

The Hotel de Ville is the city hall of Paris. The very large square in which it is situated has a peculiar history, being anciently, and down to the time of the revolution, the place of execution of noted criminals. In the first revolution the thud of the guillotine knife was heard here during all hours of the day. It was in the hotel that the revolutionary leaders of 1789 had their headquarters, and from its steps Louis Blanc proclaimed the revolution of 1848. During the seige by the Germans it was the seat of the government of the defence and later the headquarters of the Communists. In May, 1871, a few days before their overthrow, the ringleaders stored gunpowder and petroleum in the building, which they had strongly fortified, determined to destroy if they could not hold it. After a fearful struggle in the Place and surrounding streets, lasting twenty-four hours, the Communists were defeated; in their rage, firing the neighboring buildings and killing the occupants. In their haste the Hotel de Ville was fired while still occupied by 600 of their own number, who either perished in the flames or were mercilessly shot down by the national troops. The destruction of the building and the terrible massacre which accompanied it, as related to me by an eye-witness, who pointed out the localities where the incidents occurred, is almost too terrible for belief. "No more communism, *or anything tending in that direction*, on my plate," was the very American exclamation of a gentleman beside me who had listened to the story.

The Halles Centrales, or central market, is a vast iron structure, and consists of ten pavilions, between which run streets about fifty feet wide. An immense roof of iron, zinc and glass, covers both the pavilions and streets, the entire area of both being about twenty acres. The cost of site and buildings was twelve million dollars. Each pavilion contains over 200 little stalls, about five by eight feet, a few being twice this size. They are in rows close together, with a passage way of about twelve feet between. The trade is classified, one section being for meats, another poultry and game, another fish, another vegetables, etc. Opposite each subdivision is a place where the same class of goods is sold at wholesale, and auctioneers and clerks were busy making sales to wholesale customers. Whole hogs and sheep, and quarters of beef were sold rapidly in this way. In the butter department a lively business was being done. It is wholesaled in lumps of forty or fifty pounds; the purchasers come armed with tasting probes and sales are quickly made. Hundreds of these lumps lay on cloths on the pavement, were passed along rapidly by the dealers and removed by porters to the wagons outside. If the Tower of Babel was worse than the jabbering I heard at these salesrooms, I am glad I was not there. In the retail department things moved more deliberately. In several of the meat stalls the word "Cheval" informed me that it was horse meat. My attention being thus called to it, I could see that it was of a slightly different color from beef; had it not been for the sign I doubt if I should have noticed the difference. There are 1,200 apartments in the cellar below the market where goods may be stored, and tramways extend, partly underground, to the railroad that runs entirely around the city just inside the fortifications.

The garden of the Tuileries adjoins the Place de la Concorde on the east. It is about 60 by 140 rods, and open to the public during most hours of the day. The site was formerly used as a brick yard where the tiles, *tuiles*, used in Paris were made. Both the garden and palace have retained the name of Tuileries. It sounds grandly, to English speaking people, but when translated tile-yard the glamor is all gone, and one wonders at the taste which suggested it. The garden is handsomely laid out with fountains and water basins, and numerous marble and bronze statues. One of the walks has on each side a row of orange trees, some of them said to be 400 years old. On the south and west sides are terraces, and walls surmounted by gratings, with gilded tops. On each side of the central walk is a grove of trees, under the shade of which are two marble semi-circular platforms, built in r793, by order of Robespierre, for the accommodation of the Council of Old Men, who had been selected to preside over certain games. At the east end of the garden stands the ruins of the great palace, burned by the Communists in 1871. Its foundations were laid and the building commenced under the wicked Catharine De Medicis, and in it she gave a fete in which were introduced scenes intended to prepare the popular mind for the massacre of St. Bartholomew, which took place four days later. Louis XIV. resided here until the completion of the Palace of Versailles. During the revolutions which have taken place in Paris many exciting scenes have occurred at the Palace of the Tuileries. In 1792 the palace was attacked by an armed mob of revolutionists. The king and his family secretly quitted the palace, which was defended by a Swiss guard of nearly 2,000 men, most of whom were put to death by the mob. Napoleon as first consul and emperor resided here and enlarged and improved the building and grounds. It was again captured by the mob in the revolution of 1830. In 1848, at the approach of the revolutionists, Louis Philippe and family fled in the night time to St. Cloud, and the palace was for ten days in the hands of the scum of Paris, who celebrated their success by orgies of the vilest kind, carrying off or destroying many precious works of art. Under the last Napoleon the Tuileries was occupied by the imperial court, and in a part of the garden, at that time reserved from the public gaze, the unfortunate prince imperial rode his velocipede and followed his toy train of cars, watched by the eyes of a fond father and mother, who saw in him the future ruler of France. But there came still another revolution and when in September, 1870, the news of the surrender of Sedan was received in Paris, another mob invaded the palace, but this time a peaceful one. The emperor was n captivity, the empress had fled for shelter and protection, under the guidance of an American friend, and the mob satisfied themselves by painting caricatures on the walls, cutting the curtains and pictures and writing "liberty, equality, fraternity" over the doors. During the siege by the Germans the palace remained uninjured. After the German evacuation and the seizure of the city by the Communists, the palace was used for military purposes, and when their cause became desperate its destruction was decreed by a council of their leaders. Gunpowder, petroleum and other combustibles were placed in all parts of the building, and while the national troops were storming the barricades in the vicinity the Palace of the Tuileries was set on fire and destroyed.

The Place du Carrousel is east of the Tuileries and separated from it by an iron railing. It derived its name from a tournament held here by Louis XIV. It is open now to the public for general traffic, is a very busy place, and contains the Arc du Carrousel, built by order of Napoleon to commemorate his victories of 1805-6. It is an imitation, but on a smaller scale, of the Arch of Severus, at Rome. It has three arched passage ways, and is tastefully embellished by Corinthian columns, and reliefs, showing the victories of the emperor. The arch was originally surmounted by the celebrated quadriga from St. Marks, in Venice, brought here as a trophy, but sent back by the Emperor of Austria while the Allies occupied Paris in 1814. It is now crowned by a quadriga designed by a French artist and erected by order of Louis Philippe.

The palace of the Luxembourg is south of the Louvre,

on the other side of the Seine, and was built, in 1615-20, for Marie de Medicis. It was used as a royal residence till the revolution of 1791, when it was turned into a states prison in which Beauharnois and his wife, Josephine, afterward wife of Napoleon I., Desmoulins, Danton, Robespierre, David and others, were confined. It was used by the directory and afterwards by the consulate. Under the first empire it was used as a senate chamber and after being devoted to other purposes it is now used as a senate chamber and the official residence of the president of the senate. Part of the building is used as a museum of art, to which the public are freely admitted. The rooms are beautifully decorated and contain paintings, sculptures, drawings and engravings, mostly the work of living artists. Ten years after the artist's death the works of the most distinguished masters are transferred to the Louvre or to provincial galleries. The ambition to have his work exhibited in the Louvre, ten years after death, may animate a Frenchman to do his best; I doubt if the average American could draw much inspiration from a source so remotely and indefinitely in the future. I am delighted with the pictures and sculptures of the Luxembourg, all new and clean, and all dependent on their merits as works of art, and not on a distinguished name. Some members of our party have the habit of collecting around every "Corregio" or "Titian" or "Rubens," even if every trace of beauty and design had long since faded out of the canvas, seeing wonderful "effects" where the painter himself, if alive, would fail to discover anything except that it needed re-painting. I cannot lie about it; I confess the clean white marble and bright colors and fresh varnish just suit my fancy, and I console myself with the thought that after the bright colors have faded and the marble become blackened and stained, the "utterly utter" in art of future generations will worship at the shrine of many of these paintings and sculptures at the Luxembourg.

The garden of the Luxembourg is beautiful; its marble fountains, balustrades and steps, make it resemble an Italian scene. It is rich in modern statuary, largely mythological; but I noticed on one of the terraces an interesting series of twenty statues of distinguished and good-looking French women, *they look best in stone*, that seemed to possess more interest to the gentlemen of our party than the gladiators or Mercury or fawns. This garden seems to be more frequented than any other in Paris. Under the shade of its trees I have heard two of the best military bands. These open air concerts draw a very large crowd, mostly women and children. I rented a chair for the moderate sum of two cents and greatly enjoyed the music, as apparently did everybody else; indeed, enjoyment seems to be the sole purpose of the laughing crowd. Cakes and gingerbread and small shows of the Punch and Judy order, on the outskirts, gave to the scene quite a holiday appearance. I was amused at the method used to restrain French children. Nurses kept boys, two or three years old, in check by a ribbon about four feet long, one end attached to the boy's waist and the other held in the nurse's hand. I asked a western gentleman what young America would think of such an arrangement? He insisted that a bed-cord and hitching-post would be necessary in his State, which probably resembles Michigan in the character of its small boys.

The place in Paris where its richest treasures of antiquity and art may be found is the Palace of the Louvre, adjoining the Tuileries on the east. It is built on the site of a former fortress and palace, of which, however, no trace remains. The foundations of the south wing of the Louvre

were laid by Francis I., in 1541, and completed under Henry II., but first occupied as a residence by Catharine de Medicis and her son Charles IX. From that time to the present every monarch and government of France, the revolutionist excepted, has enlarged or beautified the Louvre. The first Napoleon expended large sums in its restoration, while the additions made by Napoleon III. alone cost fifteen millions of dollars. It has been the scene of many important events. It was from a window of the south wing that the signal for the massacre of St. Bartholomew was given, on the night of August 24d, 1572 ; and as the bell of the church of St. Germain, opposite the Louvre, gave the preconcerted signal, by its tolling, the guards marched from the court below to murder Admiral Coligny, the first Huguenot victim. A window is shown from which it is said Charles IX. fired on his doomed subjects collected below. In 1871 the Louvre was fired by the Communists, the wing next to the Tuileries being badly damaged by fire, and 90,000 volumes and many precious manuscripts destroyed.

The eastern front of the Louvre is, I think, unequaled by any building in Paris. Its great colonnade is considered the finest remaining specimen of architecture of the age of Louis XIV., and is composed of twenty-eight double Corinthian columns. The gateway in the center and the bronze gates made by order of Napoleon, impress me as being more beautiful than anything of the kind I have seen in Paris. This front, known as the Colonnade du Louvre, is so frequently illustrated in books and so common in stereoscopic views that many of my readers must be familiar with its appearance. The Louvre proper is a perfect square, each front 525 feet long, and has a large and beautiful inner court. Its older part has been used as a museum of fine arts since the revolution of 1789. In 1793 the more precious works of art, distributed among the palaces and chateaus belonging to the crown, were gathered here. During the wars of the republic and first empire, the choicest gems of art in Europe were collected by the armies under Napoleon and placed in the Louvre. What is now known as the Museum of the Louvre is divided into sixteen departments, containing miles of galleries and shelves, and is in many of its departments unrivaled. I can give but the briefest sketch of an entire day spent among the treasures.

The galleries contain about 2,000 paintings, by the great artists of the world, and are to most visitors the chief attraction. In no other place can Raphael be so well studied, and Titian is almost equally well represented; indeed, a catalogue would be a list of the great painters of the world. Before a painting can be admitted to the Louvre, a competent jury must decide that it is worthy of that honor, and if the work of a Frenchman, the artist must have been dead at least ten years. I noted some of the paintings which most impressed me, among them Raphael's "Holy Family," and "Madonna and Child;" a "Beggar Boy," "Holy Family" and "Immaculate Conception," by Murillo, the latter painting purchased of Marshal Soult, probably stolen in Spain, for $135,000; Rembrandt's "Supper at Emmaus;" twenty-one large paintings by Rubens, a series painted for Marie de Medicis? "Holy Family," by Da Vinci; Correggio's "Jupiter and Antiope;" Titian's "Entombment of Christ;" and "Marriage at Cana," by Paul Veronese. Among the French painters Claude Lorraine, Poussin, Vernet, Le Brun, Le Suer, David and Delacroix, are most largely represented. The glory of the Louvre is not the number or size of its paintings, but that all are gems of art.

The Egyptian department contains a very large and varied collection of remains, among them a number of sphinxes, one of them marked as ante-dating Noah's flood by at least two centuries. On its sides has been added in later times the name of the Pharaoh of the Exodus, whose army perished in the Red Sea, and the name of Shishak, who conquered Rehoboam. There are statues from 500 to 1,500 years before Christ; among them a colossal statue of Setis I., son of the Pharaoh before mentioned. There is a large collection of reliefs, some of them finely colored. The sarcophagus of Rameses III., 1,300 years before Christ, is shown, and a large number of later date, beautifully ornamented with sculptures. There are quite a number of monuments to sacred bulls, with the date of their death, and name of king reigning at the time,—said to have been of great importance in fixing Egyptian chronology. Two male and one female figures, with their hair painted black, are, according to the received French chronology of the period, assigned by the Bible to the creation of man, and conceded to be the oldest portrait figures in existence. There are several rooms filled with statues and reliefs, illustrating the religious belief and forms of worship of the Egyptians; marbles and papyri with interesting inscriptions, statues of gods and sacred animals, ivory caskets, gold mummy masks, fine linen goods, sandals, household implements, articles for the toilet, etc. I was interested in a statuette of an Egyptian scribe, with large and life-like eyes of rock crystal, and ante-dating the flood by several hundred years.

There are several rooms of Assyrian antiquities, and rooms devoted to Phœnician remains; rooms of ancient sculptures, not classified, and rooms devoted mostly to statues of the early Roman emperors. The Salle de Phidias contains gems of art of the age of that greatest of Grecian sculptors, and there are quite a number of rooms devoted to earlier and later sculptures—as a whole, undoubtedly one of the finest collections in the world. Among them is a room dedicated to the Venus of Milo, claimed to be the most precious treasure of the Louvre. On the same principle that people ignorant of music insist on becoming enraptured with ear-splitting and horribly murdered music, entirely beyond the comprehension of singers or audience, I suppose I ought to have gone into ecstacies over this disfigured and dilapidated old statue. The confession may be ruinous to my reputation, but I could really see nothing about it to especially admire. There are six rooms of modern sculpture, containing some beautiful works of art. Twelve rooms are devoted to mediæval antiquities, consisting of ivory and wood carving, terra cotta busts and reliefs, medallions in wax, glass, and porcelain ware, bronzes, Italian majolica paintings, Florentine terra cotta reliefs, vases, tapestry of the sixteenth century with scenes from the book of Judges, and a statue of Peace in massive silver, presented to Napoleon I. by the city of Paris.

The Galerie d' Apollon, over 200 feet long, is the finest room in the Louvre. The ceiling, decorated by Le Brun, Delacroix, and others, has nine large allegorical paintings; and the panels of the walls are adorned with portraits of twenty-eight celebrated French artists, and Gobelin tapestries with portraits of St. Louis, Francis I. and Louis XV. The beautiful furniture in this room is mostly of Louis XIV. The glass cases contain articles of antiquity, relics, gems, and the largest and most valuable collection of enamels in the world. Among the objects of interest in these cases may be mentioned a casket of St. Louis, with gold reliefs; a vase of jasper by Cellini; the crown of Louis XV., but now containing imitation jewels; a casket of Queen Anne of Austria, in gold filigree; an imitation of the crown of Charlemagne, worn by Napoleon I. at his coronation; sword and spurs of Charlemagne; steel armor of Henry II.; helmet and shield of Charles IX.; mirror, and candlestick adorned with emeralds and cameos, presented by the Republic of Venice to Marie de Medicis. From the articles I have mentioned, almost at random, some idea may be formed of how interesting this large room, full of just such things, must be.

The Salle des Bijoux contains a large collection of ancient jewels and ornaments, largely Grecian and Etruscan, over which days might be spent in examination and description.

In the Salle des Caryatides, Henry IV. married Margaret of Valois, and here his body was placed after his assassination. It was also used as a theater by Moliere, who acted here in some of his own plays. It is a very beautiful room, and contains some fine paintings and sculptures.

Nine rooms are devoted to the Musee Campana, purchased in 1862, of the Papal Government. It consists principally of Egyptian, Babylonian, Grecian and Phœnician statues, terra cottas, pottery, vases, caskets, gold ornaments, etc. There are also four rooms devoted to Chinese curiosities.

I doubt if my attempts at describing palaces and museums will be of much interest to my readers, and yet I have endeavored to be very brief, lumping off dozens of rooms in less than as many lines. A hundred volumes would not describe in detail the treasures of the Louvre. I have omitted whole departments, noticing only a few of the things that most interested myself.

The Place de la Bastille is a large square, in which formerly stood an ancient fortress surrounded by a moat, and afterward converted into a state prison. Its inmates were usually noblemen, politicians or authors who had incurred the displeasure of the king or some of his favorites, and were incarcerated here without being informed of their crime, or of the duration of their imprisonment. It was here the "Man with the Iron Mask," whose identity has caused so much discussion, and will probably ever remain a mystery, was imprisoned. It was destroyed in 1789, at the beginning of the revolution, "Down with the Bastille!" being the first rallying cry of the revolutionists. Its massive walls, ten feet thick, and its eight heavy towers, were torn down and removed, so odious had it become to the people. Napoleon I. ordered the erection of a colossal bronze elephant in the centre of the square, but Waterloo interfered with the accomplishment of his design. The column now standing here, and known as the "Column of July," was erected in honor of the men who fell in the revolution of 1830. It was completed in 1840, is 150 feet high, thirteen feet in thickness, and rests on a massive pedestal of white marble, intended by Napoleon to support his bronze elephant. The column is of bronze, in five sections, and fluted; and on it, in gilded letters, are the names of over 600 of the victims of July, 1830, who are buried in its vaults. On the top is a figure of the Genius of Liberty, standing on a globe, and holding a torch and broken chain. The Place was one of the strongholds of the Communists, who barricaded every street leading to it, and made preparations to blow up the column, if forced to retreat. It was saved by their holding out long enough to use up all their powder.

The Porte St. Martin is a triumphal arch, about sixty feet high, erected by the city, in 1674, in honor of Louis XIV. Its reliefs and inscriptions commemorate the victories of that monarch. The Port St. Denis is a similar arch, but larger, being eighty feet high, and in honor of the same monarch. Both these arches have been the scene of some terrible fighting in the revolutionary struggles, especially in 1871. The bullets of the Communists have left numerous marks on these arches. In passing through the streets of Paris, in the presence of the buildings destroyed or injured, and by the graves of its victims, I have been led to wonder at the ferocity and thirst for blood that has marked its revolutions. I am passing in the streets, and sitting with, in the omnibuses, the men and women who witnessed and took part in the horrible scenes of ten years ago. It was French against French, and the disciplined troops of the Versailles government were as inhuman as the leaders of the Commune. Somewhere, and not far from the surface, there must lurk in the deferential and polite Frenchman, and woman too, for they were as cruel as the men, the instincts of the tiger. which passion can arouse to murderous activity—and yet you wouldn't think it to look at them.

The Column Vendome is an imitation of Trajan's column at Rome, erected by Napoleon in 1806–10, to commemorate his victories over the Russians and Austrians in 1805. It is of masonry, 142 feet high and thirteen feet in diameter, and covered on the outside with continuous plates of bronze, forming a spiral scroll over 500 feet long, on which are represented scenes from the campaigns it is designed to commemorate. Twelve hundred Austrian and Russian cannon were used in making these plates. The statue of Napoleon, on the top of the column, was removed in 1815. It is said the Allies, when in Paris in 1815, made several unsuccessful attempts to pull the column down. The Communists in 1871 succeeded in overthrowing it, and trampling in the dust, or rather on a manure heap, the statue of the great emperor which had been restored by Napoleon III. The column has been re-erected, and the restored statue of the general whose victories it was designed to commemorate appropriately decorates its top.

The government manufactory of Gobelin tapestry is in a building almost entirely destroyed by the German bombardment. Fortunately some of the most valuable tapestries had been removed. Since 1662 the manufacture of Gobelin tapestries has been carried on exclusively by the government. It was found it did not pay, but the authorities have prided themselves on being able to produce finer fabrics than any other nation in the world. We were permitted to pass through the entire building, seeing the process of weaving and the beautiful specimens when completed. There were four rooms devoted to the exhibition of tapestries; some of the specimens are quite old, some of them very fine, among them a number of valuable fragments saved from larger pieces burned by the Communists. The looms are simple and easily understood. The part of the work on which the workman is engaged is outlined in chalk on the stretched threads, while the picture he is to copy is at his side. In front of him is a basket of fine woolen threads, of every conceivable shade of color, from which his practiced eye selects the shade to be woven into the design. Two and a quarter inches square is considered a day's work; on portraits and difficult designs it is still less. Many years are necessary for completing the large designs, which are valued from $10,000 upwards. I have seen nothing finer from the brush of the most celebrated painters than some of these Gobelins. Of course they are never in market, being worked for the government and used in the decoration of public buildings or presented to foreign courts or persons of distinction.

The Morgue is a place where the bodies of unknown persons who have perished in the river or otherwise are kept for three days if not sooner identified. It is on a much frequented thoroughfare, and its open doors invite the passers by to the hideous sights within. Stone slabs recline against the walls, and on them were the bodies of a man and woman naked to the waist. Around the room were numerous pieces of clothing, sometimes a mere shred taken from bodies that have been exposed here. A curious crowd were passing in and out and we were soon pointed to the door to make room for others. How strange that gay and lovely Paris should furnish so many suicides. During the past year 750 bodies have been brought here for identification.

In Paris fires are almost unknown, the buildings being really fire proof. With us high buildings and Mansard roofs are supposed to greatly increase the risk. The buildings in most parts of the city are five or six stories high, with Mansard roofs, and yet there are few fires of importance; indeed, I am told the fire is usually confined to the story in which it originates. The Communists tried to destroy the public buildings and the residences and stores in the best part of the city, but the conflagration rarely extended beyond the building fired. The Hotel de Ville and Tuileries were filled with petroleum and other combustibles and their destruction assured, but with little damage to the adjoining buildings. I noticed that even the ordinary outside blinds are of iron. The plans and specifications for all new buildings are submitted to a government board of inspectors whose approval is necessary, and whose duty it is to see that they are carried out in detail, and who *do their duty*. A similar board might do much to prevent the large fires so common in America.

There are thirty-three different omnibus lines, and with an omnibus chart of the city it is possible to reach almost any point in this way. These omnibuses will accommodate from thirty to forty persons, half of them on the outside, the top being reached by a stairway practicable for ladies. There are, besides, thirty-nine lines of tram-cars, running mostly to the villages on the outside the fortifications, and the cities of Boulogne and Versailles. The fare on the outside to any point within the fortifications is three cents. An omnibus may be hailed at any point and if not full will stop. If taken at a regular station you receive a number, and if the omnibus is not full before your number is reached you are assigned a seat; if full, you wait till by another arrival your number is reached; the rule "first come first served" is invariable. When the number for whom seats are provided has been seated the conductor hangs out a card with the word "Complet," meaning full, and no more are admitted. The American idea that "an omnibus is never full," has not been adopted in Paris.

Although I have described none of the theaters, except the Grand Opera House, Paris has about seventy theaters. Some of the best are sustained in part by the government, and all are well patronized by the people. The French seem to delight in shows—even the cheap out-door performances at the Cafe Chantants draw large crowds of people. In the gardens and parks are numerous shows of the Punch and Judy order. An accordeon, sometimes reinforced by a violin, furnishes the music, and the people seem never to tire watching the puppets on the mimic stage. The roars of laughter with which their sayings are greeted lead me to think, that like the "end men" at a minstrel performance, new and local hits are indulged in.

The educational facilities of Paris seem to be very extensive, beginning with the academy, with its ninety professors, and the college of France with thirty professors; supplemented by special schools of military, mining, art, Polytechnic, normal, musical, etc. Some of the buildings used for educational purposes are very fine; among them may be mentioned the Ecole Militaire, Sarbonne, Institute de France and the Palais and Ecole des beaux Arts. The Academy alone is said to number 8,000 students. All the schools and colleges and most of the palaces have extensive libraries, but the great library of Paris is the Bibliotheque Nationale, probably the most extensive in the world, containing about two million volumes. Its departments of manuscripts and engravings, coins and medals, are very complete.

## TAXATION.

The answer I have received to my inquiries about taxation would indicate that pretty much everything is taxed. The holders of real estate do not, as with us, bear nearly all the expenses of local government, permitting those rich in money, or acquiring money, to go almost scot free. Carriage stands pay nearly a million dollars yearly for the privilege; each omnibus and tram-car pays two hundred dollars tax; balconies, signs and lanterns attached to buildings are taxed; cafes pay for the use of the sidewalks for their customers. All provisions entering the city are taxed; I am assured that twenty million dollars is realized from this tax, but it seems a large sum. Trade licenses produce three million dollars, market rents two million, water supply one million, theaters half a million, and even the street Punch and Judy shows pay a tax amounting to ten thousand dollars. Even in death the government does not relax its claims. The cemeteries are public property and graves must be purchased, or, as is usually the case, rented for five years. All funerals in Paris are conducted by a company of undertakers, who pay to the authorities for this exclusive privilege one third of all moneys received for funeral ornaments aud fifteen per cent. of all other receipts. Supposing this company's charges to be on the American scale, the revenue to the city must be enormous, and after paying over one third of the receipts for the useless paraphernalia of mourning, and fifteen per cent. on things essential, the poor company's profits must be reduced to 200 per cent. or less, which seems hard on the company.

The fountains of Paris are very imposing, though, as nobody drinks water, they are not of so much utility as in America, where there are some water drinkers left. The Fountains des Innocents, de Medicis, Moliere and Notre Dame are among the finest, but seem designed more for ornament than use.

The Parisians have a great fondness for flowers and the flower markets are numerous. Even in the poorer quarters of the city every window to the sixth story has its flowers. The trees are tenderly cared for and if a large tree dies it is replaced by another of the same size so as to preserve uniformity. In the paved streets or stone walks a circular iron grating surrounds the tree for two or three feet, admitting air and moisture. It seems a sensible arrangement and I have never seen it before.

I had almost forgotten one of the things on which the Parisians pride themselves—tbe great hospitals. Over 20,000 patients are constantly under treatment and there is accommodation for a large number more. Some of the buildings are of immense size and of imposing appearance. More than one-fourth of the births are illegitimate and foundling hospitals are maintained by the government, where the unfortunate little ones are cared for. The cost of the hospitals and other charitable institutions for the poor is over five million dollars yearly.

What Paris is to be, it would be difficult to conjecture. The fortifications seem to limit its extension, and the demolition of thousands of buildings to make room for its grand squares, large public buildings, and wide boulevards has not ceased. Whole parks like the Buttes Chamonts have been formed on ground formerly occupied by the narrowest streets and most crowded tenements. Boulevards have been run through that part of Paris, occupied by what are known as the dangerous classes, and the asphaltum pavements, though expensive, are regarded with complacency as not affording paving stones for the erection of barricades. There is something in the air of Paris hardly compatible with earnest, consecutive thought—nobody seems in earnest, everybody seems to be enjoying themselves. Compare the streets of Paris with those of New York or Chicago and what a contrast. Imagine the sidewalks on Broadway or State street set with tables and chairs as if for a picnic ! The noble parks, beautiful gardens, the finest museums in the world—all that wealth and art can do has been done to make Paris attractive, and for the poorest as well as the rich. The working man on Sundays and holidays can enjoy all these without cost and with the same sense of proprietorship as the rich. Paris will probably remain as now, the pleasure ground of the civilized world, and attract to herself the wealthy and pleasure seeking of all nations. No other place so beautiful, or made so interesting and enjoyable, or that so freely and lavishly displays its treasures.

## CHAPTER X.

### SWITZERLAND.

Paris to Berne—Berne—The Cathedral Terrace—Alpine View—Organ Concert—The Streets—Swiss People—The Bears of Berne—Lake Thun—Interlaken—The Jungfrau—Swiss Houses—Religious Service—Sunday Afternoon—Lake Brienz—Brunig Pass—Lake Lucerne—Lucerne—A Fine Organ—The Lion of Lucerne—Vitznau—Rigi Railroad—View from the Summit—William Tell—Protestant and Catholic—The Common Pasturage.

I left Paris by the Lyons and Mediterranean rail road for Switzerland. There was no sleeping car attached to the train, but my traveling companion and myself, by a small fee to the conductor, secured an entire compartment to ourselves, and by a judicious placing of the cushions and baggage improvised a sort of Pullman arrangement that answered the purpose remarkably well. I awoke about daybreak at Artelot in France. The country looked very much like the hilly portions of New England. It is very sparsely settled, the houses are but one story, cover a good deal of ground and present an astonishing amount of roof. Potatoes are in blossom, and the farmers are cutting a very light crop of grass. They seem to cure their hay before cutting it, indeed, it looks like old hay as it falls from the scythe. About six o'clock we stop at Pontarlier thirty minutes for refreshments, which consisted of excellent coffee with rolls and butter. Coffee was served in a bowl with a tablespoon to sup it. Total expense of meal sixteen cents, and it is the best the establishment affords. In America, the minutes would have been reduced, and the dishes and cost multiplied. As we near the Swiss line we see large fortifications in course of repair or of erection, by the French. We entered

Switzerland by a long tunnel, but emerged into daylight and fine scenery, and soon reached Vallorbes, where for the first time I stood on Swiss soil. Here is the Swiss custom house, but our baggage was not examined or any questions asked. As we proceed the scenery becomes more interesting, bearing some resemblance to that between Island Pond and Gorham, with which many of my readers are familiar. Villages and small hamlets occur frequently in the cultivated portions, the tops of the hills being bare unless where covered by very small pines. Soon the snow capped mountains of the Bernese Oberland are seen in the distance and we enjoy magnificent views of Swiss scenery. Reaching Lausanne, we find cars on the American plan of a central passage through the car lengthwise, but with the American couplings which are inferior to the French or English. Lausanne has a population of about 25,000 and is finely situated on the Lake of Geneva. For miles in either direction are vineyards sloping gracefully from the very tops of the high hills to the waters of the lake. On the other side of the lake, which is narrow here, are hills and mountain ledges presenting the most diversified forms as we pass. A bright sun lights up a scene of beauty which is seldom surpassed. The next place of importance is Fribourg, with a population of about 11,090. From Fribourg to Berne the country is mostly capable of cultivation, and the crops look better than nearer the French line.

Berne, the capital of Switzerland, is on the river Aare which bounds it on three sides, and has a population of about 40,000. On entering my room at the hotel, the first thing which attracted my attention was a new arrangement of the bed—two ticks filled with feathers, the sleeper expected to lie between. As a summer arrangement it did not strike me favorably. In fact it seemed as if the second bed might be dispensed with. It looks very much like running a large coal stove the year round.  I proceeded at once to the Cathedral terrace, delightful as a promenade, but especially famous for its fine view of the Bernese Alps —described by Humboldt as "one of the finest panoramas in Europe."  Before me and much more irregular and broken in their outlines than my fancy had painted them, stood in solemn and impressive grandeur the snow capped Wetterhorn, Eiger, Jungfrau, Silberhorn, Doldenhorn, Stockhorn, and others of this range.  I recalled the words of the poet:

> " Who first beholds the Alps—that mighty chain
> Of mountains stretching on from east to west,
> So massive, yet so shadowy, so etheriel.
> As to belong rather to heaven than to earth—
> But instantly receives into his soul
> A sense a feeling that he loseth not,
> A something that informs him 'tis a moment
> Whence he may date henceforward and forever !"

The terrace is finely shaded by luxuriant chestnut trees, and the rapid Aare flows by its base, more than a hundred feet below.  It is a favorite resort for the citizens, who, seated in the shade of its trees, indulge in wine, coffee, ice-cream—and Alps.  My guide book informs me that a celebrated traveller "wept at the sight" which greeted his eyes from this terrace.  I didn't, but, the day being very hot, took ice-cream with my Alps, with results entirely satisfactory.

In the evening I went to the cathedral to hear the large organ, played nightly for the benefit of tourists,—and of the organist.  It is a very powerful instrument, and some of the stops are said to be peculiar to it.  The concert closed with the famous "Storm, calm, and thanksgiving" piece.  It was finely done.  The calm and thanksgiving were beautiful, and the thunder natural enough to sour milk, but too loud for thunder.  By some ingenious management the wind and rain were given by the organ, and so naturally, that at first, and until I discovered their source, I was regretting the absence of my umbrella.

An early morning walk proved interesting. Everybody seemed to be active and busy. The streets were being carefully swept, and by women. At about a quarter to seven I began to meet large numbers of children with books and slates, on their way to school. A cleaner, healthier looking, better behaved lot of young people, I never saw. On inquiry, I found that the forenoon session commenced at seven o'clock, and closed at eleven. If the young people of America are being injured by long hours of study at school, as I have heard intimated in that country, we should expect a race of invalids in Switzerland. Just the reverse is the fact. Some other reason than the *number of hours in school* must be found for the nervousness and ill health of children in America. The Swiss people I meet in Berne impress me very favorably. I have met very few women dressed as showily or expensively as the average servant girl of America. But they look healthy, clean, helpful, dignified, and self respecting. The men are like them in these respects, and though reserved in manner, are exceedingly accommodating in helping strangers to find objects of interest for which they may inquire. It seems to me that everybody in Berne is engaged in earning a living by some useful occupation, and *don't care who knows it.* Berne is said to have better preserved its ancient characteristics than any other Swiss city. The principal business street is about a mile long, the buildings each side extending over the sidewalk, their fronts supported by a row of columns on the inside of the curbstone. In the morning the sides of the street are used as a market for provisions, fruit, etc., presenting a busy and crowded appearance. Several old towers stand in the streets. One, of peculiar form, is known as the "Bird Cage Tower." Another is the "Clock Tower;" and has in it a very large clock, about twenty-five feet from the ground. On one side of the dial is a rooster, who crows three minutes before the hour. In another minute a Merry-Andrew above the dial rings two bells. A king, on the opposite side of the dial from the rooster, when the hour arrives turns over a large hour glass which he holds in his hand, and counts the hours as the clock strikes, keeping time to the counting with his scepter. During the striking, a procession of bears is passing in and out of the tower. Another crow of the rooster ends the performance. There are numerous fountains in the streets, used largely as places for gossip, and affording opportunities for admiring the simplicity of Swiss life and manners.

Berne is known as the "city of bears," for which various reasons are assigned. But of the fact that the bear is an object of veneration, there can be no dispute. On all the public buildings are bears, on every fountain, and they are numerous, may be found bears, and defending all entrances to public gates are bears—bears in effigy, I mean. Beside the statue of one of their great men stands the statue of a bear, bearing in his paws the great man's hat. In the shop windows are prints, lithographs, engravings and chromos of bears, and bears in wood, stone, and all the metals, besides gingerbread and candy bears. In the toy shops may be seen bear schools, bear soldiers, intoxicated bears in custody of bear policemen, bear orchestras, etc., etc. Desiring to bear home with me some trifle purchased in Berne, I decided of course to purchase a bear,—in the form of a gold charm—and for this purpose visited a large establishment devoted to fancy goods. After making my purchase I sat down in a chair to rest for a moment, while the salesman was putting it in a box. Suddenly, and to my astonishment, a lively Swiss air began to waltz out of my coat tails, while a small bear, hat in hand, stepped in front of me. I had sat down in a musical chair! By the river Aare is a *Barengraben*, or bear's den, where in magnificent quarters are kept a number of bears, of a peculiar breed. During the French wars the bears of Berne were captured, and taken to Paris. The loss of the bears was regarded as a public misfortune. After the restoration of the Bourbons in France, the Bernese demanded, and received back their bears. The reception given the exiles on their return, is said to have equalled in enthusiasm that given to the greatest warriors or statesmen.

From Berne to Thun is nineteen miles, by railroad. It is a picturesque and ancient town, of 5,000 inhabitants, charmingly situated on the river Aare. From Thun to Scherzligen is about a mile; and here we take the steamboat on Lake Thun for Darligen. This lake is about ten miles long and two miles wide, and is surrounded by fine scenery. On the hill-sides are picturesque villas and gardens, and the vine is cultivated on the slopes. Fine views are obtained of the Bernese Alps, which appear in a continuous chain in the distance. Landing at Darligen, I took the cars for Interlaken, about a mile distant. It derives its name, Interlaken, from the fact that it lies between Lakes Thun and Brienz. It also lies between two ridges of mountains, not much more than a mile apart, and is more resorted to by tourists than any other place in Switzerland. It is known by travelers as the village of hotels, of which there are twenty-five or more; and besides, almost every house takes boarders. Some of the hotels are large, and finely kept. At the *Hotel des Alpes*, where I stayed, about 130 persons sat at dinner in the large dining hall. The hotels unite in sustaining an institution known as the Cursaal, where the drinking of whey is practiced at certain hours of the day, by invalids and others. The Cursaal is finely kept, has a library and reading room, and a good orchestra of about twenty-five performers. Music is furnished three times a day for all who desire to attend. Not noticing a single case of spectacles, or long hair. I conclude the musicians are unpretending amateurs; they play well, however. Interlaken affords a remarkable view of the Jungfrau and Silberhorn. Looking south, between two of the mountains which enclose the village, the snowy tops of the Jungfrau and Silberhorn rise in their majestic whiteness :

> "Vast as mysterious, beautiful as grand,
> Forever looking into heaven's clear face."

The effect is startling; the lofty mountains, nearly 13,000 feet high, appear as if within musket range, but are nearly eighteen miles distant. I stayed at Interlaken over Sunday and made a somewhat extended climbing and wandering tour on foot. The small villages and hamlets of the peasants in this vicinity, as indeed in almost the entire canton of Berne, are wretched looking. Hardly a roof appeared as if it would keep out the rain, and most of them are covered with large stones to keep the roof in place. Under the eaves, or under sheds, might be seen the little stock of hardwood seasoning, to furnish material for wood carving. Occasionally by a small stream I would find a saw mill, the most primitive and diminutive I have ever met with. It is a fact which cannot be denied that these rambling old houses, where one cannot tell where the house ends and cowshed begins, look much more picturesque and satisfactory, in every respect, in a lady's album or in a picture gallery, marked "Scene in Switzerland," than they do on the spot. The houses inside gave no indications of what Americans would call comfort. They had, however, one redeeming quality; no matter how poor, they were clean. Several times I quenched my thirst with milk procured at these places, and never saw anything that destroyed my relish for the milk, no matter how poor the place. Most of

IN SWITZERLAND.

these people earn a living by whittling and carving wood, at which they are remarkably ingenious. The products of their labor may be found in every Swiss city and village, and are purchased largely by tourists as well as for exportation. On Sunday morning I attended the service of the Free Church of Scotland. I found a most remarkable state of things religiously. The nave of the old church, with which a monastry was formerly connected, is a Roman Catholic Church. The choir is used by the Church of England. The sacristy is used by a French Protestant Church and by the Free Church of Scotland. The sermon by a genuine Scotchman from Edinburgh, was very good. The singing was congregational, led by a small harmonium, located back of the little pulpit and out of sight of the congregation, such things being of doubtful propriety, and barely tolerated in the Free Church. About thirty-five persons, all strangers and mostly Scotch, were in attendance. The simple, tender, fervent prayer for "President Garfield, if still alive," touched the hearts of at least two Americans, who did not expect in that far off land to find such hearty sympathy for the unfortunate president. Sunday appears to be observed here till noon, when a half holiday begins. The stores on the principal street, the Hoheweg, are opened and promenading and shopping begins. The thousands of visitors, speaking almost every European language, mingling with the Swiss peasants in their Sunday attire, presents a scene both novel and interesting. The most remarkable thing about my hotel experience here was an item in my bill of one franc for "coal tax." I should have liked to argue the question with the proprietor, who had furnished no fires, on the double basis of "taxation without representation," and taxation without coal, but as the train was just ready to start I had to forego the pleasure.

Leaving Interlaken, I took the cars for Bonigen, about

a mile distant, and there take the steamer on Lake Brienz for the village of Brienz, at the other end of the lake. This lake is about ten miles long by one and one-half miles wide. The borders of the lake are mountainous, but occasionally relieved by a charming slope cultivated to the water's edge. Indeed, the scenery on both Lakes Thun and Brienz resembles a section of twenty miles of the Hudson River near West Point, magnified of course, as the rocks and mountains here are much higher. At Brienz the diligence is waiting to convey us over the Brunig Pass to Alpnach, twenty-five miles distant. Five horses were attached, and the journey, to be made in seven hours, requires an ascent of 3,396 feet to the summit of the Pass. The road makes directly for the mountain, and the ascent at once becomes steep, the way winding to the right and left up the mountain side. The road bed is good, being cut in the solid rock. The view, downward, from the side of the diligence, gets to be immense, say 2,000 feet perpendicular. At one point where the mountain projects over the valley, a shelf is cut in the mountain side for the carriage way. The overhanging mass of rock above looks to a timid traveler as if it couldn't hold another minute, and yet the driver persisted in stopping right under the center of it, on the pretext that it afforded a fine view of the valley of the Aare. The Pass is a favorite one, and carriage parties numerous. Swiss boys and girls, with small baskets of blackberries and raspberries, now just ripe on the mountains, approach us at every resting place. Swiss women stand by the road side ready to furnish the traveler delicious Swiss milk. The descent proved to be more gradual than the ascent, and passing the villages of Lungern and Sarnen, on lakes of the same name, we reach Alpnach. The drive from Brienz to Alpnach, over the mountain, is interesting and exciting. I intended to give my readers a detailed description of its interesting scenery, but ran short of appropriate and forcible adjectives long before I reached the summit of the pass. I must therefore leave undescribed Swiss scenes and scenery to which no words of mine can do justice.

At Alpnach we take the steamer for Lucerne. Lake Lucerne is usually described as the most picturesque and beautiful in Europe. It is cruciform in shape, Lucerne being at the head, and is surrounded by mountains, towering in imposing grandeur, five to seven thousand feet above its level. Most of these mountains are covered with cedar trees, except where cleared for human habitations, and one is led to wonder at the cottages far up their sides, apparently unapproachable except by wings or a balloon. Near the tops are seen large buildings with flags, evidently hotels, and it is claimed that during the season of travel more than 2,000 visitors stay over night at these hotels among the clouds.

The city of Lucerne has about 18,000 inhabitants and is charmingly situated in a natural amphitheater at the outlet of the lake. The river Reuss runs through it like a mountain torrent, on its way from the lake to the Rhine. The whole length of the quay is a broad avenue, shaded by chestnut trees, and fronting on this avenue are the great hotels. The background is made up of quaint old houses, and the ancient walls and watch-towers. The view from Lucerne is still more imposing. From my window, the Rigi group in the east, and grim and rocky Pilatus in the southwest rise in the foreground, and between them, in the distance, I can count nearly forty snow clad Alpine peaks. The public buildings of Lucerne are good, but not imposing. The principal streets are in modern style and there is less appearance of poverty than in any place I have seen in

Switzerland. The cathedral is of the seventeenth century, and has a remarkably fine bell. Its greatest attraction however, is its fine organ, the best in Switzerland, and the finest I have ever heard. It is played every evening and the concerts are well patronized by tourists. It differs principally from the organ at Berne in being of a smoother and softer tone. Its full organ is really much more powerful than that at Berne, but as played seems to make less noise, yet gives you a feeling of subdued power that is very impressive. The "Storm, calm and thanksgiving" piece, was performed here also, but with much finer effect. The thunder really seemed to be out doors, and to die away in the distance. The moaning of the winds, increasing fitfully in gusts, till it reached the roar of the hurricane, the pattering rain drops followed by a pouring rain, the rushing noise of the swollen mountain streams, the notes of the Alpine horn and tinkling of the cow bells were all imitated so perfectly as to seem real. But the storm began to abate, the distant convent bell rings, and soon the sweet voices of nun's chanting is heard; it is increased by male voices till all the parts are given, and a magnificent choir seems to be offering a song of thanksgiving. Gradually the music seems to die away in the distance till all is still. It required great faith in the wonderful vox humana stop, for which this organ is so justly celebrated, to believe that all these choral effects were produced by the organ. It was certainly the most remarkable musical performance to which I ever listened.

The great lion of Lucerne, to which all visitors are directed, is a lion cut in the solid rock, after Thorwaldsen, to commemorate the Swiss who fell at Paris in 1792, defending the Tuileries and royal family. The dying lion is transfixed with a broken lance, and is in the agonies of death sheltering the French shield and *fleur de lis* with its paws. The figure is cut on the smooth face of a high perpendicular rock, with a pool of clear water at its base, and surrounded by trees. The collossal proportions of the affair may be judged of by the fact that the lion measures thirty feet in length.

From Lucerne to Vitznau is a pleasant steamboat ride of about an hour, and here the cars are in waiting for the ascent of the Rigi. Lake Lucerne is 1,434 feet above the level of the ocean, and the highest peak of the Rigi is 4,472 feet above the lake. The north side of the mountain is precipitous, the east and west sides partially so; but on the south are broad terraces and gentle slopes, covered at this season by green pastures,—which I am informed sustain over 4,000 head of cattle. The term Rigi is usually applied to a single peak on the north side, which rises abruptly from the Lake of Lucerne. It commands a view of 300 miles in circumference. From its nearness to Lucerne, and the fine view from its summit—probably the finest in Switzerland—it has for more than a century been much sought after by tourists. The project of a railroad to the top of the Rigi, to supersede the slow ascent by horses and sedans, was first proposed in 1868, and in 1871 the road was completed from Vitznau to the top of the mountain. The road consists of the usual rails, and of about the usual width. The rails are bolted to the ties in the most secure manner. Each tie is built in a quarry-stone foundation, and at each end of the tie runs an iron bar, to which the ties are bolted. In the middle of the track is the "cogged rail," consisting of two very heavy bars of iron, between which are inserted the cogs on which the cogged driving wheel of the engine acts. The cogs are large, and of wrought iron, and the ends of each cog are riveted through the longitudinal rails. The utmost care seems to have been used in the construction of the road, and each train is preceded by signal-men, to see that no stones or other obstructions have lodged in the cogs of the centre rail. Each locomotive drives but one car, holding about fifty persons. The car, both in ascending and descending, is above the locomotive, and is not fastened to it in any way. A very perfect system of brakes is depended on to stop and hold the car on the track, in case of accident to the engine. I examined with much interest the mechanical arrangements, and in view of the importance of the center cogged wheel, resolved never again to speak disrespectfully of the "fifth wheel of a coach," or use it as a synonym for uselesness or surplusage.

The ascent on the principal grades is from one foot in five, to one in four. The first long grade by which the ascent commences, is from almost the water's edge, one of the steepest, and tries the timid ones severely. It is easy to say "one foot in four;" but just test it by taking a rod four feet long, and elevating one end of it twelve inches from the level; look up it and see how soon you strike the top of a house or church steeple. Continue the range to—if in Michigan, an imaginary point, half a mile distant, and suppose yourself, if you can, looking down from that elevated plane to the level from which you started. You may then get some idea of the ascent of the Rigi. I observed no levity among the passengers on the Rigi railroad; indeed, if the countenance may be relied on as a true index of the inner workings of the mind, I should say that many good resolutions were formed during the first quarter of a mile. On reaching the summit we have the full view of a scene of which we had caught occasional glimpses while ascending. On one side are the mountains of the Oberland, extending in a continuous chain for 120 miles, and covering almost half the horizon. The Rigi, though projected in the foreground, forms a part of this wonderful mass of mountains, so that on one side it is *all* mountains, and more than 200 peaks are in sight. The magnificent Bernese Alps, with their wild and irregular shapes, and eternal snows and glaciers, form the background. On the other side is the most beautiful panorama my eyes ever rested on. For more than fifty miles in distance, and extending over more than half the horizon, is an undulating plain, dotted with cities, villages, lakes, rivers, hills and fertile plains. At the base of this mountain, and so near that it seems as if one could drop a pebble in their waters, are Lakes Lucerne and Zug, with their cities. Nearly a dozen other lakes sparkle in the morning sun, and numerous small rivers, like silver threads, streak the carpet of emerald green which forms a background for this scene of beauty.

I descended the Rigi regretfully, not expecting to find again on earth a place affording such visions of the beautiful and sublime. A distinguished American has spoken of it as "the spot on earth which seems to me nearest heaven!" I regret much my inability to give my readers even a faint idea of the charms of this mountain, and of Lake Lucerne and its scenery :

> "Such beauty, varying in the light
> Of living nature, cannot be portrayed
> By words, nor by the pencils silent skill,
> But is the property of those alone
> Who have beheld it, noted it with care
> And in their minds recorded it with love."

. Lake Lucerne was formerly known as the Lake of the Four Cantons, and on its borders have occurred most of the great struggles for freedom in Switzerland. William Tell was born here, and his chapel, to which pilgrimages have been made by all Switzerland for centuries, is on the east shore of the lake. It may do in America to question the apple story, but not in Switzerland. At Zurich they show you the cross-bow with which it was done; and at Altorf the 150 paces are measured off, statues indicating where stood father and son; the apple, I believe, is not exhibited. Half a century ago, some irreverent sceptics at Berne ventured to publish a book, treating as mythical the shooting of the apple. This was more than the people could bear. The authorities were aroused by the startling heresy. All copies of the book were collected, and publicly burned, according to law; and since that time doubters have been careful not to rush into print—in Switzerland.

I shall leave Switzerland with enlarged ideas of the country, and an increased respect for its people. Some of the cantons are largely Catholic, and others largely Protestant. In Lucerne but one in fourteen are Protestants; in Valais, one in 100; in Ticino, but one in 300. In Berne but one in seven are Catholic; in Zurich, one in eight; and in Zug, but one in seventeen. In some of the twenty-two cantons, they are of about equal numbers. There seems to be no jealousy or lack of unity among the Swiss, on account of religious differences, as in some other countries. Where else can you find such a "happy family" arrangement as at Interlaken, where Roman Catholics, Church of England, French Protestants, and the Church of Scotland, all worship in one old Catholic church?

I had an impression, how formed I do not know, that Alp meant rock, or mountain. Here it is used to designate the common pasture, where every inhabitant is entitled to the pasturage of one cow. The average price of a cow is about $100, a large sum in Switzerland; and it is said there are in the country more than 1,000,000 cows. They are of good size, and usually of a dark or gray color. The average milk of one cow is estimated at thirty five pounds per day, and of cheese 225 pounds per year. It is said the best cheese is made from pastures over 3,000 feet above the level of the sea.

## CHAPTER XI.
### GERMANY—BELGIUM.

Lucerne to Strasburg—Strasburg—The Cathedral—The Famous Clock—A Legend—St. Thomas' Church—Streets and Fortifications—Mayence—The Cathedral—Market and Streets--The Rhine—Cities, Villages, Castles, and Scenery—Cologne—The Cathedral—Shrine of the Three Kings—St. Ursula —Bones and Relics--Brussels—Hotel de Ville—Statues and Streets—Waterloo--Antwerp—The Cathedral--Rubens' Famous Picture—Antwerp to London.

The railroad from Lucerne to Strasburg lies, for nearly all the way, through a fertile plain. We pass Lake Sempach, where five centuries ago Winkelreid
"Made way for liberty, and died."
Zoffinger, Olten and Liestal are passed and we reach Bale, near the French and German lines, a beautiful city of 60,-000 inhabitants, and capital of the Canton of the same name. The Rhine is here a very rapid stream, and about a thousand feet wide. The old town has an ancient appearance, but the newer portions of the city are very fine, and more public improvements were in progress, and more buildings in process of erection than in any place I have seen in Europe. We pass Swiss houses, with immense roofs and numerous dormer windows, the sides covered with very small shingles—say two by four inches—and looking very much like fish scales. In the fields are two-wheeled plows to which horses or cows are attached, women driving the animals and sometimes holding the plow. Indeed, women seem to be doing the greater part of the farm work, of all kinds. On the left are the Vosges mountains, on the right the hills of the Black Forest; and as it begins to grow dark, we pass the fortress of Kehl and enter the city of Strasburg, capital of the German province of Alsace and containing a

population of about 100,000. For 200 years Alsace was a French province but wrested from that power by Germany in 1870-1. It was in the former year that Strasburg sustained for six weeks, its memorable siege, evidences of which are yet to be found in almost every direction. The people do not even yet take kindly to their German Rulers, but Strasburg has been strongly fortified, contains a whole army corps, and will be held as long as Germany is able to hold it.

I took an early stroll through the streets, and found them narrow and very crooked. In fact it is quite as easy to get lost in Strasburg as in Boston. The only landmark is the tall roof and spire of the cathedral, but in trying to reach it I found the streets which seemed to lead to it led me in a different direction. The streets, which are kept quite clean, were being swept by women. On the river are anchored a large number of washing establishments. I am told that all the dirty clothes in the city are taken to the river to be washed, and from the amount of it being done I can easily believe it. The floating wash-houses are open at the sides, each containing about thirty women who at this early hour are hard at work in view of the passer-by.

The principal attraction of Strasburg is its great cathedral. It is one of those wonderful monuments of religious art beqeathed to us by the middle ages, and is erected on a spot which has been from the remotest times devoted to worship. Here have Pagan rites and orgies been held and sacrifices, even of human victims. The first Christian Church, was erected by Clovis about the year 570. This church was destroyed by lightning in 1007, and the present building commenced in 1015, the interior being finished in 1275. The spire was not completed till 1549. The ablest masters in the art of building, superintended its construction for about four centuries. The interior is 362 feet in length, 135 feet wide, and 99 feet high. Its spire is 465 feet, or the height of the great pyramid. Its facade contains a rose window of the finest stained glass thirty-two feet in diameter, and three entrances. These three portals are considered at least equal to anything of the kind in existence, and are covered, as is almost the entire front, with statues and groups illustrating Scripture scenes. In the niches are some equestrian statues dating from 1219. I tried to take in its vast dimensions from the outside, but found no point quite satisfactory, and wished myself Emperor of Germany long enough to order the demolition of two rows of houses, which would afford a fair front view. The interior is grand beyond description. Western readers will more readily comprehend its great size when given familiarly as eight by twenty-two rods! The supporting columns are of immense size but fine proportions. As I entered, the full organ was being played and soon the voices of a choir directed me to the place where service was held. I passed around among the pillars and side chapels to catch the music as it echoed through the lofty building, producing sometimes fine and even startling effects. The organ built by Silberman was struck by a shell during the seige and greatly injured, but is said to be quite as good as new since having been repaired. The pulpit, erected in 1486, is a fine specimen of wood carving, adorned by over fifty little statues representing Scripture characters and scenes. During the bombardment the building was very much injured, but the conquerors have made haste to repair all damages. The view from the top of the cathedral is very fine and takes in the Jura mountains, Baden, the Black Forest, and the Rhine.

    Almost every person has heard of the great Strasburg clock, and every day at noon a crowd collects to see it strike the hour of twelve. Several priests are in attendance to preserve order and give any desired information. The clock is on the ground floor, and seems to be about thirty feet high. The case was made in 1574 for an older clock; the machinery of this was completed in 1842. The first of these famous clocks was made in 1354, and all have been master-pieces of mechanical ingenuity. The present clock shows true and siderial time, the motions and relations of the planets, indicates by a perpetual calendar all movable feasts and holidays, eclipses of the sun and moon for all time, precession of the equinoxes, signs of the zodiac, and other things too complicated for the ordinary mind to take in. Immediately over the dial is a skeleton figure of Death which strikes the hours. Around him are figures representing Childhood, Youth, Manhood, and Old Age. Childhood strikes the first quarter, Youth the second, Manhood the third, and Old Age the last. The first stroke of each quarter is struck by one of two Genii seated above the calendar, the four ages striking the second. While Death strikes the hours, the second of these Genii turns over an hour glass which he holds in his hand. At the hour of noon two doors open, an image of the Savior steps out, the twelve apostles pass bowing before him, while with uplifted hands he blesses each one. A rooster flaps his wings and crows three times—the best mechanical crowing I ever heard.

Being in Germany, the clock has a legend, which is of course received as gospel, by the masses, and, as told by the guide, is about as follows: The maker of the original clock had a beautiful daughter, whose hand was sought by one of the magistrates of the town. Her heart, however, had been given to an apprentice of her father, and the old man had consented that their union should take place, as soon as the clock was finished. Its completion excited general curiosity, and it was bought by the city, to be placed in the great

THE GREAT CLOCK AT STRASSBURG.

cathedral. The authorities of Bale hearing of its wonderful mechanism, ordered one just like it, for that city. The magistrates of Strasburg endeavored to extort from the maker a promise that he would not make another clock like it, which the old man refused to give. The magistrate who had been refused by the old man's daughter, persuaded the others to order that his eyes should be put out, so as to prevent him from making any more clocks. Sentence was pronounced accordingly. The clockmaker requested that it might be carried out in the presence of his much loved clock, which he said required a few finishing touches for its completion. His request was granted, and in the presence of the magistrates and townspeople, who had gathered to see sentence executed, the old man busied himself for a few moments with the machinery. His eyes were put out, and at that moment a noise was heard—the weights fell to the ground ; the old man had ruined his clock, which could not be repaired, and remained useless for two centuries. It is needless to inform novel readers that the cruel magistrate was deposed, the young couple married, etc.

St. Thomas' Church contains a monument to Marshal Saxe, by a celebrated sculptor who is said to have worked on it for over twenty years. The marshal is represented as descending into a tomb, opened for him by death, while a female figure, representing France, is endeavoring to detain him. On the left is a lion, eagle and leopard, with the broken flags of England, Austria and Holland, intended to represent the marshal's victories over those countries, in the Flemish wars. There are many other monuments, some of them quite fine. In a side chapel are two mummies, a duke of Nassau and his daughter, who died over 200 years ago. The clothing is in good preservation. The remains of the duke may be looked at, but the daughter should be buried at once.

One of the singular exports of Strasburg, is called *pate de fois gras*, or, vulgarly, goose liver pie. This luxury is obtained by abusing the poor goose, in some way, so as to give it the liver complaint. The enlarged liver is encouraged by experts till it gets to weigh several pounds, and when cooked, is considered by epicures a delicious and toothsome delicacy, for which they are willing to pay a large price. During the siege, while the people of Strasburg were suffering by famine, the gourmands of Europe were suffering for their pie ; the geese, however, while any of them remained, were permitted to enjoy good health.

I examined the fortifications carefully, and was surprised to find how much labor can be expended in protecting one city. The inner line of earthworks is continuous, the city being entered by gates of great strength. In these earthworks are galleries, vaults, and bombproofs, on a most extensive scale. Three or four miles outside is a line of forts, as strong as military science can suggest, and between these and the city there is room for a large army to encamp. About 20,000 troops were in Strasburg yesterday, but they had mostly left for a grand review, some ten miles distant. I saw several regiments as they marched out of the city. The men were of good size, and marched finely. The bands were excellent. The martial music was new to me, consisting only of drums and trumpets, played alternately, and was of a character to almost lift a man off his feet. I have seldom heard anything more inspiring. In the streets one becomes interested in the curious and ancient looking houses and public buildings. *Brand Strasse* is pointed out as the place where, in 1349, 2,000 Jews were burned, to arrest the ravages of a plague. I was surprised at the great number of storks to be seen, and at their building their nests, unmolested, on the chimney tops ; but learned that they are held in great esteem by the people, who regard their selection of a chimney top as bringing good luck to the dwellers in the house. In Guttenberg square, one of the finest in the city, is a statue of Guttenberg, who made his first experiment in the art of printing in this place. Also a fine statue of Marshal Kleber, in a square of the same name.

From Strasburg to Mayence the railroad passes through the valley of the Rhine, which is an extended plain and under fine cultivation. We catch frequent views of the river as we approach the ancient city of Mayence, containing a population of about 50,000, It is on the left bank of the Rhine, nearly opposite its junction with the Main. A Roman fortress, part of which still exists, was built on the site of the present citadel of Mayence fourteen years before the Christian era. After the introduction of Christianity Mayence became the residence of the Archbishops of Germany. Later the archbishops became electors and Premier Princes of the German empire, presiding at diets, and at the election of emperors. Mayence was the birthplace and residence of Guttenberg, the inventor of moveable types, and the site of his first printing office 1443-50 is shown. The city is strongly fortified and has been independent, French, Prussian, or German, as the chances of war determined. Its principal street which is on the river's bank contains some fair residences and quite a number of good looking hotels. The other streets are narrow and crooked, terminating unexpectedly in open spaces or squares, and making it difficult to find the way in any direction. There are many fountains and monuments, among them a remarkably fine bronze statue of Guttenberg, by Thorwaldsen, and one of Schiller. In a stroll through the city at night I lost my way in a manner I did not expect In so small a place, but on going over the ground again in the morning to see how it was done I was not at all surprised at it. I visited the market near the cathedral at an early hour and found about as primitive arrangements as one could desire. Small carts drawn by the family cow were bringing in farm products, and the most German looking old ladies I ever saw, in stiffly starched and very clean two story caps were arranging their little stalls for the business of the day. Those whose supplies had not yet arrived were redeeming the time by knitting, gossiping the mean while with each other. It was about such a picture of German life as I have occasionally seen in engravings, and wondered if anything so primitive were possible in this century.

The cathedral forms one side of the market ground, is of red sandstone, and looks exceedingly old. The style is called pure Romanesque, and is unlike most German churches. It was founded in 988; the oldest part of the present building dates from 1136, with additions made in 1239-91. I was greatly surprised to find in it more and finer monuments than in any continental church I have yet seen, principally of archbishops and electors. The archbishops of Mayence had the right of placing the crown on the heads of the German emperors, and their monuments represent some of them in this act. One who died in 1320 is surrounded by the emperor of Germany, king of Bavaria, and king of Bohemia. The archbishop is life-size, the emperor and kings are only about half life-size, giving them the appearance of boys, and presenting a somewhat ludicrous appearance. Another queer monument is that of General Lamberg who died in 1689. The general is somewhat corpulent, wears a very large wig and is represented as being squeezed down into his bier by death. Two ancient chalices of the tenth century, and a font of the fourteenth century in which Guttenberg was baptized, are shown. An interesting relic is the brazen doors on the north side of the cathedral, of the tenth century. In 1125 the emperor of

Germany imprisoned the archbishop of Mayence. The citizens seized the emperor and held him as hostage till the archbishop was released. On these doors the grateful archbishop caused to be engraved an edict granting special privileges to the town and its citizens.

I took the steamer for Cologne, with high anticipations of a day's pleasure on the far famed Rhine. The river has an eventful history as a great national highway, as the scene of important historical events, and the theater of many deadly conflicts. Its entire length is 870 miles and from Bale to its mouth, 570 miles, it is navigable. Its fine scenery, of which I have heard from childhood, is found between Mayence and Cologne, a distance of 118 miles. Our boat, a sidewheeler, and very much like an American river steamer, carried over two hundred passengers. I had the good fortune to meet with a German gentleman thoroughly familiar with the river, who spoke fair English and kindly pointed out to me objects of interest on the way.

We soon pass some celebrated vineyards, Winkel, where Charlemagne kept his wine cellar, Eltville, Rauenthal, Erbach and Oestrich. We also pass the chateau and vineyard of Johannisberg the property of Prince Metternich. Wine drinkers the world over, who have smacked their lips over the "genuine Johannisberg," may be interested to know that this celebrated vineyard contains nearly seventy acres, and produces forty butts of wine per year, nearly enough to supply Prince Metternich and his numerous friends. A number of handsome villages are passed and we reach Bingen, "fair Bingen on the Rhine." It is a village of 7,000 inhabitants, beautifully situated at the mouth of the river Nahe. The scenery now becomes interesting and we soon reach the "Mouse Tower," built on a rock in the river, where according to a popular legend the rats took vengeance on the wicked Bishop Hatto; they

> " Whetted their teeth against the stones,
> And then they picked the bishops bones."

As we pass the tower an English lady read aloud Southey's beautiful poem, to many interested listeners. We now pass through the Rheingau a famous wine district. The sides of the hills and rocks are covered with vines. Every available foot of ground on the river's bank is devoted to vine culture; even rocky steeps, where I can see no way of approach except by a step ladder or balloon, are cultivated and said to produce the choicest wines.

We pass the precipitous rock, two hundred and fifty feet above the river, where

> " Cliff-anchored Rheinstein lifts its walls."

The castle has been completely restored, and gives one a good idea of how these old strongholds used to look. The German flag floats from its highest turret, and an old fashioned crane supporting a basket swings from one of the towers.

Ruined castles become monotonous. We pass Falkenburg, Sooneck, Heinsburg, Nollingen, Sanerberg, Furstenberg, Stahleck, Pfalz, Gutenfels, Schonberg and reach the celebrated Lurlie Rock, perpendicular and bare, rising 400 feet above the Rhine. On this famed rock in olden time sat the beautiful siren, who, by her fine singing, lured the boatmen to their destruction in the whirlpool at her feet, till at last overcome by love she herself plunged into the treacherous waters. Poets and painters have made the most of this legend. But, alas! for romance—a flagstaff bearing the prosaic German flag occupies the siren's seat, and from a tunnel in the fabled rock an express train was emerging with a whistle that would have astonished the beautiful sorceress. Between Mayence and the Lurlie we have passed the villages of Eltville, Schlangenbad, Oestrich, Geisenhaim, Rudesheim, Lorchhausen, Baeharach, Caub and Oberwesel, all ancient looking and picturesque. We

RHEINSTEIN, ON THE RHINE.

## STOLZENFELS.

soon pass St. Goar, near which is the ruins of the magnificent castle of Rheinfels, We also pass the castles of Katz, Reichenberg, Thurnberg, Sterenberg, Liebenstein, Waldenburg, and Lahneck. Three miles above Coblentz:

> "O'er the river's level current Stolzenfels leans wondrous fair,
> Like a sunset cloud in summer, pillowed on dissolving air,
> With its burnished towers and balcons, and its bannered
>   State and pride,
> With fantastic battlements, sun-illumined, glorified."

The beautiful castle of Stolzenfels, of which the frontispiece is an illustration, is on a rocky eminence four hundred feet above the Rhine. After being a ruin for centuries, it was restored by the king of Prussia, and is now used occasionally as a royal residence. It would be difficult to find a more charming situation or finer scenery.

Coblentz, at the mouth of the Moselle, is a handsome town of 25,000 inhabitants, and is strongly fortified. On the opposite bank of the river is the fortress of Ehrenbreitstein, the "Gibraltar of the Rhine," on a rock almost perpendicular and 400 feet high. Its precipitous sides are covered with batteries and towers. It will afford shelter to 100,000 troops or can be fully manned by 5,000. Its magazines are calculated to store food and supplies for 5,000 men for fifteen years. It is used also as a German arsenal for war material of all kinds. It was once starved out by the French, who on abandoning it blew up its principal fortifications, and at the end of the war paid the Prussians $3,000,000 toward its restoration. Below Coblentz the river widens, the shores become level, ruined castles are not so common and thriving villages and towns are more frequent. We reach Drachenfels, one of the seven mountains, where, eight hundred and fifty feet above the river, on its vine-clad height,

> "The castled crag of Drachenfels
> Frowns o'er the wild and winding Rhine;
> Whose breast of waters broadly swells,
> Between the banks which bear the vine."

Passing the university city of Bonn, which from the river seems quite attractive, we reach Cologne, where my Rhine journey ends.

While I must confess its natural scenery did not quite meet my expectations, the history and associations of the famed Rhine interested me very much. Born amid the glaciers of the Alps, fed by mountain torrents, and draining a thousand valleys, it has, after lending the charm of its presence to the most wild and picturesque scenery, become a sluggish stream, winding its useful way from Cologne to the flat and unromantic coast of Holland. Probably no other stream in the world is so interwoven with the traditions, the history, the patriotism, the aspirations, the affections of a nation as the "German Rhine." Its real history bids fair to be lost in its countless legends. The titled robbers who for centuries levied blackmail on its commerce, and built the picturesque strongholds, the ruins of which line its banks, to enforce their demands, are rather remembered as the heroes of some love adventure or fairy tale, than as the piratical freebooters they really were.

I was much surprised at the lack of interest manifested by my fellow passengers in the river scenery. A passing tug or raft would engage their exclusive attention while passing places of the greatest interest; and the movement of trains, which run on both banks of the river through numerous tunnels, excited general attention. At noon I felt as if I could have dinner most any day, but never again a view of Rhine scenery; with most of the passengers it was different, and eating and drinking was the absorbing occupation on deck rom Mayence to Cologne. From the number of alpenstocks on board most of the passengers must have visited Switzerland. It is considered quite the thing to provide one's self with this badge of Swiss travel, and all travelers in Switzerland must resist temptation or buy an alpenstock. It is a staff five to six feet long, with a spike at one end and hook at the other. Its possession is supposed in some way to indicate wonderful adventures and hair breadth escapes on mountain and glacier. The names of the mountains ascended are usually branded on the sides, and even on Rigi, which I ascended by a railroad, a dealer insisted on selling me an alpenstock marked "Rigi!"

The city of Cologne is on the left bank of the Rhine, and is strongly fortified. It is connected with its suburb Deutz, on the opposite side of the river, by a bridge of boats 1,400 feet long, and also by a most imposing double iron bridge intended for both railway and carriage traffic. The population is about 130,000. A Roman fortress was built here in the time of Tiberius. Agrippina, the mother of the Emperor Nero, was born here in the camp of her father, Germanicus. During the reign of her son she sent a colony of Roman veterans, and named the place for herself, Colonia Agrippina. The Emperor Constantine built a bridge across the Rhine, the pillars of which can be seen at low water. It afterwards became a principal city of the Franks, whose king, Clovis, was crowned here. The streets are narrow and very crooked; the side walks, where there are any, will not average over two feet in width. The stores look well and make a fine display of their wares. Most persons are familiar with Coleridge's epigram :

"Ye nymphs who reign over sewers and sinks,
The River Rhine, it is well known,
Doth wash your City of Cologne;
But tell me nymphs, what power divine
Shall henceforth wash the River Rhine?"

To my surprise I found the city quite clean, with no smell to disturb the traveler unless foolish enough to employ his nose in a vain endeavor to discover the "original and only genuine Cologne water," of which there are said to be forty makers, more or less, in the city. This popular cosmetic, known in almost all civilized lands, was first made by one Jean Marie Farina. The family name of "Farina" has not been permitted to run out, and "Jean Maries" are numerous. The guides, too, seem possessed with the idea that the traveler's sole object in visiting the city is to purchase cologne water, and their persistence in recommending their favorite and only original Jean Marie becomes annoying.

The great attraction of Cologne is its famed cathedral, considered by many the finest gothic structure in the world. It is of vast dimensions; leangth 512 feet, width at the transepts 282 feet, and ceiling 200 feet high—or roughly, in western measurement, seventeen by thirty-one rods on the ground, and twelve rods to the ceiling! Its towers are 512 feet high, the farthest point from mother earth, at present reached by any work of human hands. It was commenced in 1248, and hardly yet completed. A building so vast can only be appreciated by an examination of its parts in detail. Take for instance the porches—that at the south end was built by the present emperor of Germany, at a cost of over half a million dollars! The west front is still more imposing; it has two towers and three porches, the great central porch being ninety feet high and thirty feet wide. To describe the wealth of carving and statuary that ornament this grand entrance, the work of centuries, would require volumes—and yet it is only one of the entrance ways! To give the vast building its finishing touches, has, it is said, cost during the past forty years five million dollars. I was not, as at Strasburg, impressed with the exceeding beauty and gracefulness of the structure, but rather overpowered by its immensity. From a stairway inside I reached the level of the ceiling; looking down, the worshipers seemed like pigmies. The windows correspond in size with the building, and are of finely stained glass. The walls are decorated with glass paintings and frescoes. Round the choir stand fourteen colossal statues of Christ, the Virgin, and twelve apostles, sculptured in the fourteenth century.

But it is not the great wealth of decoration in the interior that impresses one; it is the massive columns and arches supporting the lofty ceiling, which seems but a lower sky. There is a legend about the plan of the cathedral: The architect was walking by the bank of the river in despair of finding any design of sufficient grandeur, and sketching in the sand such designs as occurred to him, when his Satanic majesty appeared and informed him that he could suggest something much finer, and pulled from his pocket the plan of Cologne Cathedral. Surprised at the apparition, and knowing well that his soul would be the price demanded for the design, the architect cunningly inquired as to all the details, treasuring them up in his memory. Having done this, he coolly informed the devil that it did not suit him and he would not take it. The evil one saw that he had been outwitted, and exclaimed in a rage, "You may build it according to my plan, but you will never finish it." It would almost seem as if the devil might be reckoned among the prophets, as after six centuries it is not yet quite completed.

A small chapel back of the high altar is known as the shrine of the three kings. A large silver case is said to contain the bones of the wise men who came from the east to find the infant Savior. Their skulls are shown crowned with gold and precious stones, their names "Caspar," "Melchior," and "Balthazar," being worked in with rubies. These remains are said to have been brought to Constantinople by the Empress Helena, and afterwards were taken to the City of Milan. When the Emperor Barbarosa captured Milan he caused the precious relics to be removed to Cologne. The remains of St. Englebert are preserved in a shrine made of silver, and weighing 149 pounds. There are shrines of less value, Episcopal crooks 800 to 1,000 years old, the sword of justice borne by the electors of Cologne at the coronation of the emperors, ancient vestments, vessels, monstrances, etc., also some very fine carved work in ivory. The value of the gold, silver and precious stones in this chapel, is estimated at nearly two million dollars.

I made an early morning visit to the Church of St. Ursula, and found a large congregation in attendance. A priest was reading in German, the people heartily responding in the same language. It seemed to me very much like the method of the English Church. I heard here, for the first time, congregational singing in a Roman Catholic Church, and it was very fine. The solemn music of the Mass sounded peculiarly mournful and tender, as its minor strains, taken up by hundreds of male and female voices in unison, echoed through the lofty arches. Seeing an old lady with white, starched cap, sitting by one of the doors, I tried to find where the interesting relics, for which this church is famous, might be found, by pointing around the walls, and repeating the words "bones," and "virgins," several times. She seemed to understand me, and rising, deliberately walked up to the altar, and held conversation with one of the priests, who immediately walked down the long aisle towards where I was standing. I was startled and annoyed at the audacity of the woman, and felt very much like making a hasty retreat. I was, however, at once reassured, by the priest saying to me in a pleasant tone, and in good English: "The service will be over in about ten minutes, when I will show you the relics."

There is a legend, that, some 1,400 years ago, St. Ursula went up the Rhine on a pilgrimage to Rome, accompanied by 11,000 virgins. Returning, they were all murdered by the Huns, for refusing to break their vows of chastity. Their bones were gathered together, brought to Cologne, and buried in a common grave, over which the present Church of St. Ursula was built, more than 850 years ago. The bones were afterwards exhumed, and brought inside the building. Nearly 2,000 skulls, with bones innumerable, are exhibited in receptacles all round the church. Many of the skulls are adorned below the forehead by beautiful embroidery and needle-work, made by pious hands. But the chief interest centers in the room known as the treasury, into which, as soon as the service was over, I was conducted by the priest. It is about thirty feet square, and contains over 700 skulls. The walls, which are high, are entirely covered with bones, ingeniously and symmetrically arranged. Imagine wreaths and bouquets of finger bones, pious inscriptions worked out in small bones, with leg bones for the capitals, crosses and symbolical designs in which all the bones are utilized, etc., etc. A silver box, holding about a half peck of teeth, beautiful and white, as virgin's teeth should be, was shown me. I was somewhat amused to observe the familiar, yet tender care with which the priest touched or handled the bones and skulls, as if he had known them all in their lifetime, and as if a skull or leg bone was the most natural and pleasant memento in the world. In special glass cases may be seen the skulls of St. Ursula, her lover, Conan, and some of the principal virgins, the bones of St. Ursula's arms, and of one of her feet, a finger bone of St. Stephen, the first martyr, and a part of the chain with which St. Peter was bound at Rome. I had also the privilege of examining one of the "water pots" used by our Savior in performing his first miracle at Cana of Galilee. One handle is gone, the edges are worn by the pouring out of water, indeed, in some places it is worn so thin as to be nearly transparent. It holds about four gallons, and is evidently very old. I was also shown three thorns from the crown worn by our Savior on the cross, a piece of the true cross, and other relics.

Cologne has many other places of interest, among them at least a dozen fine churches. Some of these I visited. At St. Peter's Church I saw Rubens' famous picture of the crucifixion of St. Peter. The apostle is represented as crucified head downward, and I never looked at anything so horribly suggestive of human agony. It may be a very fine painting, but the briefest examination was enough for me. The house in which Mary of Medicis died and in which Rubens was born, was pointed out, also an old Roman tower, in excellent preservation. The public buildings are substantial structures, and look well. They are to-day decorated with many flags, this being, I am told, the tenth anniversary of the surrender at Sedan. I have seen dogs harnessed in carts, but no where so extensively as in Cologne. Most of the dogs are harnessed *under* the cart, as assistants, the owners accepting the position between the shafts. The dogs are very large, and pull with all their might. They are said to be very vicious, and are kept muzzled when on duty. The ancient style of the buildings, and the strange customs one sees, make walking through an old city like this very interesting.

Leaving Cologne for Brussels, the railroad passes at first through a level country, the absence of fences giving it the appearance of a western prairie. It is thickly settled, and well cultivated. The first city of importance is Aix-la-Chapelle, called by the Germans, Aachen. It has a population of 80,000, and is known as the city of Charlemagne, who was born, and who died here. Over thirty German emperors were crowned in this city, and several important treaties have been negotiated here. Passing the German line, we enter Belgium near the small town of Herbesthal, and soon reach the city of Verviers, a place of 40,000 inhabitants. Here I expected to pass a customs examination, but was disappointed. I have now passed, satchel in hand, into Switzerland, Germany, and Belgium, without a question in regard to my baggage. It is only in England and the United States that I am suspected of being a smuggler. At Verviers we change cars, and find the Belgian much inferior to the German cars of the same class. Leaving Verviers, the country becomes more rolling, and we enter a mining region, frequently passing the tall chimneys of manufacturing establishments. We reach Liege, a city of 100,000 inhabitants, largely engaged in iron manufacture, and smoky enough to rival Pittsburg. The next large town we pass is the old walled city of Louvain—population 30,000—formerly famous for its great university, consisting of over forty colleges, with nearly 7,000 students. There are now less than 600 students, and the city is at present principally famous for its beer, of which more than 200,000 casks are exported annually. The Belgian farm-houses look uncared for and untidy; Belgian women and children—ditto.

The city of Brussels, the capital of Belgium, is on the river Senne, fifty miles from the sea, and contains a population of about 300,000. The newer part of the city has some wide and fine streets. The ancient fortifications have been removed, and in their stead are beautiful boulevards and promenades, planted with linden trees. The public buildings are very fine. Among the finest are the Palace of Justice, Mint, Museum, and Parliament Houses. The new Bourse is a beautiful building. Gigantic columns, representing a rose-colored marble, support its fine dome, and smaller columns, of exquisite workmanship, support the outer walls. The pavement is mosaic, and the interior decorations are exceedingly fine. Desiring to see how such things are done in Belgium, I deliberately walked in and took my place among the financiers of Brussels. I expect my impudence protected me, as no one objected to my presence. I found the same wild excitement that I have witnessed at the Board of Trade in Chicago, and the Stock Exchange in New York. The public park, or Palace Garden, is very finely laid out, and has some beautiful fountains and statues. It is surrounded by four streets; at one end is the Palace of the Nation, or Parliament House, and at the other the Royal Palace. The latter is a plain building, but very large. A sudden shower caused me, in common with many others, to seek shelter under its balcony, which extends over the sidewalk. A soldier in a sentry-box near by, seemed to regard it with indifference. I doubt if it would have been permitted in any other European capital.

But the most interesting building in Brussels, is the Hotel de Ville, situated in the older part of the city. It fronts on the Grande Place, and is seen to good advantage. The facade, completed in 1450, is a beautiful specimen of Gothic ornamentation. The tower is of Gothic openwork, is of stone, and 370 feet high. At the top of the spire is a gilt figure of the archangel Michael, sixteen feet in height, which serves as a vane. In the upper story is a large hall, finely decorated, with a carved oak ceiling. I had read more than once that it was in this hall that the Duchess of Richmond's ball was given, on the eve of the battle of Waterloo, and from which the allied officers were summoned to the field. My favorite "speaking piece," at school, was Byron's poem on this subject, and I commenced to repeat it from memory to a gentleman who was with me :

"There was a sound of revelry by night,
And Belgium's capital had gathered there

> Her beauty and her chivalry, and bright
> The lamps shone o'er fair women and brave men;
> A thousand hearts beat happily; and when
> Music arose with its voluptuous swell,
> Soft eyes look'd love to eyes that spake again,
> And all went merry as a marriage-bell;
> But hush! hark! a deep sound strikes like a rising knell!
> Did you not hear it?---No; 'twas but the wind,
> Or the car rattling o'er the stony street;
> On with the dance! let joy be unconfined;
> No sleep till morn, when youth and pleasure meet
> To chase the glowing hours with flying feet—"

A voice, unmistakably Yankee, interrupted me at this point: "This haint the place; the ball was held in a house in the Rue Royale." I regarded this as a sufficient introduction, and entered at once into conversation with the skeptic who had so rudely broken the scene my fancy had painted, and became convinced that he was right; and that, in order to see the place in which the ball was held, I must visit the Rue Royale—which I did.

There are many fine statues of distinguished Belgians in the public squares and streets, in which, as an American, I felt but little interest. The Martyrs' Monument, in the Place des Martyres, is quite elaborate, and is in honor of the Belgians who fell in the battles with the Dutch, September 23–4, 1830. It contains the names of 448 men, who fell at that time. In front of the church of St. Jacques, is a fine equestrian statue of Godfrey of Bouillon, who is said in 1097 to have addressed the people of Brussels on this spot, exhorting them to join him in the crusade. The most famous statue is near the Hotel de Ville, and is known as the Manikin. It forms part of the Manikin Fountain, is about three feet high, and so perfectly natural as to excite the attention of passers-by. Indeed, the great charm of the fountain, is its *naturalness*. The Manikin is held in great veneration by all classes, is provided at the public expense with a valet, and has eight complete suits of clothing, some of them royal gifts, in which it is attired on fete days and special occasions.

Most of the streets in the newer part of the city are quite wide, and the display of wares in the windows is very fine. The finest arcade I have seen, is the Galerie St. Hubert. It is eighty feet wide, fifty feet high, and over forty rods long, is brilliantly lighted, and contains some of the finest retail stores in Brussels. The prices of the articles exhibited in the windows are usually affixed in francs and centimes, and all kinds of goods seem to be very cheap. I passed several stores claiming to sell "American goods," of which small clocks, and occasionally the cheaper grades of American watches, were the principal items. I was much amused at seeing a lot of brass "knuckles," sometimes carried by our roughs and plug-uglies, exhibited for sale—a large card informing me that they are "defenses Americaines!"

In front of the cafes are chairs and small tables where wine and beer are drank as in Paris. Getting hungry, I entered a fine looking establishment in the old town which resembled very much a first class fancy bakery. An intelligent looking middle-aged lady, and two young ladies who appeared to be her daughters, sat behind the counters. I addressed them in English, but to no purpose. They replied in language neither French nor German, and which I have since learned was Flemish, which it appears is largely spoken in the old town. I was bound to have a supper, and looking in one of the show cases saw a small package marked "chocolat." I pointed to it and to some cups and saucers on one of the counters. The ladies took the hint and I sat down while they prepared for me a pitcher of delicious chocolate, which was set on a small table with a cup and saucer. I took a plate, went behind the counters and helped myself to such buns, cakes, tarts, etc., as I thought sufficient for a hearty meal, the ladies enjoying immensely my efforts at selection, and occasionally signifying by signs that something that I had omitted was especially good.  I had an excellent supper, the ladies chatting and laughing with each other at the oddness of the occasion, and I expect admiring my wonderful appetite.  The meal ended, I took from my pocket a handful of silver change and held it out, from which one of the ladies carefully selected a franc and a half, about twenty-nine cents, and I laughingly bowed myself out.  It may be inconvenient sometimes not to understand the language, and yet it is sometimes very amusing, and so far on the continent nobody seems disposed to cheat me.  I am told that in Spain or Italy it would not be advisable to hold out a handful of silver, and I certainly could not honestly recommend a foreigner to make the experiment in the United States.

Being limited as to time, I was compelled to choose between visiting the museums and picture galleries of Brussels, or the field of Waterloo.  Having seen so many miles of paintings and acres of museums in the past few weeks, I decided to take in the battlefield, and leaving Brussels by an early train I soon arrived at Braine Laleud, about twelve miles distant, and near to the field of Waterloo.  I had procured in Brussels the official accounts of the battle, and a large map showing the position and movements of the troops at various stages of the engagement.  At Braine Laleud I succeeded in securing a guide who had been recommended to me as intelligent and well informed.  He proved to be a Belgian, speaking good English, whose business it has been, for nearly forty years, to show visitors over the field— and as good as recommended.  His sympathies were with Napoleon and he endeavored in every way possible to excuse the result of the battle.

About the center of the allied line, and on the spot where

the Prince of Orange fell, the Belgians have erected an immense mound, I should say two hundred feet high. On the top is a huge lion weighing twenty-eight tons, made from captured French cannon. It is known as the "Lion Mound," and from its sides and summit may be obtained a good view of the battlefield and of the surrounding country. The first thing that impressed me was the small space occupied by the contending armies—the allied line a little more than a mile long, the French about a mile and a half, and the lines about a mile apart. In this limited space on the 18th day of June, 1815, 150,000 men engaged in deadly conflict. It is said that military history fails to record an engagement of such magnitude in so small a space. Napoleon had 240 cannon, Wellington 156, and the artillery was posted less than a mile apart when the battle began. Afterwards the principal batteries were advanced to less than half a mile, and in the afternoon the German legion was cut down by cannon not twenty rods distant. Headley says that on this small field "10,000 men an hour were slain for four hours!" It is probable that the killed and wounded numbered about 40,000, but the engagement lasted over seven hours.

The allied position was chosen as covering the road to Brussels, and is on a rising ground or ridge. The French line was on an opposite ridge, nearly parallel, and apparently as strong a position, if assailed, as the allied. Smaller ridges and hollows between would afford shelter for small bodies of troops. The position and movements of the armies can be easily understood. The farm houses of Hougomont, Mont St. Jean, La Haye Saint, Papillote and La Belle Alliance still remain, and taken in connection with the configuration of the ground clearly indicate the position of the contending forces. The allied force engaged was British 25,389, German Legion 6,793, Hanoverian 10,995, Brunswickers

6,303, Nassauers 2,926, Netherlands 17,488; total 69,894.

The French are estimated at 80,000. Of the Allied forces the Hanoverians were mere militia and the Belgian portion of the Netherlanders unreliable, breaking and making for the rear at the first attack. The French were mostly veterans, accustomed to victory on many battlefields. Waterloo is a small village nearly two miles in the rear of the allied position, from which the Duke of Wellington dated his dispatches announcing the victory. By the Prussians it is known as the battle of Belle Alliance, and by the French as the battle of Mont St. Jean.

In the movements of the days preceding the battle, Napoleon would seem to have outgeneraled the allied commanders, striking before their troops were concentrated and forcing Blucher and Wellington to give battle separately. After the battle began I cannot see what strategy had to do with it. It was a murderous hand to hand fight such as the world will never see again. Probably no battle has provoked more discussion and criticism. Who defeated Napoleon—Wellington, Blucher, or Grouchy—will always remain a disputed question. After reading more than a dozen accounts of the battle, and now surveying the ground, I am more than ever disposed to give the credit of the victory to those troops mainly composed of English, Irish and Scotch regiments, who for seven hours bravely maintained their ground against the best soldiers of France, commanded by her greatest general. The men who composed those hollow squares that successfully resisted the impetuous charges of the mail-clad Cuirassiers, and who at 7 o'clock in the evening drove the hitherto invincible Old Guard, headed by Ney, off the field, I think deserve the honors.

I visited the chateau of Hougomont, consisting of a farm house, outbuildings and orchard surrounded by a brick wall. This was the point first attacked by the French and its capture would have given them the victory. The contest here was terrible. It is said 1,500 French fell in the orchard alone in less than half an hour! Several times they forced their way into the yard and were as often driven out with the bayonet. The house, and brick wall surrounding, show the marks of the French bullets so plentifully showered upon them. I have gratified what some may consider a morbid curiosity, by traveling on foot over the field, examining in detail the various localities which recall the scenes of that terrible day. The result is a more intense hatred of the cruel trade of war. When we consider how in time of peace a single murder will stir a community or a nation, while the killing in war of the tens of thousands who fell on this field is considered a matter of course, a sort of national business affair, one begins to realize how debauching of the sensibilities is war. While some of the best minds are devoting themselves to the work of devising and introducing milder methods of punishment and better care for convicted criminals, the inventive genius of the world is still employed in devising more effective methods for human destruction to place under the control of Christian men with which to destroy each other. I am not much given to moralizing, yet I turned my back on the historic field and returned to Brussels with a fervent prayer for the advent of the reign of the Prince of Peace, when "Nation shall not lift up sword against nation, neither shall they learn war any more."

From Brussels to Antwerp is twenty-six and a half miles. About half way we pass Malines or Mechlin a place of 36,000 inhabitants and noted for its fine laces. Antwerp, on the right bank of the Scheldt, contains a population of 125,000, is strongly fortified, and is the chief port of Belgium. Its citadel is on the opposite bank of the river. It was, in the fifteenth and sixteenth centuries, the great center of

European commerce and had a population of over 200,000. It is said that 500 vessels entered its port daily. Even now it is the third commercial city of Europe, ranking next to London and Liverpool. Its docks are of great extent and present a very busy appearance. The first Napoleon spent vast sums of money in their construction, making Antwerp his grand naval arsenal. The last seige of Antwerp was by the French and Belgians, who in 1832 captured it from the Dutch. Since that time the fortifications have been greatly strengthened, and it is now the true *military* capital of Belgium.

The streets in the older portion of the city are very irregular, and the better class of houses have a stately and antique appearance. The public buildings are very fine, especially the Exchange and the marble Hotel de Ville. The people of Antwerp look different from any I have seen. They are as a rule of low stature and awfully homely. A peculiar "Dutchy" look, with flat heads and large round eyes, seems to prevail among both men and women. The cathedral of Antwerp is a magnificent building. It is 250 by 400 feet and its Gothic tower, containing a carillon of ninety bells, is over 400 feet high. A more beautiful tower I have never seen. Charles V. said of it that it should be kept in a glass case, and so fine is its ornamentation that Napoleon I. compared it to Mechlin lace. Dr. Bellows poetically describes it as "the lovely laced work spire, that airiest of all structures ever hung in stone and iron so near the stars." But the cathedral is chiefly celebrated for the treasures of art which it contains. Here are Rubens' Assumption of the Virgin, Elevation of the Cross, Descent from the Cross and The Resurrection. The Descent from the Cross is Rubens' masterpiece and one of the world's most famous pictures, admired by art pilgrims from all lands. After reading page upon page describing in detail its beauties and fine points, I feel incompetent to attempt a description of my own and shall not inflict a borrowed one on my readers. Indeed, the impression was not that of a picture or a work of art to be admired. I forgot the painter. No art terms, no hackneyed phrase of descriptive laudation occurred to me. I was looking at the descent from the cross. In the three Marys, Joseph, Nicodemus and the others, I saw real people, and the fair but bloody corpse of the Man of Sorrows, excited my sympathy as never before by any painted canvas. There is also a fine head of Christ by Leonardo da Vinci, and many other pictures of merit, besides a profusion of the finest wood carvings. Rubens' pictures are covered during the forenoon, when the cathedral is open for service, and are only uncovered from twelve to four o'clock, when an admission fee is charged, which is said to afford a large revenue to the church.

Near the cathedral tower is a well with a beautiful iron canopy, made by Quentin Matsys, the "blacksmith of Antwerp." He fell in love with the daughter of a painter, who refused to bestow her hand on any one but an artist. Matsys laid aside the apron and hammer, took to the brush and easel, became a famous painter, and—"married the girl."

The steamers plying between Antwerp and Harwich are far superior to those on the New Haven and Dieppe Line. They are larger, much cleaner, and well provided with berths. We passed half way down the Scheldt by daylight. The scenery is unique. On either side may be seen the roofs of high houses and the tops of tall trees, relieved occasionally by a church steeple or windmill of huge dimensions. The peculiarity of the scenery is owing to the fact that the banks of the river are dikes erected to prevent inundation and much higher than the country on either side. It is not just the kind of prospect one would sit up late to see, so I retired and had a good night's rest, the North Sea being smooth as a Swiss lake. On landing at Harwich the passengers were notified that we had reached a higher civilization by handbills placed in the hands of each, warning them of the penalties for smuggling. The customs officers left but little chance for escape, the search being quite thorough. A pleasant ride of sixty or seventy miles through the lovely rural scenery of the county of Essex brought me again to London.

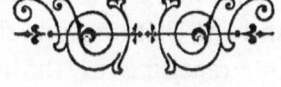

## CHAPTER XII.

### LONDON.

An English Sabbath—Spurgeons' Tabernacle—The Great Preacher—Tower Hill—Royal Exchange—Bank of England—Mansion House—Guildhall—Bow Church—Smithfield—Hyde Park—Parks and Gardens—St. James' Palace—Buckingham Palace—Apsley House—Underground Railroad—Cabs—Omnibuses—St. Giles'—Houndsditch.

Reaching London early on Sunday morning, I had an opportunity of comparing the English Sabbath with the Continental, and the contrast is striking. Every place of business is closed, and the streets deserted; even the omnibuses have a part holiday on Sunday morning, and have not yet resumed their trips. The persons I met were Roman Catholics returning from early mass, prayer book in hand. Nor is there any change till at half past ten, when the ringing and chiming of the church bells for general service seems to wake up London, and for half an hour the streets are full of church goers. On reaching my hotel, longed for letters from home, which had accumulated here, during my absence on the continent, are received and devoured with an interest that only those with a similar experience can understand. All Americans I have become acquainted with in Europe seem to be troubled with forebodings of ill news from home. The distance gives a sense of isolation and helplessness. Even should the telegraph flash in an instant news of the sickness of a loved one, and the dispatch be received on the instant of its arrival, there is the ten or twelve days that must, under the most favorable circumstances, elapse before the bedside of the sufferer could be reached—and what may not happen in those ten days!

I had wondered how London would seem to me after my Continental experience, and again seated myself under the dome of St. Paul's with some misgivings as to the result. The building seems dirtier and dingier than before, but even when compared with the cathedrals of Paris, Strasburg, Cologne, Brussels and Antwerp, has lost none of its peculiar and substantial grandeur. The other London churches look insignificant, and it requires all its sacred historical associations to give to Westminster Abbey that consideration which some of the Continental churches receive on merely architectural grounds. But the Houses of Parliament, so often disparagingly spoken of, do not suffer when compared with any public building I have seen elsewhere. It may be through the perversity of my nature in wanting to disagree with other people, or from lack of capacity to judge, but I am disposed to accord much more honor to the architect of the Parliament Houses than most people. Newspaper criticism has, I think, done him great injustice.

During the day I managed to see the interiors of a number of the churches and looked in for a few minutes on several of the Sunday schools. The scholars seemed to belong mostly to the poorer class, and I remembered that when Sunday schools were established in England it was for the instruction of those too poor to attend school week days. Desiring to know if the Christian parents of England turn over the responsibility of the religious training of their children to Sunday school specialists with their cunning devices, as in America, I made some inquiries of an English lady at the dinner table, who assured me that they were still maintained in great part for the poor. In the simplicity of her heart she told me that in some parts of the city children of ten or twelve years old were frequently admitted who could not answer the question, "Who made you?" For the benefit of a gentleman who had just been airing his infidel sentiments rather offensively, I assured her that such children had reached the very highest point attained by scientists and were abreast of the best scholarship of the day, and fitted for teachers rather than scholars. The dear woman looked puzzled and annoyed, but probably regarded it as one of my American eccentricities.

Desiring to attend service at Spurgeon's Tabernacle, seated on the top of an omnibus, I crossed Blackfriars Bridge to the south side of the Thames, and reaching an old hotel, the "Elephant and Castle," at a place called Newington Butts, found myself within a block of the tabernacle. A Methodist preacher aecompanied me, and although more than half an hour early we found a large number of people waiting for the opening of the outer gates. By putting a contribution to the church in envelopes furnished us by an official, we received tickets which admitted us at once to the building by a side door. An old gentleman, occupying a pew near the platform, kindly invited us to sit with him. As we sat down I remarked to my companion, "This church is more than twice as large as Mr. Beecher's." "Are you Americans?" quickly inquired the old gentleman. On being informed that we were from the United States, he invited us to visit with him the several parts of the building in the half hour that remained before service. He conducted us through the galleries to the platform, and to the library and parlors. In the basement we passed through the Sabbath school room, and prayer rooms, in one of which a young peoples' meeting was in progress, and gospel hymns sung with great fervor. He took us into a large room, where we found more than fifty persons at tea. These he told us were people living at a distance, some of them poor, who found it convenient to remain at the church for evening service; and for all such a plain tea is furnished every Sunday evening.

We passed through the various other rooms, getting an

interesting account of the church and its remarkable growth, and answers to our many questions as to its methods and its widely celebrated pastor. Returning to the audience room we found it fast filling up. There are two tiers of galleries which run entirely around the building, the platform being in front of the lowest gallery and about on a level with it. The seats and all available standing room were occupied before the hour for service, and the doors closed leaving many outslde, and yet the building when thus crowded holds over 7,000 persons. Exactly at the hour, Mr. Spurgeon stepped quickly on the platform, and at once commenced the service by reading a hymn. He is a short, thick set man, with short neck, round face, and, I am sorry to say, his hair parted very near the middle. He is not the man you would select for a pulpit orator, or indeed as remarkable in any respect; in fact, to be honest about it, he is a very ordinary looking person. His voice is remarkably fine— full, flexible and pleasant, it is equally well adapted to denunciation or entreaty. He reads excellently, especially the hymns; his style is quite dramatic, almost what in America we sometimes call, by way of disparagement, "theatrical," and yet with him it seems perfectly natural and does not suggest in the slightest degree an attempt at oratorical display or a studied effort of any kind. (By the way, I have often wondered why ministers don't learn to read. The first question to an applicant for orders should be, "Can you read?" If, on trial, he reads a hymn of Watts' or Wesley's as ministers usually do, he should be kindly but firmly shown the door and advised to learn to read before calling again.) After reading the hymn clear through he "lines" it out, a verse at a time, and in such a way as to prepare the audience to sing the words understandingly. During the service four long hymns were sung by the vast assembly, without an instrument of any kind either to lead or accompany.

I had heard and admired the grand choir at Westminster Abbey, and the exquisite music at St. Paul, both fine in their way, but either, as worship to God, seem the merest mockery as compared with the grand songs of praise by "all the people" at the Tabernacle. An interesting feature of the service was the scripture reading, with a running comment, mostly explanatory, and in a conversational tone. The large congregation seems made up mostly of the middle and poorer classes, and Mr. Spurgeon preaches so as to reach the lowest. His text was: "Though these three men, Noah, Daniel and Job, were in it, they should deliver but their own souls by their righteousness, saith the Lord God." His theme was—"Individual responsibility to God," and he used wonderful plainness of speech. Some expressions seemed almost uncouth, as, for example: "You won't be *lugged* into Heaven by the ear;" and another: "You are not to be saved as if you were *horses* or *cats.*" And yet he knows his hearers and how to reach them, and is evidently not disposed to fall into the error, so very common among ministers, of preaching for the few professional or literary men in their congregations, apparently under the impression that such men want to hear speculations and abstractions from the pulpit. Such men have usually enough of that sort of thing during the week, and are as likely to desire the "sincere milk of the word," and restful, helpful Bible teachng, and quite as willing to forego hair-splitting, as the women and children of the audience. Mr. Spurgeon is not, in the American sense of the word, a "sensational" preacher, but is a very earnest one and has done a great work. His training college, and the many helpful charities he has originated, occupy a large portion of his time. As to his "ability" as a preacher, which, with many persons, is of more importance than his usefulness, there can be but one opinion. He is in the largest and truest, as well as in the narrow and technical sense, a great preacher, and is so regarded in London.

Desiring to carry out a plan I had arranged for visiting the places of interest in London, I went again to the Tower, and from thence walked to the place of public execution on Tower Hill, outside the walls. The site of the ancient scaffold is now in the centre of Trinity Square, and used as a small public garden or park. Here flowed some of the best blood of England—Fisher, More, Essex, Howard, Surrey, Seymour, Somerset, Dudley, Strafford, Sydney, Monmouth, and scores of others. The Royal Mint, formerly in the Tower, is now on Tower Hill, and is quite a large building. Turning again towards St. Paul's I pass Mark Lane, with its Corn Exchange, and Mincing Lane, with its great Commercial Salesroom, into Eastcheap, which leads me again to the statue of William IVth., at the head of King William street. By the way, this statue occupies the site of the ancient "Boar's Head Tavern in Eastcheap," made famous by Shakespeare as the scene of Falstaff and Prince Henry's roysterings, and where Falstaff drank such an "intolerable quantity of sack to but a haporth of bread." King William street leads directly to the square, or open space on which fronts the Royal Exchange, Bank of England, and the Mansion House. No place that I have seen in any American city presents such a crowded appearance. It is regarded as the commercial centre of the old city, as well as of the world. Into the 632 acres known as the old city nearly a million people pass daily from their suburban homes. Blackfriars, Southwark, and London bridges afford passage from the south side of the Thames, the metropolitan or underground railroad pours out its thousands from the Mansion House station, and several lines of omnibuses terminate at the Bank of England. It is estimated that London bridge alone, and but forty feet wide, accommodates 20,000 vehicles and 100,000 pedestrians daily.

The Royal Exchange is a remarkably fine building, facing on the square, with Cornhill and Threadneedle streets on each side, the latter street separating it from the Bank of England. It is an open quadrangle, with a large statue of Queen Victoria in the central square. The portico of the west front is said to be the finest in Great Britain. The eight columns supporting it are over four feet in diameter and more than forty feet high. The cornice is massive and the pediment ornamented with interesting groups of statuary. This building is on the site of an older Exchange, and was opened in 1844. The cost of its erection was four and one-half million dollars. At the east end, up one flight of stairs, is "Lloyd's subscription rooms," headquarters of the underwriters and of merchants and ship-owners generally.

The Bank of England consists of a series of buildings, squatty in appearance and without any apparent architectural design, covering an area of about four acres, with streets on each side. The bank receives the government deposits from taxes and customs, and disburses the interest on the national debt—is in fact a sort of treasury department, but managed entirely by a corporation. It also does a general banking business and is largely a depository for trust funds. Its vaults usually contain about one hundred million dollars in specie, and its notes circulate to the amount of seventy-five million dollars, the smallest note being twenty-five dollars. It never pays out its notes but once; if returned to the bank they are cancelled. These returned notes are kept for five years, and so perfect is the system of registration that in a few minutes any of the seventy-seven million notes received by the bank during the past five years can be produced and the source from which the bank received it determined. When I arrived in Scotland I received notes of the bank of England for my bills of exchange, and found when I went to pay them out that the careful business men and money-changers wanted my name on the back of the notes; it is always best, however, to have a good endorser. I stepped into the general banking room and watched the counting of bills and weighing of specie by an army of clerks; 1,000 are employed in the various parts of the building. All gold taken at the bank, if light by a fraction of a grain, is cut in two and a discount of eight cents on each sovereign charged the depositor, that sum having been found sufficient to cover the average loss on light coins. I passed through several halls looking into the offices and rooms, and no one interfered with me; but standing in the doorways and halls were the porters of the bank, in livery, and I found but one spot where I was not followed by watchful eyes—the garden! Yes, opening a door I found in the bank of England a garden, with trees and shrubbery! I must confess I was surprised to find this "bit of nature" amid such surroundings. It indicates that even here the spirit of Mammon is not supreme, as it must cost a round sum to devote ground in such a place for such uses.

The Mansion House, residence of the Lord Mayor, is nearly opposite the Royal Exchange and was built in 1741, at a cost of $350,000. Of course it is a very large and very fine building. The city police court is held in one of the rooms and is in session daily, presided over by the Lord Mayor or one of the Aldermen. I have dropped in several times when passing, and find it very much like police courts in other large cities. The Lord Mayor puts on a good deal of style, officially. At the *city* celebrations he takes precedence of members of the royal family. His salary is $40,000, but sufficient to maintain the dignity of his official position. On his installation he gives a dinner at Guildhall, costing usually over $10,000. To make the official salary meet the demands on the official purse, it would seem as if a little civil service reform might be inaugurated in England.

Leaving the Mansion House and still going west, we pass through the Poultry, a very short street, and are in Cheapside, a very old business street of retail stores. Goods in the windows are well displayed and the prices attached in plain figures, a thing very common in London, and a custom that gives much confidence to the purchaser. We reach King street on our right and passing up a block are at Guildhall, a large building used for city purposes. It is the "City Hall" of London. The style is Gothic. Its principal hall will hold about 7,000 people, and at each end is a beautiful Gothic window the entire width of the hall. There are some fine portraits and statues, mostly of judges and mayors. It was here Anne Askew was tried for heresy; Surrey, Dudley and Lady Jane Grey, for treason; and the Jesuit Garner for complicity in the gunpowder plot. Here, after the abdication of James II., the Lords of Parliament met and declared for the Prince of Orange. The huge statues of Gog and Magog formerly carried in procession on the "Mayor's Show Day," as seen in old pictures, are in this hall. The library and reading room contain over 50,000 volumes. In the basement is a most interesting museum containing many relics of the Roman period, found in London and vicinity. There are tombs, monuments, statues, stone coffins, parts of the old wall, Roman tesselated pavement, bricks, pottery, shoes, latches, spoons, knives, &c., &c. I was especially impressed with the resemblance of many of these ancient things with those of to-day. A quantity of Roman nails, probably 1,600 years old, hardly differ in any respect from the nails common now. The original sign of the "Boar's Head" in Eastcheap is here. Several of the London Trade Guilds exhibit historical collections showing the changes and improvements in their particular line of business. Among them I found a large show case belonging to the "Most Worshipful Company of Clockmakers," and filled with watches showing the progress of invention from the first rude attempts, almost as large as some modern clocks, and through all the various forms of "bulls-eyes," to the watch of to-day. The collection is very valuable and complete, and I studied it with the interest that might be expected of a *reformed jeweler*.

Passing back to Cheapside, I continue westward, and soon reach Bow Church, on the south side of the street, where hang the famous "Bow Bells." To be born within the sound of these bells is to be a Cockney. One of the books of my earliest juvenile library was "The true story of Whittington and his Cat;" and as I reached Bow Church, admiring its beautiful spire, 225 feet high and built by Wren, the bells began to ring. I tried to fancy that as of old the burden of their chiming was

"Turn again, Whittington, Lord Mayor of London."

But it is more than forty years since I read the story and I failed to recall very vividly its incidents. There is an English ecclesiastical court of which I have frequently read, and its decisions are often quoted, called the "Court of Arches" and sometimes "Arches Court." I have often wondered why it should be so named, and have to-day learned that Bow Church was formerly known as St. Mary's of the Arches, to distinguish it from other St. Mary's, and from the fact that it was built upon arches. The old ecclesiastical court formerly held its sessions in this church and was called the Court of Arches, and retains the name, even officially, till this day. Since my return to London my saunterings seem to be on familiar ground and I have revisited many of the streets and lanes in the city that recall historic names and incidents. I believe if there is any place on earth where a man feels his littleness it is in London, and how lonesome it is! The fact that one is isolated from the busy, surging multitudes that crowd the streets, who care no more for him than if he did not exist, makes it a social wilderness. To be "alone with nature" means companionship, to be a stranger in London, means to be alone, and counting but as a grain of sand in the desert, or a drop in the ocean. In the case of Americans this feeling of loneliness is aggravated by the absence of the familiar profanity to which his ears are accustomed. A few oaths, round or square as you may please to term it, varied by occasional sons of———,would do much to relieve the feeling that one is a stranger in a strange land. I do not now remember hearing an oath on British soil. There is no doubt good swearing done in England, but in the streets and places where I have been I have not heard any. I have witnessed altercations between cabmen, omnibus drivers, porters and others, hot enough to have called forth the whole alphabet of profanity in an American city. In such cases they adopt a system of "chaffing," a peculiar kind of wit, of great severity, which seems to answer their purpose. If our English friends would cultivate public swearing and vulgarity, it would do much toward making Americans feel at home among them.

A few rods from my hotel in a place interesting to leaders of English history, Smithfield. I pass it every day, and as I pass, the wood-cut in the old spelling book occurs to me, showing "the good and pious John Rogers" chained to the stake in the midst of flames, while his wife and "nine small children, with one at the breast," are looking on. Smithfield had been associated in my mind with a cattle market, and I expected as I approached the vast building pointed out to me as Smithfield Market, to hear the "lowing of the kine." I find that the Cattle Market, though centuries old, was abolished in 1862, and where stood in dirt and mud the pens and sheds, is now an immense building of red brick with glass roof, and four handsome towers. It covers about three and-a-half acres. The roof is about thirty feet high, and supported by heavy iron columns, and lights up every part of the building. Under the market are the tracks of the uunderground and two other railroads, and trains pass every two or three minutes. The interior is not subdivided into minute cages of five or six square yards like the Halles Centrales, at Paris, the whole interior being partitioned off into but about one hundred and fifty stalls or places of business. I had been for several days puzzling myself as to how it was possible to supply the millions of London with food. After passing through Smithfield one wonders how such immense quantities of beef and mutton and poultry and game can be disposed of. The place of execution during the reign of Mary, was opposite the entrance of St. Bártholomew's Priory. The condemned were chained to a stake with their faces toward the gate where stood the Prior, the chief ecclesiastic present on such occasions. The ancient gate still remains, and on the spot assigned by tradition as the site of the stake, charred human bones, and stones blackened by fire, were dug up a few years ago in excavating for a sewer.

The hero of Scotland and of the favorite novel of my boyhood days—"The Scottish Chiefs," was executed here. After being dragged at the tails of horses through the streets of London, Sir William Wallace was here beheaded, and in accordance with the cruel custom of the times, his head was placed on London bridge. His body was here divided into four pieces and sent to Scotland for exhibition. The sight of his mutilated remains and the desire for revenge lost Scotland to the English, and Bannockburn atoned for the tragedy at Smithfield.

About two thousand acres of modern London are laid out in parks and pleasure grouds. Those most visited are Hyde Park, St. James' Park, Green Park, Kensington Gardens and Regents' Park. Hyde Park contains nearly 400 acres and is the great resort of the higher classes for carriage and horseback riding. No *hired* vehicle, however pretentious, can enter Hyde Park. "The line must be drawn somewhere, you know," and it is drawn across the word *hired* and not between different styles of carriages. A bridle road from Hyde Park Corner to Kensington Gardens has received the singular name of Rotten Row, and is devoted to horseback riding. Splendid looking horses, largely of the race-horse pattern, are pacing up and down this aristocratic course. The principal carriage road is called the Ladies' Mile, and my visit being late in the afternoon, it was fully occupied by the equipages of the nobility. Beautiful carriages with coroneted panels and liveried servants, are common as farmer's buggies at a county fair. Mounted policemen preserve order and keep the carriages in line. The occupants of the carriages are largely ladies, of fine appearance and richly dressed. The young English-woman is usually comely and among the higher classes not infrequently beautiful. They differ from most American young women in having broader shoulders and more substantial feet. They also know better how to use their feet, not walking daintily or trippingly, but planting them squarely like professional pedestrians. The middle-aged English-woman does not fade or wither like so many of her American sisters, but grows redder and stouter. At this stage there is frequently something about their appearance that is to me unpleasant; they look—yes, I say it boldly, they look "beery." When comely English women do not assume this appearance, they make the finest looking elderly ladies in the world.

The gates of Hyde Park are imposing specimens of art, especially at Hyde Park Corner, and Cumberland Gate, at the west end of Oxford street. The latter is known as the Marble Arch, and was set up originally before Buckingham Palace. I will not describe its form or its sculptures, but its cost, $400,000, will indicate that it must be a grand affair. The cost of its removal to its present site was over $50,000.

Kensington Gardens contain over 200 acres, and are a fashionable resort, but for pedestrians only. This pleasure ground is separated from Hyde Park by a narrow body of water called the Serpentine, but is connected with it by a bridge. St. James' Park contains nearly 100 acres, and the Green Park about sixty acres. All these parks are at the West End, the fashionable quarter of London, and all may be visited by crossing a bridge or street separating them from each other. Regents Park is north of Hyde Park and distant about half a mile. It contains nearly 500 acres. In this park are the Royal Botanic Gardens and the Gardens of the Zoological Society.

Bordering on St. James' Park are the royal palaces, and some of the palatial residences of the English nobility. St. James' Palace is built on the site of an old hospital that dated from before the Norman conquest, and dedicated to St. James. Henry VIII. turned out the inmates, pulled down the building, and erected instead a palace for his own use. It was enlarged by Charles I., whose children were born here, and from this place he walked, guarded by soldiers, through St. James' Park, to the place of execution at Whitehall, where he was beheaded. After the burning of the palace of Whitehall, in the reign of William III., this palace was used as the residence of the court when in London, and the British government became known as the "Court of St. James." Even when residing at Buckingham Palace the queen has held her "drawing rooms" here, it being better adapted for the purpose. The exterior of the building is far from being attractive, but it is rich in historical associations. About half past ten every forenoon the guard is relieved by a company drawn from Wellington Barracks, accompanied by the fine Guard's Band, who, on arriving at the east court of the palace, give a short open air concert lasting about twenty minutes. I several times had the pleasure of walking with this band, the best in England, from the barracks to the palace, listening to their fine music.

Clarence House adjoins St. James' 'Palace on the west and was built for the Duke of Clarence, afterwards William IV. It is now occupied by the Duke of Edinburgh. Marlborough House is near to St. James' on the east, and was built by Sir Christopher Wren for the hero of Blenheim. It is the residence of the Prince of Wales.

South-west of St. James' Palace and distant about sixty rods is Buckingham Palace, built on the site of Buckingham House and completed for the occupancy of her present majesty, who still resides here when in London, in 1837. With its grounds it occupies about thirty acres, and is separated from the Green Park by a road known as Constitution Hill. This road was a favorite riding ground of the queen and prince consort, and here the queen has been three times fired at by would-be assassins. Near the upper end of Constitution Hill Sir Robert Peel was thrown from his horse and killed in 1850.

Having passed up Constitution Hill we reach Hyde Park Corner, with its fine gate, in front of which is a statue of Achilles, cast from cannon taken in the Peninsular war, and presented by the women of England to the Duke of Wellington and his companions in arms, to commemorate their victories over the French. Next to Hyde Park Corner, in a street known as Picadilly, is Apsley House, for over thirty years the residence of the Duke of Wellington. In front of it, on a triumphal arch, is a colossal statue of the duke, by Wyatt, cast from cannon taken at Waterloo. He is represented as on the battle-field, seated on his favorite horse, "Copenhagen."

The liveried servants one meets in these parks, and in the vicinity of these palatial residences, are, as a rule, more consequential and important looking than their masters. Indeed, but for the gold lace and gilt buttons, no fellow could find out the relative position of the parties—that is, by looking at them. To-day my attention was attracted to a wonderfully important looking person in the livery of a footman, posing with folded arms on the box of a carriage, in front of the Apsley House. It seemed to me a marvel that the Duke of Wellington was rich enough and influential enough to control the services of such a person. I stopped and looked at him from the sidewalk, as I would at an interesting picture, but he took not the slightest notice of my ill manners. I felt piqued, and, determined to arrest his attention, I walked clear round the carriage; but he never as much as winked. I began to wonder if he were not another statue, cast from Waterloo cannon, when a lovely woman, wearing a pleasant smile, and who actually looked at me, entered the carriage. A few passers-by had stopped as the lady appeared; one of them informed me that she was the Duchess of Wellington. One of the effects of travel is to lead one to distrust appearances. Come to think of it, the most perfectly dressed man, with the best fitting coat and most immaculate shirt bosom and cravat, that I have seen in Europe, brought me lunch on a Rhine steamer, and accepted the small piece of silver extra which I placed in his hand, with a bow that would have made the fortune of an American dancing master. I pay little attention to dress, and in the magnificent Rhine scenery would not have noticed any person's peculiarities, but had my attention called to this elegantly dressed waiter by a person with a decided English accent, who exclaimed with a touch of envy in his tone, "My G—! did that coat grow on that man?" Yes, and come to think again, the finest dressed woman I have seen, was in the streets of Paris. She was got up in wonderful style, yet our guide actually winked at her, and after she had passed, informed us that she was no better than she should be. Alas ! for appearances.

An American said to me : " What an easy place London is to get around in." He had reference to the many facilities for travel in the metropolis. The river affords such facilities, and at a cheap rate ; small steamers are constantly passing up and down, crowded with passengers. There are fourteen terminal stations on the lines of the great railways, which enter the metropolis from all directions. The Metropolitan, or as it is more frequently called, the Underground railroad, is in the form of an irregular ellipse—not quite completed at the east end, where work is in progress—forming a belt around inner London. Its stations are numerous, and conveniently located, approaching almost all the great lines of railroads that enter the city, and forming sub-stations where trains may be taken for any point. In entering London, the well-informed traveler can be transferred so as to reach any station on the Metropolitan road. The road is not always underground, and glimpses of daylight are introduced wherever possible. It does not follow streets, but takes its course without regard to what may be on the surface. It is a great triumph of engineering skill, passing under sewer and water pipes, dwellings, stores, warehouses, etc., which have been skillfully undermined to give it passage. Take a single example—the Blackfriars station is large, and, like nearly all stations, underground. The arches sprung over it have to sustain two busy streets leading to Blackfriars bridge ; have to hold up the line of the Chatham and Dover railroad, which crosses it, and also sustain a huge six-story warehouse. The arches, pillars, buttresses, girders, beams, etc., necessary to hold up such a roof, and the skill displayed in their design and construction, are a wonder to behold. Passing into one of the Metropolitan stations, you purchase a first, second or third class ticket, and passing down two to four flights of stairs, find yourself on the platform, in a spacious and well lighted depot. The trains run every three minutes, so a time-table is not needed. Each locomotive carries a large sign in front, with the name of the terminus to which it is going, so that mistakes are unnecessary, if you understand your route. The time made is about fifteen miles per hour, including stoppages. There is absolutely no smoke on the underground railway, the cars are well lighted, and one is just as comfortable as in a night ride on any first-class railroad. From my quarters in Charter House Square to the Aldersgate street station of the Metropolitan railroad, is but a single block, so that I am in a position to thoroughly appreciate the convenience of underground travel.

Over 10,000 cabs are employed in London, and cab "stands" may be found at almost every important point. The cabs are of two kinds, "four wheelers," and "Hansoms," named after the inventor. The four wheelers resemble very much a compressed American hack, and are intended for four passengers. The Hansoms are by far the most numerous, and are intended for two passengers. They are low bodied, resembling somewhat the old chaise; the driver, however, occupies an elevated seat behind, the reins passing to him over the top of the cab. There is nothing between the passenger and the dashboard, and the view is unobstructed. In case of a storm, there is a "boot" in front which may be closed, and communication with the driver is by a trap-door in the roof. I have never seen a more convenient vehicle for city use than the Hansom cab. The fare is reasonable—about twelve cents a mile, or fifty cents for an hour—and costs no more for two than for one. As compared with the American hackman, the cab-driver is a person of modest, even retiring disposition. On arriving at a London depot, you see a long line of cabs in waiting, the drivers seated in solemn silence on their elevated seats, as if waiting in front of a church for a funeral procession. The reason for this is that they must be employed in turn; the foremost hack takes the fare, but as the vehicles and charges are alike, it makes no difference to the passenger. The driver may possess all the brilliant qualities which distinguish his American rival, but has no motive for executing a war dance or yelling himself hoarse to attract attention. He even does not condescend to leave his lofty position, the baggage being placed and the door closed by the railroad porter.

There are over 800 omnibuses going to and fro in London. As in Paris, they are "double deckers," having seats on the outside, but here the top is reached by iron ladders in the rear, practicable for gentlemen only. The best seat for the stranger is beside the driver, who possesses a mine of local information as to places of interest on his route. They are usually communicative, and not averse to airing their stale and professional jokes at the incidents which occur on the way. These drivers are a singular class, affecting top coats, stove pipe hats,—resting usually on the nose, or thereabouts—and wonderful mufflers. They are generally middle-aged or elderly men, cultivating, as most Britons do, side whiskers, have a stall-fed appearance, the complexion ranging from a dull brick color, through all the shades of red and crimson, to a royal purple. An artist desiring a model for Bardolph's nose, can readily find it among the "bus drivers." First immortalized by the graphic pen of Dickens, they have ever since been used as pegs on which to hang whole chapters of alleged wit,—I pass them lightly. The omnibus fare is graded according to distance, ranging ordinarily from two to six cents.

The eastern part of London, sometimes called St. Giles, is

the abode of the poorer and criminal classes. Whitechapel is a long and wide street, running easterly through this part of the city, and has a line of tram-cars. Short excursions from Whitechapel enable one to see as much poverty and wretchedness as may be found in the same space in any other city. The drinking places are numerous, and their customers seem to belong to the vicious and criminal classes. Travelers are not in the habit of visiting this part of the city, and yet it must be seen to form a correct idea of London.

In Houndsditch, a street which enters Whitechapel, is a celebrated old clothing "Exchange." An entry way leads to a large square or open space where are booths and stalls with alley-ways between. The market is in the hands of Jews who seem to inhabit the streets in the vicinity, and the bargaining is done with all the volubility and shrewdness peculiar to the race. There is an immense trade done here, and it has its various departments and subdivisions. The dealers in old hats deal in nothing else, but can furnish any pattern in use during the present century and in any desired state of dilapidation. The dealers in old shoes are just as select, but are subdivided, as some of them sell only parts of shoes; and uppers, soles or heels may be bought like fish, by the string. The varieties of the clothing trade are numerous, from the carefully dyed and pressed, shabby-genteel garment that, handled with care, may still do holiday duty, to the veriest rags. A very large wholesale business is done, the dealers in old clothing throughout the kingdom finding here a ready market, where, having disposed of their stock, they can procure those images and trinkets and gew-gaws that shall beguile her Majesty's subjects of their cast-off clothing. I am told that colossal fortunes have had their foundations laid in Houndsditch, their owners receiving here that slight start in business which so soon enables the careful son of Abraham to become a banker or capitalist.

The worst, or rather the most disagreeable feature of the place, is its many smells, which affect gentiles most unpleasantly. Nobody has seen all that is characteristic of London life who has not visited Houndsditch and the surrounding neighborhood.

## CHAPTER XIII.
### LONDON.

Methodist Ecumenical Conference—City Road Chapel—Opening Services—Bishop Simpson's Sermon—Methodism in England—Relics—Bunhill Fields—Windsor Castle—St. George's Hall—St. George's Church—Memorial Chapel—Round Tower—South Kensington Museum—Courts and Galleries—Museum of Patents—The Crysta. Palace—Interior—English Courts—Old Jewry—Tourists—Books of Travel.

The Methodist Ecumenical Conference is in session in London. The idea of holding such a conference originated in America, and was first proposed, I think, at the general conference of 1876, but not till two years later accepted by the English Methodists. The conference consists of 400 members, representing twenty-six branches of Methodism. One can hardly call them divisions, as all profess to follow Wesley, and all hold the distinctive doctrines of Wesleyan Armenianism. The term ecumenical has been applied to those great councils of the church that represented all christendom. Its use, restricted by the word Methodist, does not seem so inappropriate when we consider the wide spread influence of the great system which the word indicates, or the fact that it is literally a gathering of nations and of races. Unlike other ecumenical councils, it has neither legislative nor judicial powers; it cannot decide questions of doctrines, or polity, or usage. It has no rights of supervision, direction or even interference. The subjects for discussion seem to have been carefully selected with a view to avoiding possible controversy. I am inclined to think too much has been conceded in this direction, and that its sessions will not be as interesting or profitable as if a wider range of subjects had been permitted. It is simply a convention of representative Christian workers from all branches of Methodism—partaking somewhat of the character of a family reunion. As promoting fraternity and co-operation it will undoubtedly accomplish great good. Its sessions are to be held in City Road Chapel, which is historic ground, having been erected by John Wesley. It was his favorite preaching place ; in the parsonage adjoining he lived for many years, and his remains rest in the little graveyard in the rear of the chapel. Many of the men best known to early Methodism—Clarke, Watson, Benson, Bunting, Newton, and other have commemorative tablets on its walls, and many names dear to Methodism, are on the tombstones which surround the grave of its founder. Its pulpit, designed by Wesley, is of mahogany, and of medium height. The chapel has seats for about 800 on the floor and 600 in the galleries.

The opening sermon was preached by Bishop Simpson, of the M. E. Church in America, and I was so fortunate as to secure a ticket of admission. I was on hand an hour before the time of service, and secured an eligible seat in the gallery, the floor being reserved for delegates and church officials. I had a good opportunity of observing the delegates, who came in early, and also of making comparisons as the delegates of each church were seated together and their seats labeled. It is but fair to say that the delegates were not selected for their good looks, or even, in the majority of cases, their intellectual appearance. The American M. E. churches, north and south, are far ahead, so far as the appearance and bearing of their delegates is concerned.

The morning service of the English Church was gone through with—they do it here every Sunday—and two long hymns lined and sung congregationally, and without accompaniment. Bishop Simpson then read from a small pocket bible known as "John Wesley's field bible," being the one he carried in his missionary labors when preaching out doors, the following text from Johns Gospel : "The words that I speak unto you, they are spirit and they are life." The sermon, taking into consideration the occasion and surroundings, could not have been excelled. American Methodists can appreciate it when I say it was one of the bishop's very best. It occupied an hour and a half in delivery and was without notes. It is the theme of conversation among the delegates from all sections, and all admit that no other man known to Methodism could have preached such a sermon.

In the afternoon the address of welcome was delivered by Dr. T. Osborne, and responses by Bishop McTiere of the M. E. Church, south, Bishop Warren of the church north, and Dr. Douglas of the Canadian church. The occasion was sadly marred by the lack of arrangement which compelled the audience for nearly an hour to hear a lesson in carpentry while the platform on which the speeches were to be made was constructed with true English deliberation, and then by a tedious calling of the roll. The responses to the address of welcome were very fine.

In conversation with English Methodists, they claim that their delegates do not represent the highest order of talent in their church, and say that men of usefulness as pastors, conservative men, "safe men," not likely to tower very loftily above their brethren, are almost always selected for positions of prominence. This may possibly account for the fact that Methodism in England is about at a stand still as to numbers. Conservatism is not adapted for agressive warfare in an age of progress. The English Wesleyans assume a peculiar attitude toward the Established church. They meekly assume the position of "poor relations" to that body, and pride themselves on the fact that the more liberal clergymen of that church occasionally afford them tokens of recognition. The fact that the high churchmen regard them unfit to associate with the "upper classes" while living, or rest in consecrated ground with "baptized persons" when dead, does not seem to disturb the spirit of humility they are disposed to observe toward the Established church. A more independent spirit would, I think, be conducive to the best interests of Methodism.

The Lord Mayor of London and Lady Mayoress are Methodists, and lend their influence in every way to the cause. They gave a reception to the delegates at the Mansion House. On day before yesterday I attended a Bazaar at Centenary Hall, opened by the Lady Mayoress, the proceeds of sales and refreshments being for some charitable purpose. Quite a collection of Methodist relics were on exhibition, among them Wesley's old clock; a large number of his letters and of his brother Charles'; Dr. Coke's gold watch; autograph letters of most of the early Methodists, etc. The most interesting relics of Wesley that I have seen are in the City Road parsonage, where, in the room in which he died is the old furniture, of excellent quality and tasteful designs, for Wesley was evidently a man of fine taste. His book case, bureau, desk, tea-pot, his favorite mahogany arm chair, in which I was invited to sit, and assured that every president of the conference from Wesley's time had sat in it, and which I observe is used by the chairman of the Ecumenical Conference.

Opposite the City Road Chapel is a noted dissenter's burial ground, known as Bunhill Fields. It contains about seven acres, and when first used as a burial ground was in the open fields outside the city, and called "Bone-hill-fields." It is no longer used for burial purposes, but is well cared for on account of its honored dead; nor is it probable that the demands of trade or population will ever disturb it. Hundreds of Non-conformist divines rest here, and I might furnish a long list of names known on both sides of the Atlantic, like Owen, Lardner, Neil, Rees, etc. Three members of the Cromwell family are buried here. The grave of that remarkable woman, Susannah Wesley, mother of John, Charles and seventeen other Wesleys is here, and near to it is a tombstone from which John Wesley frequently preached. Wesley seems to have loved the associations of the place. Just across the way he built City Road Chapel, and beside it a parsonage, in which he resided. The great hymn writer, Dr. Isaac Watts, and Drs. Stennet and Rippon, less famous, are buried here. As I stood reverently by their graves, I felt that if one other grave was here, the lovers of hymnology would need no other shrine. Charles Wesley's remains rest in the old Marylebone churchyard, where with some difficulty I succeeded in gaining an entrance to pluck a sprig of yew from the poet's grave. Every boy and girl will be interested to know that Daniel De Foe, who wrote Robinson Crusoe, is buried here, and that a monument has been erected over his grave by contributions from the boys and girls. And last, but not least, near the centre of this burial ground, under a high tomb, lie the remains of John Bunyan, of immortal fame as author of "The Pilgrim's Progress." Of this grave Macauley wrote: "The spot where Bunyan lies is regarded by Non-comformists with a feeling which seems scarcely in harmony with the stern spirit of their theology. Many Puritans, to whom the respect paid by Roman Catholics to the reliques and tombs of their saints seemed childish and sinful, are said to have begged with their dying breath that their coffins might be placed as near as possible to the coffin of the author of 'The Pilgrim's Progress." Separated from Bunhill Fields by a narrow street is a Friend's burial ground where I found the grave of George Fox, founder of the society called Quakers.

Windsor Castle is twenty-four miles from London, near the village of Windsor (a place of 10,000 inhabitants), and the finest and most interesting of all the royal residences. It was built by William, of Wykeham, for Edward III., upon the site of a more ancient castle erected by William the Conqueror. It has for eight centuries been a favorite residence of the sovereigns of England. During and since the reign of George IV. over five million dollars has been expended upon it. A fine view of the castle is had from the railway, and the approach from the village station, but a few minutes, walk distant, gives one some idea of how imposing a Norman castle of the first class can be. The great round tower is the most prominent feature of the castle, and its stronghold. The queen being absent in Scotland, the park grounds and state apartments are thrown open to the public. Tickets of admission are furnished free at the chamberlain's office, and the attendants in charge are strictly forbidden to receive any fee whatever.

We enter by a door adjoining St. John's Tower, and passing through an ante-room in which are a number of old historical paintings, we enter the queen's audience chamber. The ceiling, like most of the others painted by Verrio, represents Queen Catherine as Brittania proceeding to the Temple of Virtue in a car drawn by swans and accompanied by Ceres, Flora and other heathen deities. The walls are covered with gobelin tapestry, representing scenes in the life of Queen Esther. In this room in a richly carved frame is a full length portrait of Mary, Queen of Scots. The inscription was to me a surprise, or rather, I was greatly surprised to find it in Windsor Castle:

"Mary, Queen of Scotland, true Princess and Legitimate Heiress of England and Scotland, and mother of James, King of Great Britain, who, harassed by the heresy of her people, and overpowered by rebellion, came into England in the year 1568, for the sake of sanctuary; and relying on the word of her kinswoman, Queen Elizabeth, is perfidiously detained captive for nineteen years, and, traduced by a thousand calumnies, is, by the cruel sentence of the English parliament, at the instigation of Heresy, handed over to execution; and on the 18th day of February, 1587, is beheaded by the common executioner in the forty-fifth year of her life and reign."

The most enthusiastic defender of the unfortunate Mary could hardly frame a severer indictment of Elizabeth and her parliament than hangs in the queen's audience chamber!

The guard chamber has a large collection of ancient armor and relics handsomely arranged. Among them armor once belonging to Lord Howard, 1588, Earl of Essex, 1596, Charles, Prince of Wales, 1620, and Prince Rupert, 1635. There are fine busts of the dukes of Marlborough and Wellington, and over each is suspended the small banner, by the presentation of which, on the anniversaries of the battles of Blenheim and Waterloo, respectively, are held the estates voted those generals by parliament. Over the fire place in a glass case is a finely wrought shield, presented by Francis I., of France, to Henry VIII. It was made by Cellini, and is accounted a marvelous piece of workmanship. There are two chairs, one made from an oak that grew on the field of Waterloo, the other from an oak beam taken from "Alloway's auld haunted kirk." An interesting relic is a piece of the foremast of the Victory, perforated by a cannon ball at the battle of Trafalgar, also a bar shot that killed eight men during the same engagement. There is also an anchor and two cannon fished from the wreck of the Spanish Armada, field pieces captured from the Sikhs, muskets and round shot from Inkermann, trophies from Zululand, King Coffee's umbrella, etc.

St. George's hall is a large room, 200 feet long, and about

thirty-five feet wide, and thirty-five feet high. Its ceiling is decorated with the arms of the knights of the garter, from the institution of the order till the present time. The names of all the knights, from Edward III. and the Black Prince to Beaconsfield and the Marquis of Salisbury (1881), are painted between the windows, with a number attached to each; the corresponding number on the ceiling indicates the arms of the knight named. The walls are decorated with portraits of the sovereigns of England, from James I. to George IV. At the east end is a magnificent throne and behind it on shields are the arms of the sovereigns of the order, from Edward III. to William IV. In the centre is a very long and heavy mahogany table, and in this room was given the banquet to the Emperor Alexander, of Russia, when he visited England, on which occasion the attendant assures me there was ten million dollars, worth of plate and decorations on the table!

The other rooms I will mention briefly. The queen's ante-chamber, the walls covered with Gobelin tapestry, and fine portraits of royal princesses. The grand reception room, the walls covered with Gobelin tapestry representing the story of Jason and Medea. This room is handsomely ornamented, and contains a very large malachite vase, a gift from the Emperor of Russia. The throne room contains many fine portraits and a few pictures by West. In the Rubens room the pictures are all by the artist, and the Zuccarelli room has nine large paintings by Zuccarelli. The Vandyke room has twenty-two of his paintings, mostly portraits of kings and princes. The grand vestibule contains banners and other memorials, and a fine statue of Queen Victoria. The general impression made by the state apartments is that they have "seen better days." The furniture needs regilding and the upholstery and decorations look faded, yet there is a genuine air of gentility and good taste notwithstanding. Gaudiness has been avoided and the works of art are both fine and interesting.

Other places of interest at Windsor are—St. George's Chapel, a splendid specimen of Gothic architecture. Here and in the royal tombhouse at the east end, are buried Henry VI., Edward IV. and Queen, Henry VII. and Jane Seymour, Charles I., George III., George IV., William IV., and the Duke of Kent, father of Queen Victoria. The stalls and banners of the Knights of the Garter are in the choir, and here their installations are held. The stained glass windows are especially fine, the west window containing subjects connected with the Knights of the Garter, the east window, a fine memorial to Prince Albert. I attended the daily afternoon service and heard some good music; the chanting was especially fine. The Albert Memorial Chapel, erected by the queen on the site of an ancient edifice, known as Wolsey's Chapel, is a remarkable building. The ceiling and walls are of Venetian mosaic, and the windows of stained glass are fine workmanship. In the center is a richly carved marble sarcophagus, with a reclining figure of the Prince Consort on the top. If judged by the cost this small room would rank first among memorials, the queen having spent upon it a million and a quarter dollars. The profusion and elaborateness of the ornamentation, however, destroys the effect. There is no beauty of form or proportion, the whole interior is simply a mass of what in America is known as "gingerbread work," but of the most delicate and expensive kind. It compares very unfavorably with the bare walls which surround and beautify by their appropriate simplicity the tomb of Napoleon, at the Invalides.

One can hardly imagine a more beautiful rural scene than the park and grounds at Windsor. There is none of that artificial appearance which characterizes the French parks and gardens. Nature has been permitted to assume her loveliest forms. The view from the top of the Round Tower is especially fine. A soldier familiar with the sights passes slowly around describing the surrounding country to a group of visitors and answering questions. The castle buildings, the royal park and gardens ; the city of Windsor ; Eton with its far famed college, on the other side of the Thames and about a mile distant ; the church of Stoke Pogis, scene of Gray's Elegy ; Burnham Beeches, a noble park ; the ancestral mansion of William Penn ; Harrow on the Hill ; Frogmore ; the field of Bunnemede, where King John signed Magna Charta ; Richmond hill ; the Surry hills ; Epsom Downs ; and the smoke of distant London, are pointed out from the top of the Round Tower. The railroad from London to Windsor passes places of much interest, as well as fine parks, beautiful residences and fertile fields ; indeed, one gets a glimpse of some of England's choice rural scenery.

The South Kensington Museum is on the Brompton road, about a mile from Hyde Park Corner. It was originated by Prince Albert and founded with the profits of the Exhibition of 1851. Since that time large grants have been made by parliament, and the government now defrays its entire expenses, amounting to the large sum of a million and a half dollars yearly. Its design is the promotion of art by means of its large museum, its schools of instruction, designed more especially for teachers, its public examinations and exhibitions, and the distribution of prizes. Its design is thoroughly practical, and its buildings are of the plainest character, nothing having been expended for show. I can give but the briefest sketh of this vast collection, already rivalling the British Museum, and soon to contain its entire department of natural history. It is principally arranged in courts on the ground floor.

The architectural court contains copies of what are

## COURTS AND GALLERIES. 253

considered masterpieces of art, largely sculptures and carvings. The north wall is covered with a diagram, representing the comparative sizes of the great buildings of the world, principally churches. There is also a large display of ornamental iron work. The south court contains the Loan Collection, and is rich in ecclesiastical curiosities—crosses, mitres, chalices, fonts, cups, carvings, and enamels, among them the crown and chalice of the Abima of Abyssinia. There is also a large display of porcelain, pottery and glassware, Chinese and Japanese ware, and ornamental and other woven fabrics, etc. The oriental courts are richly decorated in oriental style and contain specimens of the art manufactures of India, China, Japan, Persia, etc. The north court ¦contains casts of fine sculptures, mostly large size, among them the Marble singing gallery, from Florence, a biga or two horse chariot from the Vatican, and two pulpits from the Cathedral of Pisa.

The ceramic gallery has earthenware, stoneware and porcelain, from all countries, and in great variety. The Prince Consort's gallery is devoted largely to gold and silver work, enamelings, carvings in ivory, etc. The library contains about 60,000 volumes on art subjects, also over 60,000 engravings and drawings and 40,000 photographs illustrating art and architecture. In this department some of the original manuscripts of Charles Dickens' works are preserved, also Oliver Goldsmith's chair, desk, and walking cane.

The picture galleries are quite extensive, most of the best English painters being represented, but are principally interesting for their mechanical drawings, and for Raphael's celebrated cartoons. These cartoons are of a very large size drawn on strong paper and chalk, and colored in distemper. They were executed by Raphael in 1513 for Pope Leo X., as designs for tapestry work. There were originally ten of these cartoons ; three have been lost, but the tapestries containing all the designs are in the Vatican. Their history is interesting—Rubens saw them in the wareroom of a manufacturer, at Arras, and advised Charles I. to buy them, which he did, for a tapestry manufactury he had established in England. Cromwell, after Charles' death, bought them for $1,500, and they remained at Whitehall, till, by order of William III., a room was built for them at Hampton Court, where they remained until recently, when the queen gave permission for their removal to South Kensington. As one studies these works of the great master it seems strange that they should have lain forgotten among the cast off patterns of a tapestry manufactory till recognized by the artistic eye of Rubens. The subjects of these cartoons may be of interest to my readers : they are Christ's charge to Peter ; Death of Annanias ; Peter and John healing the lame man ; Paul and Barnabus of Lystra ; Elymas the Sorcerer, struck blind ; Paul preaching at Athens ; the miraculous draught of fishes. Such subjects will be recognized as worthy the highest efforts of the great Raphael.

In the General Museum may be found furniture, ancient and modern, old tapestry, state carriages, sedan chairs, wood carvings, sculptures in terra-cotta, chimney pieces, etc. The Indian Museum has been recently transferred here from the Indian Office, and contains almost everything relating to Indian life and history. The Educational Museum contains models of school buildings and school furniture and apparatus. There is, rather strangely, in this department a "munitions of war collection," possibly with a view of teaching the young idea how to shoot.

More terrible than this war collection is the formidable array of musical instruments, extending from the tomtom, the three stringed lyre and Pan's pipes, to the latest horror, the Organette. Egyptians, Assyrians, Persians, Babylonians,

Chaldeans, Jews, Greeks, Romans, as well as modern nations and tribes have endured many things of the instruments represented in this large and most interesting collection, which affords materials for the study of musical progress in all ages and countries. The assortment of harpsichords, virginals and spinets is especially large, and among them I noticed a precious relic, the favorite harpsichord of Handel. Connected with the museum is the royal school; school of mining; the scientific school; and the national art training school, where pupils are trained to become teachers, the most promising receiving, if necessary, pecuniary aid to enable them to pursue their art studies.

The museum of patents contains a large number of models and pieces of machinery. I was especially interested in an ancient tower clock, made in 1325 by Peter Lightfoot, for Glastonbury Abbey, afterwards set up in Wells' cathedral, where it remained till 1854, and now running in the museum. It is of somewhat rude workmanship, and I discovered no metals in it but iron and steel. It is one of the most interesting horometrical relics in England. Arkwright's original spinning jenny, and George Stephenson's locomotive, "The Rocket," built in 1829, are here; also the marine engine of the "Comet," used on the Clyde in 1812, and the oldest locomotive in existence, "Puffing Billy," in use from 1813 till 1862, in the Wylam Collieries. A pumping engine of 1777, and a steam pump of 1775. A threshing machine made in 1802, and a reaper (resembling very much the American) used in England from 1826 till 1869. A printing press used by Benjamin Franklin. It will be seen by the specimens given how very interesting this collection of machinery must be.

The Crystal Palace, at Sydenham, is a magnificent building situated on a commanding height, surrounded by a beautiful park and extensive gardens and pleasure grounds. Although, I should judge, eight to ten miles from Charing Cross, its railroad facilities make it as accessible as if much nearer the centre of the city. The fare from London railway station, and return, with a ticket of admission to the palace, is but half a dollar. It is regarded as the cheapest and best place of amusement in London, and sixty to seventy thousand persons have visited it in a single day. The grounds contain about 300 acres, and the vast building was erected in 1853-4 by Sir John Paxton, partly from the material used in the great exhibition building of 1851, at Hyde Park. The main building is in round numbers about twenty by one hundred rods; the centre of the glass roof is usually about one hundred feet from the floor, though in some places much higher, and the towers at each end are 280 feet high. From the centre of the building the eye can take in over twenty acres of glass overhead—in all twenty-five acres of glass, weighing 300 tons, and over 10,000 tons of iron were used in the building. I cannot describe the magnificent and graceful appearance of this immense structure, but can satisfy the usual yankee curiosity as to cost (by which so many judge of value and quality), by stating that the building and grounds cost nearly ten million dollars. It is owned and operated by a stock company, and said to pay a moderate interest on the investment. It would be impossible in a reasonable space to describe in detail this building and contents. I can only briefly indicate its general plan and uses.

The centre transept is the region of music and entertainment, and under its immense dome is the Handel Orchestra, capable of seating 4,000 performers. It is used for choral performances, notably for children's concerts, where many thousands participate. In the rear of the orchestra is a great organ, built for the place and of wonderful power. A good orchestra, numbering about sixty performers, played at intervals during my stay.

INTERIOR VIEW OF THE TRANSEPT, CRYSTAL PALACE.

VITAL

The nave is divided into courts or sections, containing the products of art or industry of the countries and periods for which they are named. The Egyptian Court has at its entrance a short avenue of lions, brought from the Nile, which leads to an open court, a fac-simile of a temple of the Ptolemys, 300 B. C.; there is also a pillared hall of Karnak. The architecture, statues, paintings, decorations, inscriptions, etc., are supposed to transport one to ancient Egypt, and it must be confessed the illusion is very perfect. The Greek Court is a representation of an ancient Grecian market place, the buildings mostly Doric. At one end is a very perfect model, a little less than quarter size, of the noblest building of the Greeks—the Parthenon. The statues in this court are casts from the finest specimens of Greek art, now scattered in the various museums of Europe. In the centre of the Roman Court are interesting models of the pantheon, the coliseum, and the forum. The Alhambra Court is copied from the Moorish Palace at Granada, and contains the Court of Lions, Hall of Justice, and other apartments. The Byzantine Court, the English Mediæval Court, the Renaissance Court, the Italian Court, the Chinese Court, are equally interesting, but their points of interest are so numerous that I must omit them.

The Pompeian House carries us back 1800 years, to the Bay of Naples, to the ill-fated city of Pompeii, where lived the indolent and luxurious Roman patricians. The burial of this city in the ashes of Mount Vesuvius, has preserved for us intact a specimen of the Roman house of the period. A perfect fac-simile, to the minutest detail, has been prepared in the Crystal Palace, illustrating the mode of life, habits and customs of the people. Some of the paintings are very fine, and the court dining room, bed rooms, dressing room, bath room, etc., are richly decorated.

A part of the nave is partitioned off by a screen, and

called the tropical department. It is kept at a temperature of about seventy degrees, as being the most congenial to the tropical vegetation it contains. A large marble edged basin with fountain occupies the centre. There are some gigantic tree ferns, one of them presented by her majesty, bananas, the date palm, bamboos, india-rubber plants, sago plants, a dragons' blood tree, Japanese fruit trees, etc. In the orangery are oranges, lemons, citron trees, India figs, camelias, etc. There is also a collection of foreign birds, cockatoos, parrots, love birds, etc. In the aquarium is a rare and interesting collection of fresh and salt water fish.

A considerable part of the building is devoted to purposes of trade. There is a printing department, a factory for ivory turning and carving; indeed, I found a large lower room where second-hand carriages are kept for sale. In all the galleries and part of the nave are stalls, booths, and small rooms for the sale of books, mathematical instruments, stereoscopes and views, and indeed almost every description of toys and fancy goods, as well as dress goods, shawls, and furs. There seems to be a large trade and the prices reasonable as elsewhere. I bought a set of drawing instruments for less than the price demanded in Cheapside. The facilities for furnishing meals and refreshments are numerous and prices reasonable.

Leaving the building to visit the grounds, we step out on a great terrace, say three rods wide and a hundred rods long. On this immense promenade are a large number of allegorical marble statues, and the view is one to delight the eye. We descend by a flight of steps a hundred feet wide, and are in the midst of artificial lakes, fountains, statues, flowers, ornamental temples—indeed almost everything that could make such a scene attractive. There are also cricket grounds, an archery, shooting galleries, an angling and boating lake, besides the usual swings, merry-go rounds, etc.;

furnishing out-door amusements for those who desire. It will not be wondered at that a place whose attractions I have only hinted at should be visited by over a million and a half persons yearly.

In the English Courts which I have visited, I have observed none of the wrangling or bitterness among counsel so frequent in America. Attorneys treat each other as gentlemen, engaged in an honorable calling. More strangely still, the fact that a man appears in court as a witness does not transform him into a perjured liar to be abused at the pleasure of opposing counsel. Attending court is therefore a dull business, and as a consequence but little room is needed for spectators and the court rooms are small. This could all be changed if counsel would only indulge in unwarranted innuendos and indiscriminate abuse of all opposed to them. Gaping crowds would then assemble to witness the exhilarating scene. But there is small hope of it, the English have such a stupid prejudice against American methods. The English newspapers are utterly lacking in enterprise. I am told that an important murder trial may be in progress for weeks without a single editorial as to the guilt or innocence of the accused, a question usually determined by the American papers before the trial begins. This lack of journalistic enterprise acts injuriously on the better class of citizens, forcing them to serve as jurors in important cases. It, however, relieves the officers of the court from ransacking their counties to find dolts and fools who never read the papers, before every important case is tried.

Speaking of courts reminds me of a visit the other day to a noted legal firm in Old Jewry. The name designates a narrow street which enters Cheapside and was formerly in the Jewish quarter. Six centuries ago it had its synagogue and was surrounded by a Jewish population, who here for centuries subsequent submitted to the tortures and abuse practiced upon them by Christian kings to extort money from them for pious and other uses. A Flint law firm had intrusted me with a matter of business to transact for them in Old Jewry, for over a century the quarters of the legal fraternity, and with visions of "Quirk, Gammon & Snap" in mind I ascended the steps of the dingy law office to deliver my letter of introduction. It was an open letter, written by my friend —— —— mostly in the "cuneiform" or "arrow headed" style. Being familiar with his hieroglyphics I was able to decipher enough of it to understand that it referred to me as "judge." This brevet title cost me a new hat, as no "judge" could present himself in a battered tile which had seen service on the Florida, and stood the wear and tear of a Continental trip. A good deal of red tape surrounds the better class of English lawyers. This firm consisted of three members, employing quite a number of assistants in the shape of clerks and messengers. On entering I was referred to a clerk whose duty it is to answer enquiries, read letters of introduction and decide the question of admission to the private offices. I handed him my letters and was motioned to a seat, where for nearly an hour I awaited his pleasure. During this time at least half-a-dozen persons were denied admission to the private offices. I was at length placed in charge of a messenger and conducted to an inner office, where sat a large Englishman, fat, jolly and unlawyerlike, in the American sense, as could be imagined—just the man to fill his pockets with candy for the children, and let them ride on his back after he got home. To associate such a man with "midnight oil" or sharp practice would be impossible. I stated my business, briefly, received the most careful attention and all desired information, leaving with the impression that however high he might stand as a lawyer, he was a whole-souled

English gentleman, the barriers which surround him being no doubt intended to save from unwarranted intrusion or the thoughtlessness of friends the time which to such a man means money—and a good deal of it. I wonder what he thought of the newly-fledged-for-the occasion specimen of the American Judiciary!

Tourists, is the stylish name given to Americans in Europe. For what purpose some of them travel it would be difficult to determine. They know little of the countries they visit and cannot be really interested in the things they see. An old man and woman, with their daughter and son-in-law, hailing from the presidential state—Ohio, were with our party in Paris for two days. The plan of our conductor required three days to see the principal objects of interest, and I told the Ohioans they had better go with us another day and not miss the Louvre. "No," replied the old man, "it's cost enough now, and I reckon one place is as good as another," and, so far as himself and family were concerned, he was right. Of course I do not introduce these as typical Americans, far from it, but there are more of this class than one cares to meet. It has become fashionable to visit Europe, so much so that in the busy season the numerous lines of steamers cannot accommodate the ever increasing volume of travel. On arriving in Europe, the only key to enjoyment some of them possess in the presence of its historical shrines and its treasures of art and antiquity, is money. It is a good thing to have—wonderfully convenient, especially among strangers. The best outfit, however, is a good stock of general information and a fair knowledge of history, supplemented by a thorough course of preparatory reading in reference to the countries to be visited. This, with but a little money, will afford more real enjoyment than General Shoddy and wife can procure from the most lavish expenditures. "Rich as an American," has become a familiar phrase on the continent, and it is fair to suppose they have associated with the name the most striking characteristic of the Americans they meet. "Sensible as an American," "frugal as an American," "modest as an American (!)" have not yet become European proverbs. The cheap arrangements of the tourists' agencies, reducing the entire cost to a fixed sum, and enabling clergymen, school teachers and others of the educated classes to make the trip, will do much to change the estimate of Americans.

I have read books of travel, largely made up of the disagreeable experiences of the traveler. Quarrels with guides, extortions of landlords, troubles with railroad employes and customs officials, fleeced by carriage drivers; indigestible and insufficient food, untidiness and rapacity of servants—yes, even whole pages devoted to encounters with fleas! I have felt sometimes as if the man who could triumph over all these must be a hero indeed. My experiences have been exceedingly commonplace. I have had no quarrels, or even misunderstandings with any one; everybody has used me well. The drivers have been reasonable in their charges, the hotels good, prices moderate, and servants accommodating, officials have been polite, I have never missed a train, or a meal on land, and the readiness of strangers to afford information or needed advice has been remarkable. The result is that I have been unable to season these pages with spicy quarrels or interesting misadventures. I did not expect to find things in Europe as at home, nor did I expect my presence and example would materially affect European habits or customs. On the contrary, I have endeavored to conform as far as possible to my surroundings, and found it pleasant to do so. I also traveled with the purpose constantly in mind of economising, wherever consistent with comfort and self respect, a method I would commend to others as securing much comfort and immunity from trouble.

## CHAPTER XIV.

LONDON—LIVERPOOL.

The British Museum—Library—Books and Manuscripts—Coins—Ornaments and Gems—Egyptian and Assyrian Remains—Rosetta Stone—Elgin Marbles, etc.—Madame Tussaud's—The Thames—Greenwich—Victoria Embankment—The Obelisk—Temperance—Taxes, etc.—Liverpool—Docks—Public Buildings—Streets.

The British Museum is on Great Russel street, Bloomsbury, and covers about seven acres, its principal front having a witdth of nearly 400 feet. The starting point of the present vast collection was a bequest to the British government of the Sloane Collection, by Sir Hans Sloane, in 1753. In 1754 this collection, with the Harlein Manuscripts and Cottonian Library, were united and placed in an old building, on the site of the present museum, known as the Montague House. In 1801 George III. presented a large collection of Egyptian curiosities; afterwards the Elgin Marbles were purchased; and when in 1823, the king's library, collected by George III. during his long reign, was presented to the museum by his successor, George IV., the present building was commenced and completed in 1847. Although the government has been most liberal in purchasing objects of interest, the museum seems to be largely composed of bequests and donations. The life work of specialists; the hoards of antiquarians and bibliopoles; with the wonderful treasures of art and antiquity, gathered during the present century, by liberal and adventurous Englishmen in classic fields, have been freely poured into this vast treasury, and become the property of the nation. It is already running over; its pictures are to be transferred to the national gallery, and its vast natural history collection becomes the property of the museum at South Kensington.

The library of printed books numbers over 1,300,000. These seven figures, formidable as they appear, can convey but a faint idea of its immensity, or of its almost inestimable value, on account of the rarity and historic interest of many of the works it contains. To spend but a single minute in examining each volume would require about seven years, working ten hours per day! In the king's library are more than a dozen table show-cases, in which are arranged some of the choicest treasures it contains. There are some fine specimens of "block-books," those very rare productions printed from solid blocks, and immediately preceding the invention of the art of printing from movable types. Among these are several parts of the Scriptures and manuals of devotion ; in some of these the cuts or illustrations are handsomely colored by hand. Among these block-books is the earliest printed almanac, published at Nuremberg, in 1474, and undisputed head of all the almanacs. Here also is the earliest complete printed book known, the bible in Latin, commonly known as the Mazarine Bible, printed by Gutenberg and Faust, at Mentz, 1455. It is a fine specimen of the printer's art, and the man who can indifferently examine or pass over the first printed book, must be more stoical than I am. I confess I have seldom felt more profoundly moved, than while inspecting this first printed book—The Mazarine Bible. And how strange it seems that it should have taken thousands of years to suggest the simple idea of movable types. Hundreds of years before Christ, we find on seals and coins the most perfect lettering, from dies as perfect as can be produced by the art of to-day, and yet how many centuries it took to suggest the idea of separate movable dies for each letter! Besides this, the earliest, the library contains over 1,700 other editions of the printed Bible, almost every known language being represented.

I shall mention but a very few of the other rare books in this collection. A Psalter in Latin, being the first printed Psalter, the first book with a date, 1457, and the first example of printing in colors. A Greek grammar, printed at Milan, 1476, being the first book printed in Greek characters. Liber Epistolorum, the first book printed in France, 1470. Recuyell of the Historeys of Troye, the first book printed in the English language, printed abroad by Caxton, about 1475; also the same work in the French language, by Caxton, about 1475. In 1477, Caxton came to England and settled at Westminster, within the precincts of the abbey, where he issued the first book ever printed in England, entitled " The dictes or sayenges of the Philosophres, enprinted by me, William Caxton at Wesmestre the yere of our lorde 1477." A copy of a book by Henry VIII., of England, Assertis Septum Sacramentarum, printed at London, 1521, and for which Pope Leo X. conferred on Henry the title of " Defender of the Faith." The Great Bible of 1540, known as Cranmer's Bible—on vellum, a copy richly bound, and presented, as the title page shows, to Henry VIII. There are also first editions of Shakespeare, Milton and most other British authors. In one of the cases is a small book of prayers, used by Lady Jane Grey and containing her autograph, presented by her, as her eyes were about to be bandaged on the scaffold, to the lieutenant of the Tower. Also an indulgence, issued by Pope Leo X., for the rebuilding of St. Peter's at Rome—on vellum. This indulgence was sold by Tetzel and Samson, as sub-commissioners under the archbishop of Mentz. Luther's remonstrances against this proceeding is regarded as the commencement of the Reformation.

The cases from which I have selected these books for

mention, contain over 200 others of almost equal interest. Some have belonged to royal personages, others are regarded as remarkable for their illustrations, and others still for their rare and beautiful bindings. Many contain autographs of celebrated persons; among these are Lord Bacon; Michael Angelo; Calvin; Luther; Melanchthon; Milton; Sir Isaac Newton, etc.

The manuscript saloon is, if possible, more interesting than the library. Here are 50,000 volumes of bound manuscripts, of which 8,500 are in Oriental languages; 7,000 detached seals and casts of seals; and upwards of 100 ancient Greek, Coptic and Latin papyri. By a convenient arrangement of glass frames, many of the more interesting papers are exhibited to the public. I mention a few—a selection of Anglo-Saxon charters from Ethelred, A. D. 692; the original Articles of Liberties, demanded by the barons of King John, which formed the foundation of Magna Charta, A. D. 1215, with the great seal attached; Charters of William II. and Henry I., signed with crosses by the kings and witnesses; the original draft of the will of Mary, Queen of Scots, with corrections and additions in her hand, and dated 1577; a book wholly in the hand writing of James I., for the instruction of his son, Prince Henry; diary of John Locke. There are also, in the handwriting of the authors, Sterne's Sentimental Journey; Pope's Homer's Illiad; a Tragedy by Tasso; autobiography of Robert Burns; and the concluding chapter of Lord Macauley's History of England. Also the original Articles of Agreement for the sale of the copyright of Paradise Lost, in 1667, with the signature and seal of John Milton; and a sketch plan of the battle of Aboukir, by Lord Nelson.

There are frames containing autographs of English sovereigns from Edward IV. to George III., as well as of most of the sovereigns of Europe, during the same period. Also a large number of autograph letters of eminent men, among them, Luther, Calvin, Erasmus ; Wolsey, Cranmer, More, Knox ; Raleigh, Sydney, Bacon ; Hampden, Clarendon, Montrose ; Washington, Franklin, Penn ; Fox, Pitt, Burke; Dryden, Swift, Prior, Addison ; Michael Angelo, Durer, Rubens, Rembrandt, Van Dyck ; Ariosto, Galileo, Sir Isaac Newton ; Moliere, Racine, Voltaire ; Handel, Haydn, Beethoven, Meyerbeer, Mendelssohn, Shubert, Spohr, Rossini ; Marlborough, Wellington, Nelson. The letter of Nelson was written to Lady Hamilton on the eve of the battle of Trafalgar and found open and unfinished at his death.

There are manuscripts in Oriental languages, written on paper, palm and other leaves, bark, metal and ivory. Some of the Arabic and Persian manuscripts are finely executed and richly ornamented. A copy of the Codex Alexandrinus, being the Greek text of the Scriptures in uncial letters—on vellum, of the fifth century; presented to Charles I. by Cyril, Patriarch of Constantinople. The books of Genesis and Exodus in the Peshito or Syriac version, written in the year 464, the earliest *dated* manuscript extant of any entire books of the Scriptures. The Bible in the Vulgate Latin, as revised by order of Charlemagne, written about A. D. 840, and richly ornamented. The original Bull of Pope Leo X., conferring on Henry III. the title of Defender of the Faith, A. D. 1521.

I have mentioned a very few of the things which interested me in the library and manuscript rooms. A long lifetime might be spent in gaining but an imperfect knowledge of the treasures of literature and art which they contain. And yet on their surface they furnish to the busy traveler, who has but a few hours to spare, a mental feast, the memory of which will ever be recalled with pleasure.

In the king's library are arranged a number of cases containing electrotype fac-similes of the finest ancient coins in the national collection. They are admirably arranged, chronologically in periods, and by cities and countries, during each period; showing at a glance all that numismatic wisdom has discovered as to the dates and coinage of the ancient world. The earliest known coins are small ingots of gold, stamped (700 B. C.) at Lydia in Asia Minor, with an official mark as a guarantee of weight, making an appeal to the scales in every business transaction unnecessary. The idea of coinage spread rapidly through Greece, the first rude coins being of electrum—three parts of gold to one of silver. The coinage of silver commenced at Ægina, 638 B. C.; the first type having a tortoise in bold relief on one side and rude punch marks on the other (I have an obolus of this coinage in my collection). The earliest inscription is found on a coin of Halicarnassus, 525 B. C., and the first portrait of a king, that of a Persian monarch on a coin of Lycia, 400 B. C. It is said that in no other Greek remains can the growth, maturity and decay of Greek art be so readily traced as in the coins of the various periods; many of them as perfect as when they left the dies of the engraver. The student of mythology can here trace the conception of the Gods and heroes worshiped in the Greek world, with their attributes and symbols. They also furnish a complete gallery of the portraits of rulers from Alexander the Great to the Emperor Augustus, as well as evidence of the various political revolutions of the times. The finest coins are about 400 to 336 B. C. The rapid decadence of Greek art from 280 B. C. to the Christian era is remarkable. Some of the finest coins produced during the highest development of Grecian art, notably those of Syracuse, are finer by far than anything produced by the mints of the world to-day.

In the streets near the museum are the shops of the antiquarians; and this morning I ventured (with a due sense of my own weakness, and the prayer on my lips, "Lead us not into temptation") to look at the coins. While some of them were very desirable the prices demanded were so very much higher than anything I had paid in America, even for coins especially imported, that I was able in every case to retreat without making a single purchase. This disparity in the price of coins, between England and America, I cannot account for.

The department of zoology is the most complete in the world, nine large galleries and rooms being used in displaying the specimens. On entering this department the first thing that attracted my attention was two large cages of "anthropoid apes," being specimens of the monkeys which are claimed to most nearly resemble man. Now, I had frequently heard of these wonderful specimens in the British museum, claimed by some to almost, and by others, to quite supply the "missing link." An inspection of them will, I think, satisfy any unprejudiced observer that between the gorilla, chimpanzee or orang and the human family there is not only a "link" but a whole chain missing. My faith in the human race, as a distinct creation, will never be troubled by references to the British museum. I passed through the zoological rooms containing preserved specimens of every living thing, and of species now extinct. To tell all about this department 130 volumes, some of them finely illustrated, have been published by the museum. I must be excused from attempting to compress each volume into half a line—it can't be done.

The collection of ornaments and gems is very attractive. Here are numerous specimens of Roman, Byzantine, Anglo-Roman, Anglo-Saxon and medieval jewelry. Gold ornaments, generally quite heavy, of the Celtic period in Great Britain and Ireland. A large collection of ornaments and gems from Babylonia and Egypt, displaying great ingenuity and perfection of workmanship. The finest specimens, however, in this department are Greek and Etruscan. The jeweler of to-day will find it difficult to excel in workmanship some of the ornaments worn one, two or even three thousand years ago. The gems consist largely of cameos, and exhibit great perfection, both in design and engraving. The Greek and Roman series depend for their designs mainly on the Mythology of the times, although there are subjects from life, forms of animals, etc. There are also many royal and imperial portraits, finely engraved on stones and seals. In this room is the celebrated vase, deposited by the Duke of Portland, and known as the "Portland Vase." It was found in a marble sarcophagus, near Rome, and was formerly in the Barberini palace. Its peculiarity seems to be that the ground work of the vase is of a very fine blue glass, over which is a layer of white opaque glass; the designs and ornamentation being cut in the white glass. The scenes worked on this vase are from Roman mythology, and the workmanship is said to be unexcelled. There is also an alabaster jar found on the site of the mausoleum at Halicarnassus and inscribed "Xerxes the Great King," in the Median, Persian, Assyrian and Egyptian languages. In this room I was shown, as a favor, a fine collection of Roman and English coins—originals.

But the crowning feature of the museum is its unrivalled department of antiquities, containing interesting remains of the earliest oriental nations—Egypt, Chaldea, Assyria, Babylonia, and the later empires and states of Persia, Greece and Rome. The Egyptian remains occupy several large rooms, and one is astonished to find a collection so large and complete, running back 2,500 years before Christ, say about to the period usually assigned to Noah's flood, or earlier. On entering the first Egyptian room my attention was called to the mummy-shaped coffin, not quite complete, of King Menkara, with a part of his mummy. On opening the third pyramid (built by this king), this coffin, showing fine workmanship and inscribed with his name, with the mummy enclosed, was discovered. These remains are over 4,000 years old; had rested in the lofty pyramid more than a century when Abraham and Lot passed by, on their way from beyond the Euphrates to the Land of Canaan—five centuries before the law was given to Moses on Mount Sinai ! It almost takes away one's breath to think of it, and George Washington cents, and spinning wheels, and andirons, and shot guns of our Revolutionary period, become as of yesterday, in comparison. There are coffins and mummies a few centuries later; and numerous others representing the centuries down to the Roman period.

There is a very large collection of vases ; one of glass, and of brilliant colors, of the time of Joseph's residence in Egypt. There are numerous figures of kings and others, finely carved in bronze and ivory, and personal ornaments in gold, bronze and ivory, including many specimens of the scarabaei, or sacred beetle ; combs, hairpins, vessels of earthenware and alabaster, tiles and unburnt bricks of the time of the Jewish oppression by the Pharaohs, bronze axes, arrows tipped with flint, writing implements, ink pots, harps, flutes, cymbals, balls, dolls, children's toys, etc., etc.

The Egyptian sculptures and bas-reliefs occupy two long galleries, with a central saloon and vestibule. Memphis and Thebes have been despoiled of some of their most interesting works of art, exhibiting in detail in their paintings and sculptures the religion, the arts, industries, domestic habits and amusements of the ancient Egyptians. The main features of their religion seem to have been a belief in the immortality of the soul, and a judgment and a state of rewards and punishment after death. Strange that the Israelites do not seem to have imbibed these ideas during their stay in Egypt. Their methods of war are very fully delineated by battle scenes; the taking of cities, showing the devices employed, and the torture or punishment of captives. The industries of the people, including flax dressing, spinning, weaving, glass blowing, rope making, cabinet making, stone polishing and engraving, quarrying, brick laying, etc., etc., are given in detail. Hunting, fishing, wrestling, ball playing and other out-door amusements, and in-door games, in which appear checker boards and dice, are carved on these remains—only think of it, the game of checkers 4,000 years old! In some of the hunting scenes I was surprised to see the throwing of the lasso pictured out. I had supposed it was a more modern device.

There is on most of these remains hieroglyphic writing in the ancient Egyptian language, and in this department is the famous Rosetta Stone, by which the method of deciphering such writing was discovered. It was found at Rosetta, on the river Nile, in 1799, and contains inscriptions in Greek and in two forms of ancient Egyptian. Its construction was ordered by priests assembled at Memphis, 196 B. C., to commemorate the liberality of the king in making gifts and remitting taxes; the Greek inscription showing that the decree or act of the priests was to be inscribed in the three languages. With the fact established that the inscriptions were identical, and the Greek being familiar, it furnished the first key to Egyptian hieroglyphics, and has enabled the savants of Europe to decipher the most ancient Egyptian records. The stone is imperfect, a part having been broken off.

The Assyrian antiquities are principally in three narrow rooms, each about 100 feet long, and are mostly from Nimroud, Khorsabad and Kongenyik or Nineveh. There are seals, engraved stones, and cylinders of hard stone, with inscriptions from 2,100 B. C., to Darius, B. C. 520. There are also terra-cotta tablets, known as "Contracts," relating to business transactions, etc., from 1,700 B. C., to 500 B. C. A beautiful glass vase, with the name of Sargon, 721 B. C.

There is a very large collection of interesting sculptures and bas-reliefs from the palace of Sennacherib. Besides giving many important historical records, they give the wars of Sennacherib, his many victories, and the vast amount of spoil taken. Among these victories is that of Sennacherib over King Hezekiah, of Judea, in which he claims to have taken great spoil and treasure, in contradiction of the Bible narrative, which states that Sennacherib's army was destroyed by an angel. There is an inscription of the time of Tiglath-Pileser, regarding the receipt of tribute from Menahem, King of Israel, and another of Shalmeneser, acknowledging receipt of tribute from Jehu, King of Israel. Lion hunting and battle scenes predominate in the bas-reliefs. There is in great detail the capture of a burning city, the bringing in of the heads of the slain, and the registration, by scribes, of the spoils and trophies taken. Another shows a city with walls and parapets, a battering ram plied from within a movable tower making a breach. The besieged are trying with grappling irons to catch the ram, and are throwing fire upon the tower and its defenders. The archers and slingers are filling the air with arrows and stones. The besieged are evidently Jews, and a continuation of the scene shows the capture of the city. This immense collection is only interesting to the unlearned, like myself, as it deals occasionally with kings or scenes mentioned in Bible history.

The Elgin Marbles were obtained by Lord Elgin while embassador at Constantinople, 1801-3, by firman of the Sublime Porte, and were afterwards purchased of his Lordship by the British government at a price, considered merely nominal, of $175,000. They are mostly from the Parthenon and the Temple of Wingless Victory at Athens. It seems too bad that Athens should have been despoiled of such treasures, belonging to the best period of Greek art, 454 to 438 B. C., the sculptured decorations being executed under the superintendence of the celebrated Phidias. Although so beautiful in themselves, I could not look on them with satisfaction, they seemed so much out of place in a British museum. They should still adorn the Acropolis at Athens.

And what shall I say of the Lycian room ; the Indian sculptures and remains ; the Roman and Anglo-Roman galleries ; the Grecian and Greco-Roman rooms ; the Mausoleum room ; the Archaic department, etc., etc.? Only this, that I passed through them, so full of what I had already seen, and so tired of taking notes, that the only impression they made upon me was one of vastness.

The Thames is one of the great thoroughfares of London. From its source to the sea it is but 100 miles long, and is navigable for sea-going vessels from London bridge to the Nore, a distance of forty-five miles. Its breadth varies in the metropolis from 800 to 1,400 feet, and the tide reaches to fifteen miles above London. Small passenger steamers are passing every few minutes in either direction on this great thoroughfare. I took passage on one of these above Westminister for Greenwich, and had a fine river view of the city. Most of the buildings seen from the river I have already described, but some of them are seen to best advantage from the Thames. This is especially true of the Parliament House and Somerset' House. St. Paul's, on its elevated position, towers grandly above the surrounding buildings, its high walls and large dome giving it that massive appearance which is its characteristic feature. Lambeth Palace, for six and-a-half centuries the residence of the archbishops of Canterbury, St. Thomas' Hospital and the Albert Embankment, all on the south side, are passed before reaching Westminister bridge. We stop at Charing Cross pier, leaving which there is a fine view of the Victoria Embankment, the beautiful Water Gate, the only remaining relic of York House, Adelphi Terrace and the Obelisk. Waterloo bridge is of granite, has nine arches, of 120 feet span, and cost, with its approaches, five million dollars. It has been called "the English bridge of sighs," because of the number of suicides from it. Passing Somerset House, King's College and Temple Gardens, we reach Blackfriars bridge, and stop at St. Paul's Wharf pier, the nearest stopping place to St. Paul's. Southwark Bridge was built at a cost of four million dollars ; one of its arches has a span of 400 feet. London Bridge is the next reached, and the last on the river. Before 1750 this was the only bridge across the Thames. The old bridge had a row of houses on each side, forming a street, which were not removed till 1757. The history of London Bridge includes many important and stirring incidents in English history. The present bridge was built in 1831, costing, with its approaches, the large sum of seven and-a-half million dollars. It is more used than any other bridge in the world ; over 20,000 vehicles and 100,000 foot passengers crossing daily. At London Bridge the port of London may be said to begin, sea-going vessels ascending the river to this point. We now pass the Coal Exchange, Billingsgate, the Custom House and Tower of London, and reach the great docks, filled with the shipping of all nations. The first docks, St. Katharine's, cover twenty-four acres, and were built at a cost of ten million dollars. Twelve hundred and fifty buildings, accommodating over ten thousand people, were demolished to make room for them. London Docks, covering 120 acres, cost the large sum of twenty million dollars. The entire system of artificial docks covers 900 acres, and over 50,000 vessels enter and leave the Thames yearly. Opposite the Isle of Dogs and on the south side of the river we land at Greenwich, so widely celebrated for its hospital and observatory.

Greenwich hospital was built by William III., on the site of an ancient palace, in which Henry VIII., Queen Mary and Queen Elizabeth were born. It was built at the request of the Queen, for the reception of sailors, who were wounded at the battle of La Hogue, and was afterwards, for a long series of years, used as a residence for naval pensioners. The buildings are quite large and are at present used for picture galleries, Museum of Naval Architecture, Royal Naval College and Chapel. Having been built partly by Inigo Jones and partly by Sir Christopher Wren, it will be understood that they possess some architectural merit.

The picture galleries contain portraits of all the noted admirals of England, as well as paintings illustrating the most important naval engagements of the last three centuries, by the best English artists. In one of the rooms I found many interesting souvenirs of Lord Nelson, among them the coat and waistcoat worn by him when killed at Trafalgar. The bullet seems to have entered at the top of the shoulder, a part of the epaulet being torn away. There are blood stains from the wound on both garments. The relics of the Sir John Franklin Expedition, found on the icy coasts of the far north, are preserved here, recalling the earnest and untiring efforts of Lady Franklin in behalf of her lost husband. These sad remains, largely the personal effects of the lost—watches, knives, boxes, pieces of clothing, buttons, etc., raise again the question that has often occurred to me—What good? The sacrifice of human life and the hardships endured in polar explorations, have always appeared to me as unwise, and the would-be heroes who have perished in their efforts to get a little farther north than somebody else, as deserving no more sympathy than the acrobat who risks life and limb on the suspended wire to gain the plaudits of the gaping crowd. I am heartily in accord with the old gentleman who, on hearing of a new polar expedition, testily exclaimed, "Why can't they let the pole alone, it's working all right."

The Museum of Naval Architecture occupies a large number of rooms and seems to have models of everything past or present that has sailed on the ocean, aided in the management of vessels, or dealt death and destruction to an enemy at sea. It is said to be by far the most complete naval museum in the world. The former Infirmary of Greenwich hospital is now known as the Dreadnaught Merchant Seamen's Hospital, is for sailors of all nationalities, and is supported by contributions from all maritime countries. The Greenwich Observatory is on a hill three hundred feet high, and not far from the landing. It is not open to sight seers, but its grounds afford a fine view of the Thames and its shipping. From this observatory our longitude is reckoned and " Greenwich time " is here given to the world.

Returning, I landed at the Victoria Embankment. This great work consists of a solid granite wall, eight feet thick, and said to average forty feet in height, extending on the north bank of the Thames from Blackfriars to Westminster bridge, a distance of over a mile and a quarter. What was once a great eye sore to the city—the slimy, sloping bank, the rotting wharves and dilapidated old warehouses and coal sheds, has been reclaimed, and inside the wall is a splendid roadway, one hundred feet wide, under which runs the underground railroad. The reclaimed land north of the roadway is laid out in walks and flower beds, with trees running the entire length of the embankment. It affords a much needed thoroughfare from Blackfriars to Westminster, and also furnishes an attractive pleasure ground in the center of the city. The cost of the Embankment was over eight million dollars. The Egyptian Obelisk, known as

Cleopatra's Needle, is on the Embankment, at the foot of Salisbury street. It is a single stone of red granite, seventy feet high and eight feet square at the base. It was presented by Mahomed Ali, pacha of Egypt, to the British government, in 1819, and after lying unclaimed in the sand at Alexandria till 1877, was, by the liberality of two private but public spirited citizens, removed to England. The methods employed in its removal and in floating it, its loss in the Bay of Biscay in a storm, and subsequent recovery by a passing vessel, are familiar to most readers. One of the inscriptions on the Obelisk, prepared by Dean Stanley, gives its history very briefly, as follows: "This Obelisk was quarried at Syene, and erected at On (Heliopolis) by Thothmes III., about 1,500 years B. C. Further inscriptions were added two centuries later by Rameses II, (Sesostris). Removed to Alexandria, the royal city of Cleopatra, it was erected there in the seventh year of Augustus Cæsar, B. C., twenty-five. Transported to England and erected on this spot the forty-second year of Queen Victoria." What a history has this old stone!

One of the most interesting exhibitions in London is Madame Tussaud's historical collection and wax figures, in an extensive building on Baker street. It is the largest and finest collection of the kind in the world. The magnificent halls are crowded from morning till midnight with sightseers, and I am told that visitors, Americans especially, usually attend Madame Tussaud's more than once. It is impossible to convey any idea of the splendor of the robes and dresses worn by historical characters, ancient and modern. I was assured that at least twenty of the more modern dresses worn by ladies, cost from $250 to $2,500 each. The halls contain many groups effectively arranged. On entering, the first group is "Pope Pius IX., lying in state at St. Peter's;" among the figures are Antonelli and Garibaldi, Victor Immanuel and King Humbert. Quite interesting groups are arranged by associating the shah of Persia, maharaja of Cashmere, Yacoob Khan, Abdel Khan, Shere Ali, and other eastern princes, with a large number of British generals and governors general of India. The queen, Prince Albert and the royal family, with a host of their German relations, are quite happily arranged in groups. The Berlin congress is represented; also the lying in state of the Emperor Alexander after his assassination, showing the various members of the royal family of Russia. Whatever may have been the feeling, curiosity or commiseration, I could not help noticing the fact that Henry VIII. and his six wives, and Cetewayo and his wives (I forgot to count them), seemed to attract the most attention.

In the magnificent hall of kings are all the kings and queens of England, regnant and consort, from William the Conquerer to Queen Victoria. The likenesses are the best obtainable, and all are dressed in the royal apparel of their time; the dress alone making an interesting study. The single figures are so numerous as to make anything like a complete list undesirable, but among them may be found Chaucer and Shakespeare; Scott and Byron; Dickens and Macauley; Davitt, Parnell and Bradlaugh; Cobbett and O'Connell; Cobden and Bright; Washington, Franklin and Penn; Lincoln and Garfield; Grant and Andy Johnson; Livingston and Stanley; Wellington and Von Moltke; Wycliffe, Luther, Calvin, Knox and Wesley; Kean, Siddons and Macready; Maria Antoinette, Mary, Queen of Scotts, and Lady Jane Gray; Dr. Tooth and Mr. Spurgeon. But I must stop; add to these almost any remarkable person you think of and wind up with all the reigning sovereigns of Europe, and you may imagine how interesting the collection must be. As works of art the figures are perfect. There is none of the uncomfortable feeling that you are surrounded by dead people or that marble statues have been dressed up for the occasion. Eevrything seems natural enough to be real.

The golden chamber is devoted to relics and objects of interest eonnected with the Napoleon family, and I was greatly surprised to find a collection so complete on British soil. On entering this room I found the interest seemed to centre around two carriages, near each other, in the centre of the room. One is the military carriage of the First Napoleon, in which he made the Russian campaign; also used by him as sovereign of Elba, and captured on the evening of the battle of Waterloo, with some of the great emperor's personal effects. It was forwarded by the Duke of Wellington to the Prince Regent, and by him sold for $13,000, under guarantee that it should always remain on exhibition in England. The other is the military carriage used during the Franco-German war by the Emperor Napoleon III., and in which he was driven through the Prussian lines on his way as a prisoner of war to Germany, after the surrender at Sedan, September 2, 1870. The carriages attracted a constant crowd of visitors. Everybody seemed to want to touch them, and occasionally some one would be invited to enter and examine the inside. The principles on which the selections for this honor were made puzzled me. I solved the problem by quietly slipping into the hand of the attendant in charge, a silver coin, which said hand opened and shut as if used to such transactions. The carriage doors opened and I was invited to enter, very much to the surprise of some who were not allowed to follow my example.

In this room is the camp bedstead used by Napoleon during his seven years imprisonment at St. Helena, with the mattresses and pillow on which he died, and on which lies the cloak which he wore at the battle of Marengo. The coronation robes of Napoleon and Josephine; the train of the latter was borne by four queens. The favorite drawing

## THE CHAMBER OF HORRORS. 281

room and garden chair used by Napoleon at St. Helena. The sword worn by Napoleon in his campaign in Egypt. The flag of Elba, presented by Napoleon to the national guards at Elba, and used by him on his return to France to rally his old soildiers around him. It was captured at Waterloo, and there are three French eagles exhibited in this room taken at that battle. The atlas used by Napoleon, in which are plans of most of his battles sketched by his own hand. The cradle of the son of Napoleon, the young King of Rome, of great beauty, made by Jacob of Paris, at a cost of $2,500. There is also a fine collection of portraits, by the best French painters, of the various members of the Napoleon family, and of the marshals of the first Napoleon, and also wax figures of most of them. There are many mementoes of Napoleon, only a few of which I noted down—among them his small medicine chest, a toilet case presented to him by Maria Louisa on his leaving Paris for Russia, his coffee cup, table knife, spoon, cameo ring, etc., etc.

There are also in this room a number of relics of a miscellaneous character, of which I mention a few. The reading chair of Voltaire ; snuff box of James II. ; shoe of Pope Pius VI. ; shirt of Henry IV., of France, worn by him when stabbed by Ravaillac in 1610, and showing the blood stains ; coat worn by Nelson at the battle of the Nile ; coat and vest of Duke of Wellington ; ribbon of legion of honor worn by Louis Phillippe. There is also a coronation robe worn by George IV. in the coronation procession to Westminster Abbey, and borne by nine eldest sons of peers ; a purple or imperial robe worn by his majesty on his return from the abbey, and one used by the same monarch at the opening of parliament. These three robes contain 567 feet of velvet and embroidery, and with the ermine linings cost the enormous sum of $90,000!

The chamber of horrors is a separate room with additional

fee for admission. It contains wax figures of over fifty desperadoes and criminals. Here are Orsini, Fieschi, and Traupman; Hare, Burke and Oxford; Marat and Robespierre. In this room is the key to the dungeon of the bastille; a gallows on which several noted criminals were executed; and what is claimed by the Tussauds to be "the most interesting relic in the world"—the original knife and lunette, being the identical instrument used during the first French revolution and that decapitated over 22,000 persons, among them Louis XVI., Marie Antoinette, Madam Elizabeth, the Duke of Orleans and Robespierre, shedding the best and worst blood of France. I will touch lightly on the chamber of horrors, but will do it the justice to say that its inspection is not calculated to make crime attractive.

The temperance reform seems to make slow progress in England. There are, of course, temperance societies, a good temperance literature is being circulated, and I have no doubt there is a growing temperance sentiment, but much remains to be done. Until the English churches adopt a higher standard, there is not much hope of any great progress in the direction of total abstinence. To illustrate—an American Methodist minister, a member of the ecumenical conference, preached Sunday morning, September 11th, in one of the leading Methodist churches of London, and was offered wine in the vestry room of the church, by the official brother in charge, before going into the pulpit.

He was most hospitably entertained during his stay in London in the house of a wealthy Methodist, superintendant of the Sabbath school, and circuit steward, and a man regarded as eminently pious in the community. Beer and three kinds of wine were on the table and used by host and hostess. Every evening this brother would have his hot toddy prepared for him by his religious wife. Other delegates found the same state of affairs in the houses of English Methodists where they were entertained. The ecumenical couference, if it has done nothing else, has given the American delegates an opportunity to show their English brethren, that in America we are far in advance of them on this question of temperance. It is, no doubt, true that very many of the ministers and laymen, both preach and practise total abstinence, and we cannot doubt that as in America, the Methodist church is in the front rank in all reforms. It is this last fact, that makes it evident that the English churches have got to purify themselves very much before they can hope for a temperance revival in that country.

The English barmaid is found in all drinking establishments, from the gilded saloon to the lowest gin-shop. They are generally young and seem to be selected for their good looks. I have entered more than a score of places where liquor is sold. By making some enquiry, or looking around as if expecting to find some one, I have been able to take in the place and its surroundings, and retreat without giving offense. Among the middle and lower classes the women are to be found drinking with the men—and why not? If it is good for the husband, why not for the wife? If the young men may indulge in strong drink, why not the young women? The German who goes to the beer garden with his wife and children may consistently and honestly claim that he thinks beer a good thing. Americans who steal away behind a screen to drink, who would be shocked beyond measure to see their wives, children or sweethearts step up to the bar with them, proclaim to the world that when they call the use of intoxicating liquors harmless and all right, *they deliberately lie about it.*

In London taxes are not derived mainly from real estate. The man who keeps a carriage pays ten dollars tax for the privilege, and if he has his armorial bearings on the panels the tax is just doubled. For each coachman and footman a tax of four dollars is paid. Cabs, omnibuses, railroads and steamboats are taxed, and the markets afford a handsome revenue; indeed, almost everything that enjoys a corporate privilege pays for it. A gentleman who has made some figures for me assures me that the tax on real estate in London would not amount to the half of one per cent. on the valuation. But then for the purpose of taxation the estimated *rental* and not the *valuation* is the basis; in other words real estate is taxed according to the income which might be derived from it. Compare this with the system of taxation in America, by which one may pay on a few acres of land, not worth a hundred dollars a year for farming purposes, as much tax as on four stores renting for $3,000, and largely more tax than the owners of mortgages paying more interest than the rental of the stores. It may be that I write *feelingly* on this subject, but after learning how taxes are assessed in Europe, the American method, as practiced in the west, looks like legalized robbery.

In Paris a ragged and dirty person appearing on the street would be arrested by the police, and begging is strictly prohibited. The owners of real estate must erect such buildings as will correspond with the general architecture of the street or square, to be determined for them by government officials. The owners or occupants of buildings are compelled to keep them well painted, and to clean the pavements and windows. In London there is larger liberty, every person enjoying the privilege of being as untidy and outre in person or premises as he may desire. A London shop keeper, compelled to wash his windows at the pleasure of the police, would appeal to Magna Charta, and cause a revolution, while to treat rags and dirt as a crime would rouse to frenzy the bronze lions in Trafalgar square.

Barbers are about the same the world over. I entered a

shop in the Strand and was quickly in the hands of an English "hoperator." I missed the easy American chair, but had my hair cut and "singed," head shampooed and then brushed by machinery, followed by a warm bath. Because I did not want my hair dyed, did not purchase a bottle of hair restorer and had no corns to be extracted, I left the proprietor of the concern in a melancholy frame of mind, for which he made me feel as if I were somehow responsible. I feel bad about it yet. It seems just as if I ought to go back and make it right with him in some way, though I can't hardly make out how I have injured him; but then, as I have said, barbers are the same the world over.

In the poorer parts of the city street fights are very common and excite but little notice. You see a small crowd and know that something of interest is occurring inside, but the police regard it with comparative indifference. It is regarded by the lower orders that about the best way to settle a quarrel is to fight it out. There is no noise, no profane war of words, it is strictly "business." The corner loafers who meet to chew tobacco, talk politics, stare at ladies as they pass by and make vulgar remarks about them, I do not find. It is not impossible that persons of this class exist in London, but they have the good taste not to exhibit themselves in the streets.

I left London regretfully. Its streets and scenes had become familiar, and although I had worked hard and visited the principal places of interest, there was still much to be seen. In the time devoted to London I might have visited most places of interest in England—but where could I find places recalling so vividly the history of the nation as the Tower and Westminster Abbey; where nobler buildings than the Parliament Houses and St. Paul's; finer modern parks than at the West End, or a nobler park and castle of the olden time than Windsor. The treasures of antiquity and of art, as exhibited at the British museum, South Kensington and the national gallery, cannot be found elsewhere in England, or in the world. I have omitted scores of places which I hunted up, interesting from their association with the greatest names in English literature, for most of England's great writers have at some period resided in London. Even the names of the streets were ever bringing to mind forgotten incidents in history or in fiction. London is a world in itself. Only think of it, a city with a larger population than the six New England States. It contains more wealth, more poverty, more luxury, more wretchedness, more honesty, more crime; indeed, more that is good and more that is bad than may be found in any other twelve miles square on the face of the globe. The railroads and the national debts of the world are largely owned here, and never in the world's history was there such an accumulation of wealth; but mingled with this wealth is more of abject poverty, squalor, wretchedness and crime than was ever concentrated in any city. It is a wonderful problem as to what the outcome will be from the intimate association of such elements, and it frequently occurred to me that while this condition remains the people of England might well be excused from sending missionaries to foreign lands.

 Taking the early train on the Midland, by way of Bradford, Leicester, Derby, Stockport and Manchester, passing through some of the finest agricultural and richest manufacturing districts, I reached Liverpool in five hours—crossed central England between breakfast and dinner. Wagner dining room cars are of no use in such a small country, you can go anywhere between meals. As to Pullman sleeping cars, the deliberate Briton, after undressing and again making his toilet, would find no time for dozing on an express train, unless by a special arrangement he took the little island lengthwise.

Liverpool is one of the great commercial cities of the world, but sombre and uninteresting in appearance. It was on my arrival dressed in its gayest holiday attire, but through the gaudy decorations one could discover the plainness and dullness of the place. A complete circuit of. the principal streets failed to discover a store of the first class in any line of business. As I said, the city was in holiday attire, and as well, loyalty and patriotism at the boiling point. Miles of decorations, some of them quite elaborate and expensive, and banners and mottoes by the thousand, with crowds of people thronging the streets, indicated a great occasion. And was not his royal highness, the Prince of Wales, and her royal highness, the Princess of Wales, in Liverpool to formally open some new docks, and did not the whole city turn out to do them honor! And here let me correct an impression which I had entertained, and which is, I think, common in America, that the prince is not popular in England. The reverse of this is true; he is regarded as a. good husband and father, living in plain style, and appearing much in public to interest himself in everything that pertains to the welfare of his future subjects. I think he is quite as popular with the masses as his mother, the queen, who really seems to be more respected than loved by her people.

It was not yet noon and I went at once to the docks, and there ascertained that the boat for Belfast did not leave till midnight, being detained by the tide. On inquiring I found that the daily rising of the tide is never less than twenty feet, the spring tide reaching to thirty feet and over. Vessels can leave the docks only at high tide, so that the time of departure of the cross channel steamers is changed every day to correspond with high water. The necessity for this arrangement was explained to me in this way—the docks, which look immensely strong, have large basins in front and are connected with them by gates operated by steam power and open only at high water. In this way the water inside the docks is kept always at the same level and is not affected by the rising or falling of the tide. But for this arrangement the Mersey could not afford anchorage for all the vessels now in port, and if it could they must lay out in the stream to be loaded and unloaded by lighters. Now all vessels are floated into or out of these granite walls at high tide. I have never seen any masonry so massive and apparently substantial as these docks, and when one thinks of the weight of water, twenty to thirty feet deep, which they retain within, and the rushing tide of the Mersey outside, it will be seen that wonderful strength is necessary to maintain them in position. The docks, numbering about forty, extend along the river for six miles and furnish over thirty miles of quays. In them may be found the flags of all nations, and yet although about a third of the immense trade of Liverpool is with the United States, the American flag is comparatively scarce. By a little more "protection" to American ship builders it might possibly be got rid of altogether. It could still be exhibited to the curious at the American consulates and in European museums.

Liverpool has some fine and substantial public buildings, among them the Assize Courts, Custom House, Exchange and Town Hall. Its finest building, and next to the Parliament houses, the finest public building in Great Britain, is St. George's Hall. Its eastern front is over four hundred feet long, and has fifteen beautiful and massive Corinthian columns nearly fifty feet high. Its great hall is about eighty by 170 feet, and its organ is claimed to be the largest and finest in the world. I saw the finest organ in the world in Boston nearly twenty years ago. It is numerous in Europe, indeed I found it in most of the large cities I visited on the continent, again at the Crystal Palace and Albert Hall in London, and meet it here in Liverpool. It is as ubiquitous as

Washington's body servant and nurse. Every American knows which is the "only greatest show on earth," or can find out by inquiring of P. T. Barnum, but which is the "only finest" organ is not so easily determined. I can only say that the organ at Lucerne, with mellow bass notes and marvelous *vox humana* stop, afforded me more pleasure than any organ I have heard elsewhere.

I remained in the streets of Liverpool till about ten o'clock, seeing more drunkenness, more street walking, more of poverty and hunger, presented too in their most offensive forms, than in the streets of any city I have been in. Other cities may be worse in these respects, but they do not exhibit it in public so boldly. I was especially surprised to see so many intoxicated women. Numbers of them, comfortably dressed, and accompanied by men who seemed to be their husbands, were staggering through the streets, the husband as intoxicated as the wife. About ten o'clock I started for the boat, distant over two miles, and most of the way through a part of the city lined with gin shops, ending by a walk of half a mile beside the dead wall that encloses the docks. It was a foolish thing to do at that time of night and alone in such a place, but it gave me an opportunity of seeing how terribly depraved a great commercial city and port of half a million inhabitants can be.

## CHAPTER XV.

### IRELAND.

Ireland—The Jaunting Car—Belfast—Dromore—Anticipations and Disappointment—The Old Cathedral—Grave by the Laggan—Statistics—An Excursion—Downpatrick— Newcastle — Rostrevor— Newry — Drogheda—The River Boyne—Dublin—Its People—Public Buildings—The Castle—Churches—Glasnevin—Kingston—Athlone, etc.—Condition of the Country—Tenant Farmers—Land League—The Irish People—Notes by the Way, etc.

The steamer from Liverpool for Belfast had but few passengers, and the sea being smooth I had a good night's rest. When I went on deck in the morning we were passing the Isle of Man, and soon the rocky northern coast of Ireland, with its verdant hills and slopes, came in sight. It was about eleven o'clock when we entered the harbor of Belfast and as the boat neared Donegal Quay I recognized my surroundings. As I touched Irish soil my eyes rested on the familiar jaunting car. I hailed the driver and was soon rattling over a rough cobble stone pavement. The jaunting car is an Irish institution, and has a peculiar rollicking, dare-devil look—a sort of Irish joke on wheels. When seated on it you feel secure enough, but when it passes you at a rapid pace you expect every minute to see the passengers thrown off. It has neither back, sides, nor cover. There is a small seat for the driver in front, and the passengers sit back to back, their seats being over and parallel with the wheels, which are quite small. From the seat hangs a footboard, and when there is but one passenger the driver sits on the opposite side to balance the car. On the smooth country roads, I know of no pleasanter conveyance than the jaunting car, but when driven rapidly over a rough pavement the smallness of the wheels causes it to jolt fearfully. In fact it seemed as if my teeth would be loose when I reached the hotel.

Belfast is the seat of the linen trade, and the principal manufacturing town in Ireland. In 1841 its population was 64,000, now 207,000, and few places exhibit signs of more substantial growth. This increase of population is wonderful when we consider that since 1841 the population of Ireland has decreased about three millions, being now a little over five millions. It shows what manufacturing enterprises can do even for Ireland. The population is made up largely of what are known as Scotch-Irish, and they do not carry their nationality in their faces. Indeed, one will recognize more people in the streets of New York as of unmistakably Hibernian origin than in Belfast. The Scottish traits are predominant, both men and women being large boned and not remarkable for their good looks—especially the women; but they strike one as honest, hardy and self-reliant. I have not been able to get the figures of the recent census, but in 1871, of places of worship, the Presbyterians had fourteen, Episcopalians seven, Methodists five, Roman Catholics three, Unitarians three, besides nearly a score of chapels for offshoots of these and for minor sects.

Belfast has the substantial look of Glasgow, as well in its stores and residences as in its large manufacturing establishments. The streets are wide, well paved, and clean. Of flax mills alone there are about a hundred, with more than a million spindles in operation. The public buildings compare favorably with the provincial cities of Europe. The Presbyterian College, Queen's College, Methodist College, and Royal Academical Institution are fine buildings. The Custom House, Post Office, Commercial Buildings and Linen Hall are substantial buildings but not showy in appearance. There is also an extensive botanical garden and a fine museum. The latter was one of the first places I visited, and it afforded me great pleasure to recognize the Irish antiquities, immense deers' horns, and dilapidated Egyptian mummies that excited my wonder when a small boy. Notwithstanding its great growth, the city having more than doubled its population in the thirty-four years since I last saw it, the changes in the older and business streets are but few, the city having extended its borders rather than enlarged its buildings.

Dromore is sixteen miles from Belfast and was the home of my childhood. For over twenty years I had desired to see it again, and as the memories became more indistinct the desire increased. To visit the places where when a boy I had gathered primroses and violets, picked blackberries, went in swimming, and played base ball and tag, had been a passion with me for years, and as the train neared the old home, no wonder if I became excited. I had arranged it that I should arrive late on Saturday afternoon, and, as a stranger, take in the familiar scenes to my heart's content before surprising my old companions by introducing myself. The first place I visited was a modest two-story building, arranged in the European style as a store and dwelling, and where most of my early years were spent. I was delighted ; it did not seem changed in the least, and scenes and incidents of my boyhood days were vividly brought to mind. I next visited the churchyard, where I remained till late, by a neglected grave, recalling the sacred memories it suggested. My first disappointment was on Sunday morning, when, to my surprise, I found the old stone church had been replaced by a new brick one ; I had wanted so much to sit in the old pew by the middle window again, and at Sunday school occupy the old corner seat by the pulpit. I almost wished Methodism had not been so prosperous, that they had got along somehow with the old church till after my visit. But disappointments had only begun—eagerly and earnestly did I scan the faces of the congregation, to find one that I had known familiarly in the olden time, but in vain. Of all that congregation I knew not one. My dreams were rudely destroyed, no pleasant surprises, no grasping by the hand of old friends. I began to realize that over a third of a century had passed since the pleasant April Sunday when I last sat in the Methodist church in Dromore. I recalled the incidents of that day, the long visit to the churchyard, the leave taking at the Sabbath school which more than aught else seemed to break my heart, and the solemn prayer meeting at the close of the evening service, to pray that God would care for the widow and her son who were to leave the next morning for America. The voices of the earnest and God fearing men, whose prayers on that occasion have, I hope, in some measure been answered, seemed to ring again in my ears, and I found myself living it all over again. * * * * * * * * *

Dromore is a very old town, and but for the railroad and some factories recently established, would be a perfect specimen of a hundred years ago. It has a very perfect Danish mound, a castle of the time of Elizabeth, now in ruins, and a cathedral of the sixteenth century, in good preservation, having been recently repaired and enlarged. But to me it *seems* changed. The hills are steeper, the streets are narrower, and the public square not half as large as when I was a boy. The "mound" which I used to run up when a lad, is more nearly perpendicular, and the stream near by; once a respectable river, has become a mere brook, even the water from the old town pump seems to have changed and become insipid. And the friends of my youth, the boys I loved to play with—where are they? Gone! not one that I knew intimately in the days of old, remains. Some rest in the churchyard, some have removed to other places, and quite a number have made themselves homes in foreign lands. And yet I am not friendless, for an older generation receives me with a hearty welcome, as the son of one they respected and loved.

A more picturesque place than the old cathedral, and its surrounding graveyard, it would be hard to find. The cathedral has a massive square tower, meant for defence if need be, and its top is turreted and loopholed. In its vault is buried the celebrated Jeremy Taylor, who resided here as bishop, and many others of less notes. The beautiful river Laggan flows peacefully by the side of the burial ground, and one could desire no more quiet or beautiful spot in which to rest awaiting a joyful resurrection. Near the cathedral is a newly sodded grave, and a new and fair marble slab bears this inscription :

"Erected by Mary and William Stevenson, of Flint, Michigan, U. S. A., to the memory of a dear husband and father, Thomas Stevenson, who, after a life of singular piety and usefulness, died at Dromore, March 23, 1846, aged 44 years."

But two other places so dear to me as that grave : one a small mound in Glenwood, the other, and dearest of all, my own home. No honors or titles could afford me the satisfaction I enjoyed during the days occupied in caring for that far off grave by the Laggan.

It was the sage remark of a clergyman of my acquaintance, made over a dish of strawberries and cream, that "the Lord might possibly have made a finer fruit than the strawberry, but in His wisdom he has not seen fit to do so." I feel just so about Ireland. I would not limit the Divine possibilities in the least, but in His wisdom He has not seen fit to make a finer or more beautiful island. I have been going up and down in the northern half of it for about two weeks, by railroad and jaunting car, and also quite largely on foot, endeavoring to understand better its history and present condition, and shall try to give my readers a general idea of the country as well as of some of the places I visited.

Ireland is washed on three sides by the open Atlantic, and is separated from Great Britian by the Irish sea or channel. It has an area of 32,531 square miles, or 1,371 square miles less than the lower peninsula of Michigan. One hundred and ninety-six small islands belong to it, having an area of 246 square miles. Its mountains and highest hills are nearly all on the coast, the interior being an undulating plain. More than one-fourth of the entire island is what is known as bog land, furnishing a fuel called "peat" or "turf." The bogs, I notice, have been largely reduced; those I was familiar with in my youth have nearly disappeared, and in their stead I find cultivated fields. Were the waters of the ocean to rise 500 feet, eighty per cent of its surface would be covered with water, leaving a hundred small islands marking the coast and enclosing a shallow inland sea. Ireland has more fresh water lakes, in proportion to its area, than any other country in Europe; Lough Neagh is the largest, and one of the three largest in Europe, having an area of 158 square miles. The mean temperature is about 50 degrees, and the average rain-fall forty inches, being more on the south and west coasts and less on the north and east. There is a peculiar humidity in the atmosphere favorable to vegetation, mosses and grasses being especially luxuriant, and giving the country that beautiful and verdant appearance for which it is celebrated, as indicated by the terms "Emerald Isle," "Green Isle," etc. Its staple industry is the manufacture of linens and poplins. Woolens, silks, muslin, paper and glass are also manufactured. Its iron mines are said to be good but are not worked, owing to scarcity of coal, which when found is much inferior to the English and Scotch. Granite, marble, slate, copper and lead are found, but not worked to any great extent. There are twenty-six lines of railroad, and most parts of the country are now accessible by rail. The fluctuation in population is wonderful. In 1750 the population was 2,372,634. In 1811 it had increased to 5,937,856, and continued to increase till 1841, when it reached 8,175,124. According to the census just completed and some items of which I find in a Belfast paper, the present population is 5,159,839, showing a decrease of over three millions since 1841. The new figures as to the principal religious denominations are, Roman Catholics, 3,951,888; English Episcopal, 635,670; Presbyterians, 485,503; and Methodists, 47,669.

I made an excursion from Belfast, going south as far as Dublin and west to Athlone. Leaving by the County Down railway, and passing through a number of pretty villages, I reached Downpatrick; supposed to be the oldest town in Ireland, having been the residence of early native kings. A monastery was formed here in 432 by St. Patrick, about two miles from the town, in which St. Patrick, St. Bridget and St. Columbkille are said to be buried. Near the town is a large and interesting Danish Rath. Downpatrick has about 3,500 inhabitants, is built on a hill overlooking the river Hoyle, and although said to be the oldest, looks newer and fresher then most Irish towns.

Passing Dundrum, on the bay of the same name, I reached Newcastle, a noted watering place, situated at the base of Slieve Donard, the highest of the Mourne mountains. It has been called "the Scarborough of Ireland" on account of its admirable bathing facilities, and is made up largely, as such places usually are, of hotels and boarding houses. I wandered along the beach to the ancient quay where were several fishing vessels, picked up a number of small colored stones for which this beach is remarkable, and tried to locate the spot where, when a small boy, I first tasted salt water during a compulsory bath. Selecting a comfortable looking hotel on the beach, I ordered a fish dinner, and was met by the usual "no fish to-day" that greets one at the sea-side. But the mutton chop was excellent and the dinner a success, on the part of the cook, and an immense success on my part; eaten too by the open door of the dining room in full view of the ocean, whose incoming tide reached within a few rods of where I was sitting.

At Newcastle I took a public jaunting car for Rostrevor, distant over twenty miles, our course lying along the coast on a strip of land between the Mourne mountains and the sea. A fresh ocean breeze gave a bracing effect to the atmosphere, while the rugged mountains on one side and the rocky coast and open sea on the other, furnished a scene to delight the eye. Beside me sat an elderly gentleman, who at once opened conversation. It turned on the state of the country and we happened to agree in our political views, by the way a wonderful bond of union in any country. He informed me on all matters of local interest, and when we arrived at Kilkeel, a dull country town of about 1,000 inhabitants, and where he was to stop, he gave me a pressing invitation to go home with him, pointing to a fine mansion in the distance. On learning that my traveling arrangements would not permit me to accept his hospitality, he advised in this wise: "When you get to Rostrevor don't stop at the big hotel at this end of the town. It is run by servants, and a man without a retinue and a pile of baggage gets little attention, and *you couldn't buy comfort at any price.*" The words in italics I shall never forget, they are full of meaning and describe so many places in all countries.

Crossing the Whitewater we pass a massive square tower, built by the Anglo-Normans to protect the entrance to an arm of the sea, known as Carlingford Lough, and soon reach Mourne Park, the residence of Lord Kilmorey. A few days ago his Lordship brought his bride to her lovely Irish home, and the floral decorations with the word "Welcome," formed by evergreens, are still fresh over the entrance to the park.

It was getting dark when we reached Rostrevor, and taking the advice of my traveling acquaintance I went to Mrs. Sangster's hotel, where I found as comfortable quarters as I have met anywhere on my travels. Rostrevor is a lovely watering place on Carlingford Bay, surrounded by high hills and shady groves. Taken all in all it is the prettiest small town I have seen in Ireland. From Rostrevor to Warrenpoint, a noted watering place and the port of Newry, is but a few miles, and horse-cars, very American in appearance, run between the two places. The road is lined with fine residences and handsome grounds, while Carlingford Bay, here narrowed down and surrounded by high hills, has the appearance of an inland lake. On reaching Warrenpoint I find more stylish residences and better hotels and boarding houses than at Newcastle, although the latter place is by far the finest location for bathing purposes. Probably its railroad connection with Newry, but six miles distant and from Newry with all the world, may account for the growth and prosperity of Warrenpoint.

Newry, on the Newry River, a few miles above Carlingford Bay, contains a population of nearly 14,000. It is an old town, an abbey having been erected here in the twelfth century. It lies in two counties, the old town on the eastern side being in the County Down and on the side of a steep hill, the streets rising in terraces one above the other, while the modern town on the west side is in the county of Armagh. Vessels drawing fifteen feet of water reach Newry by a ship canal, larger vessels stop at Warrenpoint. It seems to have a large shipping trade as well as mills, manufactories and foundries, and the place has a busy appearance. There are several new churches, many elegant residences, and few if any evidences of extreme poverty in the suburbs. Newry does not at all bear out Dean Swift's description of the place :

"High Church, low steeple,
Dirty streets and proud people."

Dundalk, the next place of importance, is a town of about 12,000 inhabitants, and very much resembles Newry in business and manufactures.

Drogheda is about thirty miles from Dublin, and has a population of about 15,000, The warehouses and docks present a busy appearance, and there are a number of tall chimneys indicating the presence of manufacturing establishments. The ground rises somewhat abruptly from the river, affording fine sites for private residences in the hilly suburbs. Drogheda has been the scene of some important events in Irish history. I found in the city the remains of an ancient round tower and near to it a church on the site of one destroyed by Cromwell in the terrible siege of 1649. Three times Cromwell assaulted the city. Succeeding in the third, "by God's help," he ordered "knocked on the head" the officers of the garrison, and that none of them should be spared. In his account of it he says : "That night we put to the sword 2,000 men, and 100 of them having taken possession of St. Peter's steeple and a round tower next the gate called St. Sunday's, I ordered the steeple of St. Peter's to be fired, when one in the flames was heard to say, "God confound me, I burn, I burn !" He calls the victory "A great mercy vouchsafed to us," and declares that "It is good that God alone have all the glory." And yet Cromwell died in his bed, declaring, however, "I would be willing to live to be further serviceable to God and his people," After the restoration his remains were torn from the burial place of the kings by a mob, and although somebody in England claims to have his head, the resting place of his body is unknown. In view of the horrible massacres at Drogheda and other places in Ireland, ordered by him and executed under his personal direction, it would seem unreasonable for any person holding orthodox views as to "a material hereafter" to doubt the whereabouts of his worser part. It is not strange that with Cromwell as a specimen Puritan and reformer the Irish people should have continued to prefer another religion to that which he professed.

But there is other historic ground near Drogheda. Just above the city was fought, July 1st, 1690, the battle of the Boyne, between the forces of James II., and his son-in-law, William, Prince of Orange. Like most important battles, the numbers engaged and causes of defeat are matters of dispute. There would seem to have been about 30,000 men on each side, William having, however, a great advantage in commanding veterans accustomed to war. James, who appears to have been sadly deficient in determination as well as personal courage, ungenerously attributed his defeat to the cowardice of his Irish troops. And yet several times during the engagement the chances were in his favor. He seems to have anticipated defeat, and while the Irish horse under Hamilton were making a noble effort to retrieve the day, and William, to encourage his troops was forced to fight as if a private soldier, James started for France by way of Dublin. Histories of the battle, and most guide books, relate his encounter with Lady Tyrconnell on his arrival at Dublin Castle. He said to her "Your countrymen, the Irish can run fast, it must be owned." "In this, as in every other respect, your Majesty surpasses, for you have won the race," was the merited rebuke of the lady. The battle of the Boyne was decisive, not so much from its military results, as from the abandonment by James of the struggle, for which the loss of this single battle did not, by any means, furnish a sufficient excuse. Although nearly two centuries have passed since James quitted the field, the battle of the Boyne still continues to be fought in Ireland, and each anniversary fanatical bigots try to stir up old animosities by arraying Catholics and Protestants against each other. Although out of the season for such demonstrations, on the night of my arrival I was kept awake by martial music, the favorite tune was "Boyne Water," and an occasional profane imprecation against the head of the Catholic Church, indicated the pious zeal which prompted the music. Americans should determinedly oppose the transferring of this battle to their soil. We have, alas! battles enough of our own to celebrate without importing the battle of the Boyne.

Dublin, the metropolis of Ireland, lies on both sides of the river Liffey, about a mile above the point where it enters the Bay of Dublin. It has a population of over three hundred thousand and has been the scene of many stirring events in connection with Irish history. I expected to find in Dublin the remains of an ancient city, where centuries ago rude kings held sway, reduced to a dependency of Great Britain, though for a time holding a semblance of self-government through its local parliament, and now a provincial town in a state of decay, nursing in sorrow and bitterness the memories of its former greatness. I have, as a consequence, been more surprised at the character of the buildings and beauty of the city than any place I have yet visited. Dublin, with its fine public buildings and noble park, its elegant private residences and imposing business streets, is well fitted to be the capital of a nation and the seat of government.

In Belfast I noticed the Scotch-Irish element, indicated by a peculiar homeliness of person in both men and women. At Kilkeel and Rostrevor the Celtic element prevailed, especially at the former place, where the true Milesian beauty of the women could not be hidden by their sometimes untidy appearance. Barefooted and barelegged girls, with soft bewitching eyes and luxuriant but unkempt hair, turned out to see the car as we passed, and strolls through the villages and suburbs showed good looks to be the rule and tidiness the exception. In Dublin, among the better classes, both the Scotch and Irish elements seem to be lacking and one might imagine himself in London, were it not for the fact that in Dublin he hears the English language spoken. The clear and ruddy English complexion and English form and features meet one in the streets and stores. I met, in Dublin, more people whose appearance indicated gentle breeding than any city I have been in. In the poorest quarters the people resemble Kilkeel or Rostrevor and the provincial dialects crop out, but the purest English I have heard spoken in her majesty's domains is by the educated classes of Dublin.

Of public buildings the bank of Ireland, in College Green, is the finest. It has a semi-circular row of Ionic columns fronting on the green, with figures representing Hibernia, Commerce, and Fidelity. It is a fine specimen of Ionic architecture and was fifty-eight years in building, being completed in 1787, at a cost of half a million dollars, for the use of the Irish Parliament. The parliament met here for the last time, October 2d, 1800, when the act of union, uniting Ireland with Great Britain, was passed. What was formerly the House of Commons is now the public office of the bank. The House of Lords remains as when occupied by them and is now used for meetings of the bank directors. The old Gobelin tapestries on the walls are very good, representing the siege of Derry, and the battle of the Boyne. The furniture remains just as when it was used by the Irish Lords, the only change being that where the throne formerly stood is now a statue of George III. After the passage of the act of union, the occupation of the Irish law-makers being gone, the building was purchased by the bank of Ireland, for $200,000. A military guard is always on duty on the premises.

Opposite the bank of Ireland, on College Green, is Trinity College, founded by Queen Elizabeth in 1590. The grounds occupy about thirty acres and are in the heart of the city. The buildings are of granite, and arranged in three separate quadrangles, with an open court in the center of about 300x700 feet. There is a grave, but not gloomy air about this old college, that comports well with its uses as a seat of learning. At either side of the entrance, which is quite imposing, are statues of Burke and Goldsmith. On entering the inner court we see directly in front a beautiful Bell Tower, erected by the late Primate Beresford, at a cost of $50,000. The buildings are said to be equal in their adaptation to college uses, to any buildings of the kind in Europe, and accommodate, at present, about 1,400 students.

I had supposed, from my previous reading, that Sackville street was the crowning architectural glory of the city, and was surprised at its plainness. It is about three fourths of a mile long and the only remarkable thing about it is its width, about 200 feet. Near the center and marking the line between Upper and Lower Sackville street is Nelson's Column, a pillar 120 feet high, surmounted by a statue of the hero, and affording from its summit a fine view of the city.

Dublin Castle is the official residence of the Lord Lieutenant, and dates from the thirteenth century. Earl Cowper had left a few days previous, for England, and on presenting myself at the castle yard and expressing a desire to see the state apartments, a young woman, bearing a large key which seemed to open every door, was detailed to show me through. The council chamber contains portraits of the viceroys since 1800. The presence chamber is finely decorated, has gilded and richly upholstered furniture, and a curiously carved and ornamented throne. It is in this room the Lord Lieutenant holds his receptions. The great ball room is really magnificent. It is about 40x80 feet and forty feet high, the ceiling being decorated with fine paintings. One shows the conversion of the Irish by St. Patrick and another Henry II. receiving the submission of the native Irish chiefs in 1172. The Lord Lieutenant being absent I was permitted to pass through the various rooms ordinarily occupied by his family. These rooms are not large but finely decorated, furniture good, and paintings both good and interesting. The Royal Chapel, completed in 1814, at a cost of $200,000, is a small Gothic edifice with an exceedingly handsome interior. Here are displayed the coats of arms of the viceroys from 1172 till the present time.

Christ's Church Cathedral is a very old building and has an interesting history, running back to the time of the Danish Conquest. It looks bran new, having been recently restored, which in this instance would seem to mean rebuilt, by a munificent citizen of Dublin, who spent on it over a million dollars. Although on a week day, service was being held at the time of my visit, and I had an opportunity of hearing some fine music.

St. Patrick's Church possesses much interest historically, but is situated in the most squalid part of the city, a place apparently dedicated to junk shops, and the tenements of the poorest classes. The legend is that it was originally founded by St. Patrick, and a small and very old crypt is shown at the end of one of the aisles, said to have been built A. D. 540, and is all that remains of the ancient church. This church has also been restored by a citizen of Dublin, at a cost of three quarters of a million dollars, but great care has been taken to leave the interesting relics it contains untouched. There is a stone font of 1190, and an old chest for vestments of about the same date ; also a number of ancient stone coffins. and carvings from the old church. There is a tablet to Duke Schomberg, and suspended upon the wall the cannon ball which killed him at the battle of the Boyne. There is a monument to Swift and a tablet to Stella. The stalls and banners of the Knights of St. Patrick are in this cathedral, also a number of quite imposing memorials to soldiers who fell in India, China and the Crimea.

The Four Courts are best seen from the opposite side of the river. A Corinthian portico of six columns rises in the centre of the grand front, which is 450 feet long. On the pediment is a colossal figure representing Moses. Statues of Mercy, Justice, Wisdom and Authority occupy the angles. A great dome surrounded by columns rises behind the pediment. Entering the portico we are in the grand Circular Hall, off from which are the four courts of Chancery, Queen's Bench, Common Pleas, and Exchequer. There are statues of deceased judges, and some interesting bas-reliefs in this hall. The erection of the Four Courts was commenced in 1776, and completed in 1800, at a cost of over a million of dollars.

The citizens of Dublin take more pride in their famous Phœnix Park than in their beautiful public buildings. It has an area of about 1,800 acres, and has a People's Garden admirably laid out and cared for. It contains the Zoological Gardens, the Viceregal Lodge and Chief Secretary's Lodge. Near the entrance is a tall quadrangular stone pillar, erected in 1816 to the Duke of Wellington. It has inscribed on it the victories of the duke, and relievos representing the signing of Catholic Emancipation, siege of Seringapatam and battle of Waterloo. Not far from the Chief Seeretary's Lodge is a piece of ground known as the

"Fifteen Acres," where the "Oirish Jintilmin o' the oulden toime" used to settle their little differences before breakfast with a pair of pistols at twelve paces. The park is really magnificent, and has drives fifty feet wide and several miles long, lined with gas lights to illuminate it at night. Scores of deer are sporting on the open grass, or under the great trees, which are usually in clumps for landscape effect. It is the largest public park in Great Britain and probably the finest. There are several small parks finely kept and which add much to the beauty of the city, among them Stephen's green, Merrion Square, and Mountjoy Square.

The Cemetery of Glasnevin is outside the city limits. It is small in extent but well kept, and is the shrine of many pilgrims, who come here to visit the tomb of Daniel O'Connell. The grounds being quite level, lack that picturesque effect sought for in the location of American cemeteries. By a happy thought, almost inspiration it would seem, the monument that marks the resting place of the Great Commoner, is a column modeled after the ancient round towers of Ireland. It is a 168 feet high and surmounted by a cross eight feet in height. Beneath is a crypt containing the remains, looking through the door of which the crimson coffin is seen, strewn with flowers, thrown through the railing by visitors. In simple majesty and appropriateness I have seen nothing in my travels that compares with the tomb of O'Connell, unless it be the tomb of Napoleon at the Invalides.

Kingston is a fashionable watering place about six miles from Dublin. Previous to 1881 it was a small fishing village with the less genteel name of Dunleary. On the occasion of George IV. visiting Ireland, he embarked at Dunleary; the royal touch transformed it at once to Kingstown, and its greatness and prosperity were assured. To commemorate the grand event a monument were erected, a sort of obelisk, with a crown on the top, to mark the spot at which the monarch *quitted* Ireland—which seems to be a peculiarly Irish idea. The harbor is the finest in Ireland, but entirely artificial and built at a cost of two and-a-half million dollars. The residences are largely occupied by wealthy citizens of Dublin, who are carried by express trains to that city in less than fifteen minutes. Hotels and first-class boarding houses are numerous. The business part of the town has some fine stores, but is made up largely of small shops in almost every line of business. I shall principally remember Kingston for a delightful warm sea water bath, at an extensive bathing establishment, named for her majesty the queen, and for a very comfortable dinner in the upper front room of a modest hotel, enlivened by the ready wit of some Catholic priests and students dining in the same room. They were brim full of humor, and seemed to especially enjoy the fact that a stranger should be compelled to join in their laughter over matters to which he must of course be indifferent, but their good humor and flow of spirits was contagious.

Leaving Dublin, where I had spent three days very pleasantly, I took the cars for Athlone, by way of Mullingar. My route returning to Belfast lay through the disturbed districts, and the long train was largely occupied by soldiers and police. At Mullingar, a considerably body of soldiers stood in line at the depot on our arrival. The presence of the military on the cars and at the depots, gives to the stranger, who does not desire to mix in Irish quarrels, a sense of insecurity that is not agreeable.

Athlone, ten miles from Mullingar, is on the River Shannon, about two miles from Lough Ree, and has a population of about 6,000. It is an exceedingly quiet town, apparently sleeping by the placid Shannon, on whose smooth face I could not discover a ripple. The old castle, built by King

John, is kept in good repair and has been strengthened by additional fortifications. Athlone was besieged by the English in 1690, and at the bridge which marks the ancient ford the armies of Ginkell and St. Ruth fought. There is here an extensive fortified barracks, to accommodate 3,000 troops, with 15,000 stands of arms stored in its armory. The practising of a band, bugle calls, squads drilling and sentries marching up and down by the gates give it a very military aspect, especially when compared with the quiet town it was intended to defend.

Returning to Mullingar, I passed on my way to Belfast, stopping at most of them, Cavan, Clones, Monaghan, Armagh, Portadown, Lurgan, Moira and Lisburn. Until leaving Monaghan the presence of soldiers indicated that I was in the disturbed district. But I feel that my readers may be tired with my description of places, and shall omit the return trip from Athlone.

To spend so much time in Ireland and ignore its present unsettled condition, politically and socially, would hardly satisfy my readers, and yet, in view of the difficulties of the situation and the complexity of the subject, one might well desire to avoid the question. Dodging, however, was never my forte, and though I should differ with valued friends, I trust they will recognize my right to have my say on this as on all other questions. I yield to none of them in a strong desire for a better state of things, or a willingness to aid in bringing it about. If we differ it must be as to methods, our earnest desire as to results is the same.

I find the condition of things worse than I had been led by the newspapers to expect. While the more serious outrages become public, the minor offences are frequently concealed by the victims, who do not care to advertise the fact that they are under the ban of the League or suspected of opposition to its methods. There is an organized system of terrorism ; men are afraid to carry out their convictions in business affairs, or express their sentiments publicly on the state of the country. The fact that one is an American invites confidence, and in my goings up and down, for the past two weeks, I have had an opportunity of getting the views of all classes. I have no pet theory, no cure-all for existing evils. The statesmen of England must continue to grapple with the "Irish question" without a single ray from my intellectual rush-light to illumine their path. It is, however, possible that I may be able, by a statement of some facts which I have gathered here, to give my readers a better idea of the situation.

The land is occupied by tenant farmers who pay an annual rent for the use of the land, varying of course with its location and the quality of the soil, but averaging say $6 per acre, more or less. On taking up an Irish newspaper you read that a certain farm containing twenty acres has been sold for $800; it does not mean that the fee of the land has been disposed of, but only the "tenant right," or a right to occupy at the fixed annual rental. In this sale the owner of the land has not been consulted at all. The purchaser knows what the rent is, thinks there is money in the farm at that rate, and makes the investment. Take for example the farms on which my father and mother were born. Both have been sold twice in thirty-five years, and each is now occupied by a tenant, who, well knowing the amount of rent to be paid, bought the privilege of occupying the land and paying the rent. Should the present tenants complain that the rent is too high, it simply means that they have deliberately, and of their own free will, made what they now consider a bad investment, and there does not appear any more occasion for sympathy than in the case of any other person who finds, or thinks, he has made a bad bargain. But now suppose these tenants refuse to pay any rent, adopting the popular motto "to the tillers belongs the soil," and where does the equity come in? They purchased, one of them within five years, the right to occupy the land at a well-known rental, paying, not the *value* of the land, but what the right to *use* it was supposed to be worth, and now claim to own it! The next step of course is to fortify this position by compelling other tenants to refuse to pay rent, and here is where the lawlessness begins.

Of course I credit the leaders of the land league with the best motives, but in permitting, winking at, or failing to denounce lawless attemps at coercion, they assume a fearful responsibility. Should they force a settlement of the land question on terms much more favorable to the tenant, can they arrest at pleasure the roused evil passions of the "camp followers?" May not the men who think they are doing "God's service" by engaging in acts of violence to carry out the well intended objects of the league, continue to practice violence as occasion seems to require, on their own account? These are serious questions and may possibly account for the attitude of the Catholic clergy, who are thoroughly familiar with the situation, and actuated by the highest motives. As a body they do not approve of the workings of the league. I heard a sermon in a Catholic church which struck directly at the league and its methods. The subject of the sermon might be stated as "Christ our example when suffering wrong," and it was pointed in its application to the present state of the country.

It is claimed by some that the whole thing might be remedied by a parliament on Irish soil, and the statement is almost always made in this connection, and with great bitterness too, that the union with Great Britain was accomplished by a barefaced purchase of the last Irish parliament. Even if we admit this as a disagreeable fact, does it not bear quite as severely on the men who sold out their country as upon the foreign government that made the purchase? There should be local self government in Ireland, but I have little faith in the legislation of any parliament, English or Irish, to remedy the present evils.

Ireland has now a larger representation in parliament than England or Scotland, having 105 members. Scotland has but sixty, and would be entitled to fifteen more if it had as many members according to its population as Ireland. If England had the same representation as Ireland it would give it twenty more members than it now has. London, with a population four-fifths as large as Ireland, has only twenty-two members to Ireland's 105, and London, Yorkshire and Lancashire, with more than twice the population of Ireland, have together but ninety-two members against 105 from Ireland. It is not therefore unfair representation in the British parliament that causes the present condition of things.

The average size of the 400,000 tenant farms of Ireland is something over twelve acres each. There are of course many large farms, but the number of these serves to diminish the size of the remainder, and farms of four to six acres are quite common. The rent of a six-acre farm includes a dwelling house, and even if $7 or $8 per acre is charged, does not amount to as much as the mechanics or even day laborers of America pay for a house alone. The American laborer or mechanic, however, earns good wages and is able to pay his rent and support his family, while the Irish tenant depends entirely on his small farm for everything. This it will not supply, nor do I see how legislation can help the matter, unless the size of the island can be extended indefinitely by act of parliament. If rents were entirely abolished to-day it might temporarily check emigration, but the increase of population would soon bring matters to the same state again. The Irish women are true to their husbands, willing to bear the burdens and cares of maternity, and look with horror on the criminal methods by which the unborn babe is murdered by an unnatural parent. Large families are therefore the rule, and as the boys become men how is the little farm to be divided? Even if there was no rent to pay, how many square rods of a six acre farm would there be for each of the great grand children of the Irish farmer of to-day?

(If disposed to pluck motes from the Irish eye, instead of casting beams from the American eye, I might here interject a temperance speech. I might insist that Ireland deliberately runs up a bill for intoxicating liquors and the time used, or rather wasted, in overseeing their consumption, that would more than pay the rents of all these small tenant farms, but I forbear, and place this paragraph in parenthesis.)

To remedy existing evils the recent land act was passed. Its important provision is the establishment of courts presided over by three commissioners who determine the rental of tenant farms for all who may feel aggrieved, the rent as fixed by them to remain unchanged for fifteen years. The forms are simple, and the fees merely nominal, but the principle involved is most serious. There are landlords who have for considerable sums bought valuable leases of large tracts, subdivided among small tenants. There are also small estates, held by the widows and dependent heirs of deceased persons, and trust funds have been quite largely invested in such estates. The value of all such holdings and investments depends of course on the amount of rent received, and this is to be determined by the land commissioners. I can think of no principle of law or equity to justify the creation of such a tribunal, while the relief afforded must be but temporary. So long as the principal industry of Ireland is raising on diminutive farms hardy sons and daughters, whose honest and willing toil shall develop the resources of America, the amount of rent to be paid is a minor question.

Of the Irish people it is the more ambitious and enterprising that make their way to the new world to gain for themselves a home and a competence. The shiftless, the thriftless, the lazy, the improvident, seldom emigrate. If they can vegetate at home, barely keeping soul and body together, they are contented. The great problem in my mind is how these are to be excited to an honorable ambition for a higher style of living, and an energy of purpose that shall make its accomplishment certain. Has it come to this that the regeneration of Ireland means a plan by which the people may exist and pay their rents? God forbid. The land league served a good purpose in forcing the attention of the country to the pressing need of a radical change, and this change should mean nothing less than remunerative employment, comfortable homes and clothing, nourishing food, education for all the children, and a chance to lay up something for old age and a rainy day. I have no faith in politicians or legislation. The change is a social and industrial one, and must spring largely from the people themselves. An Irish parliament in College Green would be a good thing, but a handsome greensward by every dwelling, taking the place of the rotting dunghill, would be more to the purpose. I yield to no man in my desire for a better state of things here, but the grand idea "Ireland for the Irish," can only be carried out when the masses rise in the dignity of their manhood and show themselves capable of better things. I believe, could the present inhabitants be exported to America and the Irish in America return to their native land, they would in less than fifty years own the island, and run it as a republic, without taking up subscriptions from their friends in America either.

Belgium, with an inferior climate and soil, has nearly five times as many inhabitants to the square mile, *supported by manufacturing*, and in this direction is, I think, the only hope for Ireland. To make industrious mechanics of the shiftless small farmers is a formidable but not a hopeless task. To convince capital that it can be done to a profit may not be so easy, and until the country becomes settled and life and property secure, it will not be possible. As I regard it, every act of violence in Ireland delays the hour of her final redemption.

And what shall I say of my trampings up and down in the land, walking in highways and by-ways from morning till night, stopping at the rude cabin for a drink of water or obtaining a meal at the more pretentious farm house. It can't be told, but the experience was novel and always to be remembered. The weather has been delightful, summer weather they call it here, but it is more like the Michigan Indian summer that comes in October. I found walking a pleasure, the country roads are graveled and traveling on their grassy sides is easy. The farmers are cutting their oats and in some places the crop is marvelous. In a field near Moira, it seemed to me impossible that so many shocks could have grown in it; they almost touched each other. To satisfy myself I went to a distant corner where they were still cutting and made sure that some had not been drawn in from other fields. I never saw such a crop. Reaping machines are used occasionally, resembling very much the American reaper but heavier; indeed so heavy as to make it almost impossible for two ordinary horses to draw them when cutting. Most of the reaping, however, is done with the sickle, and as in other European countries, the women work in the fields with the men, and seem able to acomplish just as much. Remarking on the women at work in the fields to a rather intelligent farmer, he replied quickly, "An dudn't Ave, (Eve) hilp to kape the gairden?" I was not sufficiently confident of my bible lore to contradict him, or insist that Eve had devoted most of her time to playing the piano, painting saucers, attending sewing societies, shopping and making calls, so I wisely dropped the subject.

The children are a study, wading in mud puddles, rolling in the dirt, bare headed and bare-legged, seeming indeed as they rise up from the ground to shyly look at the passing stranger, as if made of "the dust of the earth," and the surplus dust used in the manufacture not yet rubbed off. And yet, as I looked at their frowzy heads, brown faces and black feet, I could not help thinking that it might not be wholly to their advantage to change places and conditions with the fragile darlings so tenderly cared for in luxurious homes.

I wish the man who invented the combined-reciprocal-self-acting house-and-pig-sty, had died with the secret in his bosom. It is altogether too handy. A division of the several parts might require more steps on the part of the family, but would comport better with American ideas about such things. And yet the dwellers in these low thatched cottages are saved from many sorrows and discomforts. They do not spend weary days and nights watching their consumptive darlings, dearer to them than life, fade away. Their sons do not become stunted little men at fourteen, and acquire all the vices before they are two years older. Their daughters do not bring down the gray heads of father and mother in sorrow to the grave by choosing a life of shame. It requires not pepsin to aid digestion or chloral to give them sleep. No torturing headaches will ever reveal to them the fact that nerves constitute a part of the human system, nor shall a single twinge of gout interfere with locomotion. I might mention scores of other ills both mental and physical from which their condition exempts them.   Poverty is not an unmixed evil;   it has its compensations.

Many other things appear on my note books which might be of interest to my readers, but I am informed by the printer that I have already exceeded my allotted space by twenty pages. The return voyage was tedious, and tempestuous, even to the point of serious danger. I spent much time in preparing a graphic description of this terrible storm, but on reading it to a friend, he remarked in the most provoking manner, " Not so good as David's." I proceeded at one to investigate and compare. The Psalmist probably described a squall encountered in a fishing boat on the little inland lake known as the sea of Galilee, or possibly a gale on the Syrian coast of the Mediterranean, in a craft not much larger, while I had undertaken to describe a hurricane in mid-Atlantic! I deliberately consigned the only piece of "fine writing" I ever attempted, to the waste basket, and give " David's : " " For he commandeth, and raiseth the stormy wind, which lifteth up the waves thereof. They mount up to heaven, they go down again to the depths ; their soul is melted because of trouble. They reel to and fro, and sta like a drunken man, and are at their wits end. they cry unto the Lord in their trouble, and he l them out of their distress. He maketh the sto.. calm, so that the waves thereof are still. Then are they glad because they be quiet ; so that He bringeth them unto their desired haven. Oh that men would praise the Lord for His goodness, and for His wonderful works to the children of men !

M186275

THE UNIVERSITY OF CALIFORNIA LIBRARY

www.ingramcontent.com/pod-product-compliance
Lightning Source LLC
Chambersburg PA
CBHW021157230426
43667CB00006B/432